The publisher gratefully acknowledges the generous contribution to this book provided by Sukey and Gil Garcetti, Michael Roth, and the Roth Family Foundation.

Race Music

MUSIC OF THE AFRICAN DIASPORA

Edited by Samuel A. Floyd, Jr.

Race Music

Black Cultures from Bebop to Hip-Hop

GUTHRIE P. RAMSEY, JR.

University of California Press

BERKELEY   LOS ANGELES   LONDON

Center for Black Music Research

COLUMBIA COLLEGE CHICAGO

Parts of this book appeared previously in different form as follows:
chapters 3 and 4: copyright 2001 from "Blues and the Ethnographic
Truth," by Guthrie P. Ramsey, Jr., *Journal of Popular Music Studies* 13,
no. 1 (2001): 41–58, reproduced by permission of Taylor & Francis, Inc.,
http://www.routledge-ny.com; chapter 6: Guthrie P. Ramsey, Jr., "Who
Hears Here? Black Music, Critical Bias, and the Musicological Skin
Trade," *Musical Quarterly* 85, no. 1 (spring 2001): 1–52, reproduced
by permission of Oxford University Press; chapter 7: Guthrie P. Ramsey,
Jr., "Muze in the Hood: Music and Cinema in the Age of Hip-Hop,"
Institute for the Study of American Music Newsletter (spring 2000),
reproduced by permission of Johns Hopkins University Press; and
chapter 8: Guthrie P. Ramsey, Jr., "African Discourse in Black Music
Pedagogy," *Black Scholar* 30, no. 3–4 (fall–winter 2000): 60–65,
reproduced by permission of the Black World Foundation.

University of California Press
Berkeley and Los Angeles, California

University of California Press, Ltd.
London, England

Center for Black Music Research
Columbia College Chicago

Library of Congress Cataloging-in-Publication Data

Ramsey, Guthrie P.
  Race music : black cultures from bebop to hip-hop / Guthrie P.
Ramsey, Jr.
     p. cm. — (Music of the African diaspora ; 7)
  Includes bibliographical references (p.) and index.
  ISBN 0-520-21048-4 (alk. paper)
     1. African Americans—Music—History and criticism.   2. Popular
music—Social aspects—United States.   3. African Americans in
popular culture.   I. Title.   II. Series.
ML3556 .R32 2003
781.64'089'96073—dc21   2002068455

Manufactured in the United States of America
12 11 10 09 08 07 06 05 04 03
10 9 8 7 6 5 4 3 2

The paper used in this publication is both acid-free and totally chlorine-
free (TCF). It meets the minimum requirements of ANSI/NISO Z39.48–
1992 (R 1997) *(Permanence of Paper).* ♾

To
Bernadette
Robert
Candace
Bridget
and to the memory of
Ethel Ramsey Batey
(1918–2002),
our matriarch and inspiration.

Contents

Illustrations

Preface

Following a recent meeting of the Jazz Study Group in New York City, Muhal Richard Abrams, the radical musician, gentle soul, and "godfather" of black music collectives, told me in a private, unforgettable conversation: "You can go anywhere, but don't never leave home."

In many ways this book is about that idea and the way Abrams chose to express it. This is not a comprehensive, strictly chronological study of African American popular music. Rather, it is a meditation on the interpretation and criticism of various aspects of its history. I attempt to forward a poetics of this music that explains some of the circumstances and consequences of its power and its relevance for specific historically situated listeners. My poetics of "race music," as I call it, speculates on how the interplay of the backgrounds of audiences, musicians, critics, and scholars might inform the creation and reception of the music.

Some of the ideas represented here took shape while I was writing a dissertation on 1940s jazz. Rather than continuing down that professional path exclusively, I have expanded my work to also include various strains of gospel, rhythm and blues, soul, and hip-hop. Throughout my life as a listener and musician I experienced these musics as closely linked to one another: in my home growing up; on jukeboxes in assorted and sundry establishments in Chicago, Detroit, and Philadelphia; and in the various musical organizations with which I have been associated. As an African American musician raised in a primarily segregated working-class environment, whenever I was listening to or performing one style of race music, it seemed that the others were never far away or totally out of earshot.

Chapter 1 takes Muhal's advice quite literally: I go home. Beginning with some of my earliest musical memories of the house party and church cultures of my youth, the chapter then winds through multiple cultural spaces and the musical styles and genres that signified within them and distinguished each. Chapter 2 builds on the first by specifying and developing the intellectual, theoretical, and methodological issues raised by the themes and scenes detailed in the previous chapter.

In chapter 3 I explore the blues musings of three important figures in mid-twentieth-century race music: Dinah Washington, Louis Jordan, and Cootie Williams. Chapter 4 goes home again, recounting the history and southern memories of my family, shedding light on the historical grounding of midcentury race music, the background of its audience, and the tensions embedded in it. In chapter 5 I provide what is perhaps the core argument of this study: that the musical, socioeconomic, and political developments in midcentury African American culture constituted an Afro-modernism that not only indexed the moment but extended into future decades. Chapter 6 accounts for some of the foundations, contentions, and declamations of the Black Consciousness era by juxtaposing three sites of cultural memory: migration narrative, historiography, and a recording by a prominent musician.

Chapter 7 moves closer to the present, to what I call the Age of Hip-Hop. Upon the foundation of the memories, histories, music, and modernisms discussed earlier, I establish hip-hop's signifying effect by focusing on musical practices in three important films: *Do the Right Thing*, *Boyz N the Hood*, and *Love Jones*. Finally, in chapter 8 I return to where I began this study: to a discussion of the equally voracious muses of hip-hop and black gospel in the contemporary scene.

While part of the story I tell here is directly tied to black Chicago, readers should understand it as suggestive of other cities in the North that experienced similar migration patterns. I should also mention that the interviews forming the ethnographic component of this study are more germane to chapters 1 through 6 than they are to chapters 7 and 8. As I argue, however, the notions of memory and history embedded in the earlier chapters form the basis for understanding the creation and the generation of meaning in African American popular music of the contemporary moment.

1   Daddy's Second Line

Toward a Cultural Poetics of Race Music

> History, because it is an intellectual and secular production, calls
> for analysis and criticism. Memory installs remembrance within
> the sacred; history, always prosaic, releases it again. Memory is
> blind to all but the group it binds. . . . There are as many memories
> as there are groups. . . . Memory is by nature multiple and yet
> specific; collective, plural, and yet individual. History, on the other
> hand, belongs to everyone and to no one, whence its claim to uni-
> versal authority.
>
> Pierre Nora, "Between Memory and History: *Les Lieux de Mémoire*"

> Cultural memory, obviously a subjective concept, seems to be
> connected with cultural *forms*—in the present case, music, where
> the "memory" drives the music and the music drives memory.
>
> Samuel A. Floyd, Jr., *The Power of Black Music*

In the summer of 1999, Stevie Wonder's hit recording "I Wish" from two
decades earlier provided the rhythm track to a rap recording by the ubiquitous entertainer Will "the Fresh Prince" Smith. The recording, a single from
the soundtrack of the film *Wild, Wild West* (based on a 1960s television
show), features Smith rapping and the soulful vocals of Sisqo, formerly the
lead singer of the hip-hop/R&B group Drew Hill. While the film *Wild, Wild
West* drew mixed reviews and proved only moderately successful, the single itself was a smash hit, without doubt bolstering interest in the movie.
Smith's gesture to revive "I Wish" in this setting speaks to more than the
tune's enduring appeal. History and memory are embedded in the original
song—in both its musical and its lyrical qualities and in its connection to a
film about a television show from the past, which was, in turn, about a key
moment in America's past.

Wonder's "I Wish" first appeared in a special double-album project titled
Songs in the Key of Life (1976). Contemporaneous audiences, historians,
and critics have viewed *Songs in the Key of Life* as groundbreaking on a
number of levels. Recorded on the conservative and historically important
Motown label, Wonder's project (and his other early- to mid-1970s work)

has been heralded for helping to expand the company's formal and formulaic approach to hit making. Moreover, Wonder's explicitly expressed cultural nationalism represented a thematic departure from his earlier body of love songs. Along with Donny Hathaway, Gil Scott Heron, and Marvin Gaye, among others, Wonder has been credited with introducing a political element into 1970s black popular music that had not been seen before. What is more, Wonder's music "crossed over" into the pop market, won critical acclaim and numerous Grammys during this period, and at the same time earned him a "progressive" artistic reputation.[1]

For all of the reputed progressive orientation of *Songs in the Key of Life,* it produced hit singles, among them "I Wish." Wonder cast the musical language of "I Wish" in a remarkably "nonprogressive" mold. Most of the recording features a heavy funk backbeat under a nonlinear chord progression (E-flat minor to A-flat 7). Despite the repetitious quality of this harmonic setup, "I Wish" propels itself forward on the foundation of a symmetrical, "straight eighths" walking bass pattern. The chords and bass movement "take it back home," sounding very much as though they were straight out of a black Sanctified Church shout—the time in the worship service reserved for ecstatic religious dancing and the visitation of the Holy Ghost. Wonder's ever-towering tenor vocals add another layer of gospel-infused excitement to the performance. The theme of the song does not convey political sentiments in the traditional sense. It expresses, rather, a nostalgic (though not saccharine) reflection on a poor and presumably black childhood: the "joy" of unanswered Christmas wish lists, boyhood pranks, spending Sunday school money on candy, playing "doctor with that girl," and schooldays discipline.

Wonder's new "political" profile, as evidenced by *Songs in the Key of Life* (and his other projects from this period), was clearly of its historical moment. He wanted his work to be relevant to his Black Power movement–era audience, stating as early as 1973 that "we as a people are not interested in 'baby, baby' songs any more."[2] Wonder wrote from his vantage point as an adult composer, choosing the modes of history, memory, and his meditations on the contemporary moment to make profound musical statements that, despite their specificity, spoke to the hearts and musical sensibilities of a very diverse audience base.

My brief discussion of this piece shows how it participated within a historically specific, socially grounded dialogue between a film and a recording, an artist and his audience, three decades, several musical genres, commercial and political interests, "folk," mass, and art discourses, sacred and secular sensibilities, and history and memory. All of these dialogues (and undoubtedly others that I have not mentioned) help audiences to generate and perceive meaning in this music. This book is my attempt to identify and explore some of the ways in which meaning is achieved in various styles of African American music.

Boiled down to its essence, the central question addressed here is, How does the music under consideration work as discourses and signifying practices at specific historical moments? I discuss several post–World War II musical genres, including jazz, gospel, rhythm and blues, and their stylistic progeny. As my title suggests, I call these musical styles race music. I have grouped these various styles under this rubric because, while each is certainly distinct, possessing its own conventions, performance practices, and formal qualities, they are yet grounded in similar techniques and conceptual frameworks identified with African American musical traditions. Most of the genres were historically marketed and mass mediated in the culture industry as "race records."[3]

My use of the term *race music* intentionally seeks to recapture some of the historical ethnocentric energy that circulated in these styles, even as they appealed to many listeners throughout America and abroad. The concept "race" is recognized in most academic circles as a "fiction" and social construction and has become almost reviled in today's cultural criticism. But the word at one time represented a kind of positive self-identification among African Americans. The black press routinely used "the Race," for example, as a generic term for African Americans during the first half of the twentieth century. Furthermore, calling oneself or being referred to as a race man or race woman became a way to display pride in being an African American and in having efficacy in the affairs of one's immediate community. I use the word *race* in these senses, not to embrace a naive position of racial essentialism, but as an attempt to convey the worldviews of cultural actors from a specific historical moment.

I weave through a number of theoretical, methodological, and intellectual concerns in this study: ethnographic perspectives, historicism, cultural memory, practice theory, and self-reflexivity, among other tools that I use to engage musical analysis, interpretation, and criticism. Taken together, they cluster into three broad modes of investigation: history, memory, and theory. Before elaborating on these various investigative modes, I want to proceed by recounting some of my own experiences with black music.

I have several reasons for including the following information in this context. The musical autobiography sketched below brings into high relief some of the theoretical and intellectual points that I will explore throughout the book. As an African American scholar and musician, I believe there is value in exploring the historical grounding of my own musical profile and revealing this to readers. The family narrative and the other cultural spaces that I discuss highlight a cultural sensibility that has undoubtedly shaped my critical approach as much as, if not more than, any academic theory has. Moreover, they provide a window of interpretation that allows me to enter into some important ideas about the cultural work performed by music in the processes of African American identity making.

I call these kinds of spaces community theaters. These community theaters or, perhaps better, sites of cultural memory include but are not limited to cinema, family narratives and histories, the church, the social dance, the nightclub, the skating rink, and even literature, or the "theater of the literary." The communal rituals in the church and the underdocumented house party culture, the intergenerational exchange of musical habits and appreciation, the importance of dance and the centrality of the celebratory black body, the always-already oral declamation in each tableau, the irreverent attitude toward the boundaries set by musical marketing categories, the same intensive, inventive, and joyful engagement with both mass-mediated texts and live music making, the private performances of class-status and gender, the fusion of northern and southern performance codes, the memories of food, sights, smells, and the ritualized spaces of what the old folks called drylongso, or everyday blackness—all these combine to form living photographs, rich pools of experiences, and a cultural poetics upon which theoretical and analytical principles can be based. By recounting these experiences in detail, I hope to give some idea about how I learned that music possesses a power; in particular, the power to mean something important about the world around me.

My earliest recollections of African American music stem from childhood. My father's immediate family was raised during the 1920s and 1930s in the "black belt" of Chicago's South Side. The neighborhood was home to many important cultural institutions such as the Regal Theater and Chicago's Savoy Ballroom. My relatives were music lovers, and jazz held an important place in their collective musical tastes. As I recall, a variety of music—jump blues, rhythm and blues, soul, and jazz—accompanied virtually every family gathering. Soul food and, most important, dance were central to these events and charged each with an air of communal celebration in which everyone—the young and the not-so-young—eagerly participated. The musical foreground of these celebrations (and of our everyday lives) comprised a broad selection of black vernacular music. We paid equal attention to contemporary and "dusty" artists: Louis Jordan, Sarah Vaughan, Cannonball Adderley, Count Basie, the Supremes, Charlie Parker,

Aretha Franklin, Dizzy Gillespie, Otis Redding, Duke Ellington, Dinah Washington, James Brown, Oscar Peterson, the Four Tops, Dakota Staton, Dexter Gordon, Archie Bell and the Drells, and Joe Williams, among many others.[4] Suave jazz aficionados, Motown-minded teenagers, blues stompers, and weekend gospel rockers partied cheek to jowl to these various styles.

And we did party. I've used this word as a verb twice, and it deserves some explanation. Everyone understands what a party is, but "to party" in this particular context means something quite specific. On a designated weekend, my father's brothers and sisters, together with their numerous offspring, would crowd into our house. His sisters, Ethel, Doris, and Inez, all small women under five feet tall, commanded the most attention. The word *jazzy* comes to mind when describing them: strong, shapely women, each adorned with hair colored somewhere from reddish-brown to downright what-you-looking-at red. "Hey, ba-a-a-a-a-by," they'd croon in that informal but hip Chi-town drawl, planting polite kisses on every familiar mouth present. The brothers, Earl, W. J., and Russell, and their families completed the picture. These men were not as demonstrative as the women, at least not until the drinking and the music stepped up a notch or two. The Ramsey brothers played the spoons, and they played them better when the party had hit its stride. Spooning consisted of holding two spoons on either side of the index finger of both hands so that the bowls could click together, back-to-back, in a polyrhythmic flurry. Flexibility, timing, and stylized facial contortions separated "wannabes" from the real article. My father, Guthrie Sr., was the resident spoon virtuoso. Once the flow of recorded music had hit a sufficiently upbeat groove, somebody would rush from the kitchen with the necessary supplies. And then the show would begin. *He-e-e-e-y* now! Hand clapping, foot patting, finger snapping, neck popping, shoulder shrugging, hip-rolling, pah-tee-*in'*!

Not that the Ramseys necessarily needed anybody else's help in the entertainment department, but on occasion, we would pay our neighbor, little Vernon Glenn, to come "do the James Brown" for the guests. Coffee tables and throw rugs were tossed aside, and "Stinky," as we called him, would go to work. Slipping and sliding across the floor on both feet, lifting one foot up and having the other dash energetically from side to side like a washing machine agitator, and then putting an exclamation point on his routine with a fake split on the downbeat. A kitchen full of food and drink, rise-n-fly bid whist, poker, loud music, jivin' and signifyin', laughing, and dancing completed the agenda. Whenever this scene and its beloved cast of familiar characters shuttled through our front door, my chest would fill with a breath-gripping anticipation. We *knew* we were going to have a ball.

Some of my earliest musical memories also include those from the Mount Moriah Missionary Baptist Church, which my immediate family attended in the mid-1960s. No matter what the temperature happened to be outside, it was always hotter within the confines of its tiny, shoebox-shaped sanctuary. The volcanic baritone voice and percussive piano accompaniments of Arbry, the church's musician, were the conduits for the spark of Holy Ghost fire each week. His gale-force rendition of the hymn "We've Come This Far by Faith" would electrify our swaying congregation, whose hand clapping, foot stomping, and other kinetic stirrings offered sacrifices of praise to God, efficiently burning the fuel of the Sunday-morning breakfast of grits, gravy, spicy Mississippi sausage, bright yellow scrambled eggs, and biscuits soaked with butter and thick Alaga syrup. Mount Moriah's musical experience took us to the mountaintop indeed, but it was only one aspect of the entire Sunday-morning ritual sights, smells, sounds, and textures: the weight of the hearty meal in your belly, the sizzle and crackle of a hot comb frying my sister Cynthia's long, billowy kinks, which was followed by the unmistakable scent of smoke and Royal Crown Hair Dressing, the firm press of my mother's perfumed hand working a smear of Vaseline into every pore of my face, and the televised images of *The Lone Ranger*, *The Cisco Kid*, and the locally produced *Jubilee Showcase*. And we weren't heathens either; there was no secular music before church. *After* church, however, was another story. The sounds of soul, jazz, and blues filtered from the most stylish piece of furniture we owned, our hi-fi. The music came courtesy of Daddy-O-Daylie's Sunday-afternoon jazz party or any one of the other local media personalities who played "the jams" right up to the early evening ham, collard greens, corn bread, and macaroni and cheese supper.

When we switched congregations to the more structured liturgy of the Colored Methodist Episcopal tradition, I experienced the black storefront. A potbellied stove heated the tiny rented space. It was cramped; all roads led to "the building fund." We needed our own church. The musical tradition differed somewhat from that of Mount Moriah. Hymns were sung more or less as written, but the gentle swing of Mrs. Dicey Perkins's gospel piano put a dash of "jive" in them, as my grandmother used to say. Many of the church's cultural activities surrounded the raising of money. Culture and capital were synonymous. Rain, shine, winter, or summer, Saturdays comprised a few of us more dedicated kids selling barbecue or barbecue chicken dinners door to door, barbershop to beauty shop, car wash to service station, until the food ran out. Sides of slaw, white Wonder Bread, and spaghetti rounded out each meal. Chitlins, when they were available, cost more. We were only eight or nine years old, but we prided ourselves on delivering hot.

The Sunday Afternoon Program, always held at 3:30, though, seemed to be the veritable cash cow. Tom Thumb Weddings, Baby Contests, Oral Recitations, and Musicals were events that rallied the church community, drawing attendance from spouses, brothers, aunts, and former members whom one rarely saw at the regular worship services.

In the preadolescent days, our choir was known as the Tiny Tots. We would later insist—with more than a hint of exasperation—that our new name was the Sunbeams, apparently with no clue whatsoever that this new rubric did not increase our "hip quotient." We sang standard hymns in unison and in tune. I think. When we became preteens and teens, we formed the Youth Choir. Our repertoire, thanks to the music minister's youngest daughter, a prodigy at singing and piano, was updated with only the latest gospel hits, including the Hawkins Family's "Oh Happy Day." As the choir director, I got my first experience in arranging music in the moment and flowing with the spirit. There were many decisions to make, and I relished the role. When should we start rockin'? How many times should we repeat the chorus? Should the soloist sing the verse again? My sense of accomplishment grew with each performance. We rested assured that our performances on second Sundays constituted the centerpiece of the church's musical output, perhaps even of the entire greater South Side of Chicago! That's how the congregation made us feel, anyway. Thunderous applause and enthusiastic "Amens!" greeted our every utterance. Occasionally, somebody would even "get happy," overcome and wringing with emotion until the fan of an alert usher calmed him or her down.

This Sunday-morning community theater shifted to another cultural space at 1:00 P.M. Art's Roller Rink, a white-owned and -operated cavern, was our teenage hangout. And theater it was. Art's featured a short, white organist who played funky blues patterns until 5:00 in the afternoon. All Skate. Backward Skate. Ladies Only. Men Only. Couples Only. Trio. Fox Trot. Collegiate. He had a set tune for each dance, propelling us to daring feats of speed and style. Virtuosity was cherished and pecking orders were established week after week. I dreamed of the day when the most popular female skaters whom I had spied during Ladies Only would agree to couple skate with me, or at least for the day when my heart would stay out of my throat when I asked. Or for the day when I could casually join in with the spontaneous slightly older group of skaters who moved in a unified, synchronized line around the rink. Their moves were in sync and complex. I could even copy the smug look they wore on their faces—they knew they were jamming. But the risk was too high. If you couldn't fall into step or, God forbid, by accident you made one of them fall or even stumble, you may as well pack up the skates for good that afternoon. Your reputation would be beyond repair. After all, when this group passed by, the other skaters parted like the Red Sea, yielding the right of way to the skilled and "the cool." At the other black-owned skating rink nearby, the operators played not organ music but James Brown records, seemingly all day long. Nobody minded, because this theater was *really* about the ritual, the style, and the high sense of drama and athletic skill every week.

"Sit down and shut up," my high school music teacher whispered emphatically. "I've gotten your name put on a very important list." Life-changing words. I had been asked to audition for the Madrigal singers, a select ensemble that performed madrigals, whatever those were. After being asked to join, I learned to perform this repertory along with the other standard fare that music educators believed would make us better citizens: Mozart's choral music, themes from movies such as *The Way We Were*, Handel's *Messiah*, arranged Negro spirituals, pop tunes such as "Home for the Holidays," and the showstopper "Boogie-Woogie Bugle Boy of Company B," which I accompanied on piano. Two of the first madrigals I learned were "Fire, Fire My Heart" and "April Is in My Mistress's Face." I loved the polyphony, the layering, the routine of practice, and especially the sense of accomplishment after a performance. Participation in this music literally opened up another world for me: the white one. At home, the strong ostinato pattern of songs such as the Ohio Players' "Fire" and Count Basie's version of "April in Paris" hung heavy in the air. In one space, P. D. Q. Bach. In the other, "Jungle Boogie." Each of these was, of course, a parody of larger musical traditions but ones that were viewed as mutually exclusive.

As the pianist in the jazz ensemble, I found some kind of middle ground but no respite from trying to negotiate the boundaries of race as I had experienced them as an adolescent musician. Primarily, white kids were asked to be in the band, because they were "better prepared." In other words, the band program in the segregated black elementary schools that we had attended had been the first to have their budgets cut, and music programs were the first to go. Boundaries, as they played themselves out in my young musical world, became more and more apparent. I chose my route, and this period is known in my family as my "white years." All-State Choir, summer instrumental and chorale camps, state contests, constant rehearsals, *South Pacific, How to Succeed in Business without Really Trying, You're a Good Man, Charlie Brown, Pajama Game*, Neil Hefti big band arrangements, piano lessons, music theory classes, faded jeans, earth shoes, flannel shirts, and, of course, the cut classes and mediocre grades that usually accompany such obsessions. Life was a never-ending rehearsal. My sister swore in exasperation that if she heard me pound out the chords of Carole King's "I Feel the Earth Move under My Feet" one more time, the earth would move, all right, when I was clocked at the piano. She couldn't appreciate that I was perfecting my C minor to F7 chord succession.

My very specific interest in modern jazz began in the late 1970s, when I kept fast company with a group of musicians who were either recent graduates or in the process of completing high school. Two prodigious brothers, Wynton and Branford Marsalis, had launched highly visible careers and seemed to be creating a renewed musical and marketing interest in jazz. Soon, my friends and I found ourselves counted among a growing number of young, African American musicians seriously studying mainstream jazz, although many of us had deep roots in 1970s gospel, soul, funk, and jazz-fusion, as the Marsalis brothers did. In this atmosphere, however, one wore absolute devotion to mainstream jazz like a badge of noble martyrdom: no "mindless" pop music shall enter these ears, thank you very much. Relentless and self-imposed routines filled the days and nights: aggressive collecting and learning of jazz standards; "discovering" and tracing the influences of important jazz artists; playing as many gigs on the chitterlin' circuit as possible; and "sitting in" on Monday nights at the El Matador Lounge and on Tuesdays at the Club Enterprise, two long-running jazz "sets" on Chicago's black South Side. The upscale North Side of Chicago also boasted several regular jam sessions with good musicians who played a lot of the same repertory; however, we were drawn to the South Side sessions, because its specific ethos seemed geared toward and welcoming to African American musicians and audiences. These weekly episodes lasted well into the wee hours of the morning, and their consistent structure, organization, and flow took on ritualistic dimensions. One of these involved the sessions' floating waitress, China Doll, an endearing term that referred to her obvious biracial (probably Asian and black) background. Without fail, she asked each week what we were drinking that night. Since none of us was old enough to be there legally in the first place, our answers never varied: orange juice and ginger ale.

We had come for the music, anyhow. Veteran tenor saxophonist Von Freeman, then a fifty-ish, salt-and-pepper-haired Gene Ammons protégé, whose breathtaking virtuosity and mix of urbane yet southern-fried patter stole any show, began each evening playing standards with his house band. Freeman's masterful musicianship—incredibly fast bebop runs, timing that pushed ahead of the beat, soulful tone, and original melodic approach—was in itself mind-boggling and inspirational. Yet despite his consistent ability to leave everybody in the house awestruck at his prowess, distractions were also part of the scene. As patrons entered the dimly lit club, those already seated would survey newcomers with more than passing interest. Of course, one could not easily ignore them, since the door was situated—in typical hole-in-the-wall fashion—directly adjacent to the bandstand. Each new arrival could bring a known musical rival, new competition, or perhaps visiting musicians who had "graduated" from their apprenticeships on our local scene and moved to New York City to really test their mettle. These musicians usually returned full of stories of how many dues they were paying. As young players we were, of course, very impressed. Not that one had to leave Chicago to pay dues, though. On the occasion of my first jazz gig and that of my steady bassist Lonnie Plaxico, I showed up equipped with a Fender Rhodes electric piano and fake book only to learn that our drummer—an older gentleman who played with a disarming Cheshire cat grin—had fallen out with his girlfriend and that she had disappeared in a huff with her car. His drums were still in the backseat. Welcome to the "jazz life."

Along with Von Freeman's performance, an important feature of these jazz nights at the clubs was the jam session proper. We all knew its starting signal: Freeman counting off a moderately fast twelve-bar blues, invariably in the key of F. "It's time to hear from my horses," he'd state coyly; "they've been chomping at the bit *all* night." With those words still hanging in the air, a palpable excitement would stir through the nightclub as a chorus of unzipping, unbuckling, and unsnapping instrument cases sounded from all corners. Although the skill level among the collective "horses" was noticeably uneven on any given night, all seemed to play their hearts out. Some were there for the practice; and still others came looking for the recognition that could—and, for many, did—lead to local and national professional opportunities. Advice flowed like water at these sessions. As a young pianist, I was often pulled aside and advised on many issues ranging from the necessity of my being able to transpose on the spot for singers, to the virtues of listening to the giants of jazz piano. All of us thrived in this after-hours cultural space, and virtually all of my associates from those years are now professional musicians.

Then I got saved. So broke that I couldn't pay attention, and funding my own college education, I began playing at a small Baptist church for something close to thirty-five dollars a Sunday, plus rehearsal. I rode public transportation to church, which took an hour and a half each way. I learned to play many of the standard hymns that I had heard as a youth but with the Baptist kick. During the annual revival one summer, a sermon from a young, Pentecostal minister who happened also to be in college convinced me that in order to avoid hell I would have to be saved and baptized with the Holy Ghost and with fire. Salvation came with impressive fringe benefits. I could also improve my financial status, provided that I developed enough faith. This was the updated, early 1980s, belt-tightening, "Reaganomics era" gospel message. God wanted me prosperous. The excitement generated by the charismatic presence of this sanctified Holiness preacher was awe-inspiring. My mainline denominational background did not prepare me for the waves of emotion fanned by the delivery and impact of the message. When I was growing up, we whispered, "She's sanctified" behind someone's back with disinterested pity. It was a suitable explanation for why someone who came from a religious family would dress out of date, or otherwise seem a little out of sync with the times. But this prosperous sanctification had enormous appeal to me as a young adult. Not only could I save my soul, but I could get the house, car, and wife I wanted as well. I soon left that church position in search of greener, "more sanctified" pastures and, of course, higher-paying gigs.

Again, musical style marked important boundaries. Music in the Holiness churches was decidedly more spirited than I had ever experienced. It possessed a mysterious power. Despite my new outlook and discernment, however, I still had designs on a career as a professional jazz musician, so I continued to frequent the nightclubs where this music was being played, and I enjoyed it. Weeknights in the nightclubs, Sundays in the church, usually behind a piano or Hammond B-3 organ. My jazz ensemble in college was sounding better. The choir I directed at Second Baptist was starting to "smoke," and life was pretty uncomplicated until my musician friend and pianist Kenny Campbell asked me when I was going to give up the night life and play for God only. I wish he hadn't said that. After debating this issue ad nauseam for a while on the street, we must have decided that I did not fashion a satisfactory response to this curious question. Shortly thereafter, I found myself visiting his family's church, the St. James Church of God in Christ.

I had never heard such a choir. The musicians formed a tight unit of piano, Hammond B-3, and drums. Sixty or so teenagers and young adults sang down the glory of God each week. Sometimes robed, sometimes dressed in standard black and white, the choir rocked, stomped, riffed, and brayed with a brassy verve unmatched on Chicago's West Side. The West Side of Chicago had always earned a reputation unto itself within black Chicago's larger history. It was rougher, tougher, and very territorial. St. James sat in the middle of "K-Town," a section of the West Side in which all of the cross streets started with the letter *K.* Kenny Campbell's older brother, Elder Willie James Campbell, pastored St. James; he had inherited this responsibility following the untimely death of their father, who had founded the church decades earlier. Elder Campbell's nephew manned the B-3; another brother played piano; his wife sang beautifully; one of his sons directed the choir; another played drums and later developed into a nationally known gospel tenor. The Campbells were one of Chicago's premier "church dynasty families": immensely talented preachers, teachers, singers, and instrumentalists in the black Holiness tradition. People were attracted like magnets to them and to the youthful energy of this church. I was no exception.

The collective created the social energy of this space, but Elder Campbell was the central *dramatis persona*. A gifted preacher and singer, he single-handedly taught the choir their three-part harmonies by rote and administrated the church's vision and finances. His reputation grew throughout the country as one of the up and rising, a man to watch. The church's musical repertory comprised a combustible mixture of congregational Pentecostal "church songs," sung prayers, impromptu ditties, compositions for gospel choir in contemporary and traditional styles (original and covers), and, of course, Elder Campbell's virtuoso preaching style, which always featured the speech-song "tuning-up" as the climax of the worship service. A-flat was his tuning-up key signature. This was the preacher's primordial "call." The Spirit entered the congregation, and the saints responded in kind by concluding each worship service with the shout—a stylized, energetic dance unto the Lord that would have made King David himself green with envy. New saints were reassured that God will "give you *your* shout," which consisted of an individualized dance, but one that nevertheless was defined by established parameters of kinetic and vocal expression. The musically mediated pacing of the entire service led to such dancing, in fact; it distinguished this type of worship from others. I cannot stress enough the depth of musical talent within cultural spaces such as these. Moreover, the musical styles combined with "the teaching" and other modes of socialization to create community primarily because of the strong sense of tradition and the higher purpose of evangelizing the world. Although our congregation was constituted of the lower socioeconomic levels, I gained numerous musical and life skills, and even a life partner, in this situation. I married one of Elder Campbell's altos.

But there existed greener, *more* sanctified pastures to explore. By the time my young family and I discovered the "Full Gospel" ministries of Liberty Temple Full Gospel Church, we were up to our hip boots in the boundary skirmishes and the territorial battles of doctrinocentric contemporary Christendom, intense and black Chicago-style. Liberty stressed "teaching" and not the powerful preaching styles of the Church of God in Christ denomination. This church, only three years old when we joined, sought to be different from the surrounding "competition," and that difference was articulated in the realm of black expressive culture.

Musical practice constituted a most notable arena of contrast. Citing instances of "church mess" in choirs, the pastor insisted that there would be no such groups at Liberty. The main musical unit was provided by the Sanctified Band, a variable five- or six-piece rhythm section (plus lead singers and backup vocals) that prided itself on professionalism, slickness, and most important, being "in the pocket." *Funky* was the watchword here. God liked funky. Funky ministered to "the people." The Sanctified Band's contemporary gospel approach is best described by way of comparison: it sounded something like the 1970s funk group Rufus with Chaka Khan or perhaps the Gap Band. The fervor of the Holiness church was streamlined and repackaged for the youthful congregation, who were weary of "tradition" and "religion." We wrote our own compositions and recorded them in semiprofessional studios. We were broadcast on local religious radio and television stations. Our reputation among Chicago churches grew by leaps and bounds, and I believe the phenomenal growth of the membership rolls had to do with the music ministry's singularity.

Another feature of musical life at Liberty sought to distance itself from the competition of the surrounding dynamism of gospel music in black Chicago. Liberty featured "Praise and Worship Music," which can be described in terms of both style and repertory. The style was modeled after that of other, white Full Gospel churches: some of it had what is known as a messianic-Jewish beat, an even boom-chuck, boom-chuck, boom-chuck rhythmic feel. Some of it sounded like placid soft rock. It could not have been more different from what one would typically hear in a black church on Sunday morning. The repertory itself also came from the white Full Gospel–type churches and was circulated and promoted via videos, cassettes, and CDs through an increasingly sophisticated distribution system patterned on that of secular music. The funky-messianic combination set this ministry apart from many others on Chicago's South Side, and it probably helped to demarcate the boundaries set by its rather cultish insularity. However, as this congregation grew into the thousands, I noticed a shift in our musical habits. Slowly but surely, the sounds of the traditional black church crept into the congregation. Although the messianic strain of music remained part of the overall repertory, we began to look and sound more like the Afro-Gentiles we really were. Notwithstanding the distinctive rhetoric of black "musical preaching," it became hard to distinguish us from any other black Holiness church.

"That's not God." I was stunned but not really surprised when these words fell out of the preacher's mouth onto his gigantic desk and rattled inside my head. My grand announcement that I was planning to begin graduate study in musicology had gone over like a lead balloon heading straight to hell but with a five-year layover in Ann Arbor, Michigan. Another boundary to cross.

When I began my study of black music as an academic pursuit in graduate school, I learned that jazz was privileged as a carefully selected part of the musical styles that played such an important role in my youth. One might apply the label "jazz-centrism" to this ideal. The "bebop only" attitude that underscored my years as a jazz crusader was in many ways shared by and reflected in the academy's approach. Boundaries were clearly marked along cultural hierarchies. Jazz, for example, had become "art": music for listening and not dancing, for the concert hall and not the family gathering; it had become music for the textbook and the lecture hall. Many jazz writers and jazz musicians have generally supported this cultural shift, downplaying or even ignoring important aspects of jazz's social history. As for the other styles of black music, they seemed to cluster around other hierarchical labels such as "folk" and "popular." My personal experiences bore witness, however, that boundaries, territories, and categories tell only part of the story of meaning.

The specific circumstances of my Chicago-based, working-class, African American background mediated my engagement with "the literature" and provided a healthy dose of skepticism for my studies. Much of my initial work involved an effort to formulate a "theoretical" position based on my empirical experience. But that task proved to be difficult. In doing research for my dissertation on bebop and pianist Bud Powell, I lacked models for the issues I wished to explore. I could not satisfy my desire to develop fully a framework that would sufficiently address all my concerns. How could I represent the vital influence of World War II on the postwar venues, discourses, institutions, and life experiences of the many writers who had already contributed to the literature of jazz and that of the other styles of African American music?

A key family event would reinforce my imperative to keep working toward that end. Just prior to finishing the dissertation, in northern New England, still questioning the validity and importance of the questions I have raised here, an urgent phone call from my brother announced that my father had passed suddenly. Within a few days I found myself back in the family circle and cultural setting that had first nurtured my love for the musical styles treated in this book. After completing all the necessary affairs, our family elected not to meet in someone's house, as had always been our custom at these times, but in a restaurant. Initially, it seemed like a sound decision: the food *was* passable; everyone *was* together reminiscing and lifting each other's spirits. But something was still missing; the circle of culture was incomplete, and I think we all sensed it. And I could not board a plane and leave Chicago without it.

A couple of days later we decided to gather in a more appropriate "home-cooked" cultural space where we could really get down to the business of "gettin' up," to begin healing ourselves through celebration. Once again we convened for some blues in the basement, albeit a stylishly appointed and finished one. The food and drink were good and plentiful, and the music was just right—a little jazz, a little rhythm and blues, a little funk, a little soul—played at a volume that caused you to raise your voice above conversational tone in order to be heard above its infectious strains. And then something happened. When the DJ, my cousin-in-law "Bobby-Love," cued up the Gap Band's "Yearning for Your Love," a familiar dusty from the early 1980s, a cultural necessity emerged among us—something larger than the event itself.

Innocently, the introduction of "Yearning for Your Love" permeated the airwaves of our cozy room without a view. The piece opens with eight bars of a Fender Rhodes, a drummer accenting two and four, a catchy asymmetrical electric guitar pattern that would unify the entire piece, and a distorted lead guitar lick—à la Jimi Hendrix. We were being set up. After a glissando on the Rhodes, the piece settles into eight more bars of the song's main medium-slow, bass-heavy groove that comprises all of the elements of the opening gesture but with some added meat on the suggestive skeletal frame of the first measures. The musicians mix in some bottom, middle, and top: a strong, ostinato bass pattern and synthesized strings. Charlie Wilson's baritone vocals, a stellar example of gospel-influenced soul singing, introduce the final ingredient in the funk recipe. When Wilson sings the first lyrics in a heavily syncopated phrase, "The time has come for us to stop messing around," no truer words could have been spoken for this moment. Although the song is from the torch tradition (a singer telling the object of his unrequited affection, "Let's do something about it"), the words also resonate with other cultural work. Some serious business needed attention, and it was time to stop messing around. My cousins Ernest and Sina started things off. As they glided gracefully into some "steppin'," an intergenerational couples social dance that has many geographical varieties but is unique to Chicago's black community, others chose partners until the makeshift dance floor filled to capacity. This activity could easily be considered our version of the "second line," a term that refers to the New Orleans jazz funerals in which mourners play solemn hymns in the beginning of the ritual but gradually celebrate in a more spirited manner as it progresses. The second line impulse not only honors the dead but also serves to "cleanse and renew the spirit of the community."[5]

So as the evening progressed, the young and not-so-young, aunts with nephews, brothers with sisters, cousins with cousins—"steppers from the new school and the old school," as one of my cousins put it—danced, played cards, "stomped the blues," and stomped our grief away with *the* blues. Auntie Ethel would refer to such events as "good times like the Ramseys *do* like," even if the reasons for the gathering were not always happy ones. And although the spoons my father would have played lay still on the table, we finished the job and partied for him. This was also jazz's "home": among the blues people, whose social, emotional, and cultural well-being depended on its power.

The cultural power and significance of my father's "second line" were not lost on me when I returned to rural New England. Musical practice had sparked a flood of memories, and I felt compelled to understand the social, cultural, historical, and material grounding of that experience. I began to think about the powerful ways in which music had informed my own personal history, how it has always signified community or some other kind of identity—be it ethnic, generational, gender, geographic, religious, professional, educational, or scholarly. My mind flooded with questions. Why was our funeral "stomp" so cathartic? Could the impact of the moment be explained through an examination of larger cultural and historical factors? What was the relationship of my lived experience to the topics I have chosen to deal with in my scholarly work? How could I use these experiences to establish a critical, interpretive voice in scholarship? And what could all of this have to do with musical meaning?

2　Disciplining Black Music

On History, Memory, and Contemporary Theories

> What does it mean when this performance (of this work) takes place at this time, in this place, with these participants?
>
> Christopher Small, *Musicking:*
> *The Meanings of Performance and Listening*

Christopher Small's question in the epigraph above has served as a guiding principle for me in both my research and my teaching. Answering the question adequately, however, has taken me to many methodologies, each shaping my interpretations of music in specific ways. I don't consider myself beholden to any one theory over others; rather, my methodological, intellectual, and theoretical premises are taken from varied sources and disciplines. In the previous chapter I tried to show how my muse has led me through many different cultural spaces. Likewise, my intellectual pursuits reflect no straight line of influence: my thinking has been inspired by a number of methodologies and concepts, some complementary, others contradictory. Throughout the many twists and turns in my early musical life, I believe that I always found myself returning to a perceived "ethnic center," for lack of a better term. Similarly, my methodological tools, while eclectic, also seek an intellectual center, despite some of the obvious tensions that are present. Black music analysis, ethnographic perspectives, cultural memory and identity, practice theory, history, and the idea and role of authorial voice in scholarship are among the more prominent issues shaping this study. I will address these issues in this chapter, beginning with the relationship of my work to previous studies.

BLACK MUSIC AND THE "MUSICOLOGIES"

Music possesses the power "to mean." While this statement might seem obvious to audiences and musicians, the idea has caused much ink to spill in academic circles. Without belaboring some of the many controversies surrounding this point, I should make clear how the idea impinges on this project. Growing numbers of music scholars now argue quite profitably that music is a dynamic social text, a meaningful cultural practice, a cultural transaction, and a politically charged, gendered, signifying discourse. Collectively, this body of work has successfully raised in musicological discussions important issues that had previously existed in more pronounced ways in other humanistic and social science disciplines.

An important distinction needs to be made here, however. For the most part, "music" in traditional musicology has meant European art music and its derivatives. The "music means something" debates are, in fact, arguing for new (and more intellectually honest) ways of studying "art" music. It is rare for scholars to actually write that popular music or African American music does not mean anything. Yet judging from the historical trajectory of musical studies in the United States, one might conclude that, until recently, few have believed that African American music has meant something worth considering seriously.

I need to make a further distinction with regard to my last claim. Generally speaking, two groups of music scholars—ethnomusicologists and African Americanists—have always contended that music means something that can be rigorously explored. The field of ethnomusicology, which developed historically with a focus on non-Western "classical" music and various kinds of "folk" music, has always advanced a two-pronged agenda. It seeks to explain the relationship between the musicological and the ethnological, between the text and the context, between the structural and the referential, between the technical and the human dimension of the musical experience. In practice, ethnomusicologists' work has tended to cluster on one side or the other of this division. As Alan P. Merriam, an important figure in the field, wrote in 1964, "This dual nature of the field is marked by its literature, for where one scholar writes technically upon the structure of music sound as a system in itself, another chooses to treat music as a functioning part of human culture and as an integral part of a wider whole."[1]

Historical debates among ethnomusicologists and musicologists (the latter group's province being traditionally the Western art music tradition) reveal further distinctions. While ethnomusicology has certainly been a more self-reflexive enterprise, as Joseph Kerman has shown in an important study, musicologists don't like to be accused of outright ignoring cultural contexts. Musicology has, with a few exceptions, generally paid more attention to the facts of musical contexts than to broader cultural and social factors.

In addition, ethnomusicology has been historically linked to a sociopolitical agenda, which Kerman characterizes as "middle-class antagonism toward conventional middle-class culture."[2] Generally speaking, ethnomusicologists themselves have maintained that their focus on "nonelite" music making, their interests in preserving traditional folk musics, and their desire for cross-cultural understanding have put them on the right side (read "left") of the global struggle against colonialism, ethnocentrism, and imperialism. Another group of music scholars, music theorists (or music analysts), has focused on the development of complex ways to explain the structural aspects of musical syntax.

It is fascinating to consider how these disciplinary divisions of labor (however theoretically constructed) have influenced the study of black music, or perhaps, better, how this body of music has influenced these divisions. If we consider the recent histories of these subfields, we see that while the disciplinary boundaries remain somewhat intact, "blackness" tends to upset the apple cart. It is typical, for example, for a musicologist, or in some cases even a music theorist, working on any form of black music to be considered at least "part" ethnomusicologist.

There are several reasons for this, in my view. First, because of its associations with the "black-folk-vernacular" constellation of ideas, black music has been easily "Othered"—that is, it has readily been slotted into the "exotic" category of human cultural production that has been the traditional focus of anthropological discourse. Next, while African American music is certainly Western in most senses, it is Western with a distinct difference and, therefore, not comfortably analyzed with the tools designed for Western art music. Another reason that black music research tends to resist the usual disciplinary demarcations is that it has been slow to shed its modern-day genesis in the politics of the 1960s Black Power movement. This era saw the birth of "the Afro-Americanist" in the scholarly realm. Thus, working on black topics has retained this political association for many scholars. I situate the present study within this latter tradition of scholarship and embrace the ways in which blackness troubles the disciplinary boundaries among the subfields of music scholarship.

CALL AND RESPONSE:
WRITING BLACK MUSIC SCHOLARSHIP AFTER THE ELDERS

In the arena of Afro-Americanist musical studies, my study is closely situated in a theoretical sense with two of the most penetrating meditations on the blues modality in African American music making: Albert Murray's *Stomping the Blues* and Samuel Floyd's *The Power of Black Music*.[3] While these books are quite different—they are products of different eras and branches of black music research—when taken together they make a bold statement about the importance of the blues modality as a fundamental paradigm for African American music at midcentury.

Certainly one of the most influential writers in what I call the "community theater of the literary" is Albert Murray, and one of his most important works is *Stomping the Blues*. Murray treats blues culture (which stands in this study as a metonym for black musical culture broadly conceived) as sprawling traditions associated with various attitudes, social customs, personalities, secret rituals, discreet and visible venues, social functions, and vibrant dance forms. Murray's insights are presented from his perspective as a participant-observer, as a "trusted insider" of blues culture.[4] But Murray also claimed membership in other communities of American thinkers. As a novelist, essayist, and biographer, Murray has become a primary actor in the theater of musical letters.

Writing in 1986, musicologist Richard Crawford identified a stream of work he called the literary approach to black music research. Writers in this group work "outside the realm of formal musical scholarship," deriving authority from their participant-observer positions and their ability to "make a reader or listener understand and *feel* the special qualities of black experience as it is reflected in black music."[5] Murray's stomp does make you feel it. He zigzags between myriad referents, between the mystical and the philosophical, and between mojos and Hamlet. Although the book works overtime to make readers believe in the "universal" qualities of black music culture, it also accounts wonderfully for the specific ethos of these expressions.

Elegantly written, Murray's musical discussion is based on his experiences of both recordings and live performances. His use of illustrations throughout is extensive, diverse, and telling. They include live and publicity photographs of musicians, famous and nondescript venues of performance, ecstatic social dancing, blues divas, jam sessions, church services, the actual record labels of commercial recordings, movie stills, advertisements, and promotional materials. This attention to the material aspects of blues culture provides a catalog of its vibrant sights, tactile sensibilities, pungent smells, and sonorous riffs and runs, which are important modalities of cultural memory. Moreover, these illustrations amount to a pragmatic celebration of the commodification of blues-based musical styles. There is no scholarly apparatus to speak of in the book, which suggests a widely cast net for readership.

Samuel A. Floyd's *The Power of Black Music* is situated in many ways on the other end of the scholarly continuum. Floyd's theory of black musical production is modeled largely on Henry Louis Gates's densely textured theory of black literary criticism as outlined in *The Signifying Monkey* (1988), Sterling Stuckey's book *Slave Culture*, and other works that focus on the presence and past of the African legacy in African American culture. Signifyin(g), according to Gates's theory, pertains to the way in which black literary works exhibit an intertextual relationship through the acts of reference and revision in both form and content. While these black literary statements may signify (and they often do) on white literature and culture, the critical signifyin(g) relationships among black texts themselves are important and frequent.

Musical signifyin(g), according to Floyd, reflects Gates's literary usage but expands it to include the use of key "figures" and gestures within a musical work. These gestures include calls, cries, hollers, call-and-response devices, additive rhythms, polyrhythms, heterophony, pendular thirds, blue notes, bent notes, elisions, hums, moans, grunts, vocables, oral declamations, interjections, off-beat phrases, parallel intervals, constant repetition, metronomic pulse, timbral distortions, musical individuality within collectivity, game rivalry, melisma, and musical forms such as 12-bar blues.[6] Floyd subsumes the rhetorical use of these tropes under the rubric "Call and Response." As Gates wrote of literary and oral Signifyin(g), Call and Response "epitomizes all of the rhetorical play in the black vernacular. Its self-consciously open rhetorical status, then, functions as a kind of writing, wherein rhetoric is the writing of speech, of oral discourse."[7] Floyd's study aims directly at deciphering that function in music, and he gives readers a sense of the capacity of black music to circulate social energy, to embody cultural work, and to express the struggles and fulfillments of existence.[8]

While Floyd's work provides the field with a much needed theoretical framework or, perhaps better, a language to talk about the salient features of black music that distinguish it as a cohesive tradition, I wish to push his theory further. If we situate it more firmly in specific historical and social contexts, we can add nuance to the provocative Call-and-Response idea. By attending to the specific historical moment and social setting in which a music gesture appears, we avoid the appearance of reifying or "essentializing" cultural expressions; their meaning and value are, after all, contingent on these and other factors. Moreover, since the social meaning of a musical gesture involves other aspects of identity besides race or ethnicity, information about gender, class, and geographic location, among other issues, should be figured into the equation of any interpretation. The presence of call and response or any other of Floyd's tropes in a piece of music is only the beginning. We need to situate these figures and gestures into as fully contextualized a setting as possible—and this includes identifying a specific audience—in order to arrive at a penetrating and convincing interpretation.

FAMILY IN "THE FIELD": REPRESENTATION, REFUSAL, AND THE CRITICAL ETHNOGRAPHIC STANCE

In the previous chapter, I suggested the importance of cultural memories in the construction of musical meaning and scholarly interpretation. The "ethnographic memoir" in that chapter moved through various sites of African American cultural memories and community theaters. We experienced the house party culture, in which a celebration impulse ruled and music making (the spoons and the dance) mixed with mass-media recordings, creating a musical mosaic of idioms that inspired varied reactions from listeners. We visited, for example, several black Christian denominations, all of them distinctively marked by the repetitions and revisions of African American religious music practice but in different ways.

Each mise-en-scène depicted intimate connections among musical practices, food rituals, bodily expressiveness, and vocal exclamations. My own development as a practicing musician and culture bearer allowed me to experience divergent cultural spaces that were related to African American culture or at least implicated by it. This look at the vernacular dancing, conducting, piano playing, singing, and skating in house and block parties, church and school choirs, jazz bands, jazz clubs, rinks, and so on, situated lived experience and cultural practice in a specific historical moment. These experiences (cultural memories) informed the scholarly viewpoint I began to develop during my graduate study. Finally, my father's second line brought the narrative full circle; it anchored the impact of a single cultural practice in a larger system of cultural "knowing."

I had two goals in mind with this method. On one level, I sought in the telling of those stories to have readers understand something about some of the sources and grounding of my own critical voice and biases. On another level, I wanted to situate the artists and the musical gestures and idioms they performed in a specific cultural ethos. The impetus behind this kind of project, as I have already discussed, is not new. Illuminating the link between race music, in this case, and race(d) identity—between cultural practice and "the people"—has been a key concern of ethnomusicology, of some musicological studies, and of anthropological work on music for decades. My desire to situate in a specific "ethnographic truth" the social energy circulating in mass-media musical texts is part of this long-standing agenda. But the ethnomemoir narrative and the subsequent inquiries and interviews that it generated beg further discussion if their implications are to be useful beyond mere personal revelation.

During 1996 I conducted interviews among some of my older relatives, African Americans living in Chicago, Illinois. The Rosses, my mother's immediate family, were migrants who had moved from Georgia to Chicago in the years immediately following World War II. My father's family, the Ramseys, were second-generation migrants, whose parents and siblings had come to Chicago earlier, in the late 1910s. As I've already stated, one of the reasons that I elected to conduct these interviews—usually very lively sessions of conversation and storytelling—was to understand and to question the historical and material grounding of my own critical biases and assumptions as a musicologist. I was seeking, in other words, to reveal to my readers something that is usually cloaked in much of the cultural criticism and music scholarship appearing in the contemporary moment.

My using "data" from my own family history goes against the grain of scholarly objectivity, upsetting one of the assumed prime directives of ethnographic writing: that one must cross some kind of culture boundary and explain an "Other" life world distant from one's own. At the same time, however, the historical grounding of my subject position as a scholar, as an African American, and as a listener with a specific, multilayered relationship to the musical legacy under consideration can be more fully understood within the web of culture revealed in the narrative here.

On the microlevel of culture, we find that during the 1940s African American domestic spaces also experienced profound changes, of which the stories related here represent specific, yet typical, examples. The information that I collected about African American life challenged many of my preciously held notions. When I began these interviews and asked why each of my interviewees had left the South and moved to Chicago, for example, I fully expected to hear horrific stories about white racism and the North being a better, more sophisticated place. Instead, the focus of their stories, like many of the rhythm and blues songs recorded in this era, concerned love and family relationships.

Scholars have recently sought to replace monolithic depictions of black culture with diverse ones that take into account the full spectrum of black life in America. These critiques of a unified blackness, such as a recent one by Evelyn Brooks Higginbotham, have shown how the notion of "race" alone can obscure more than it illuminates. She writes that "Afro-American history . . . has accentuated race by calling explicit attention to the cultural as well as socioeconomic implications of American racism but has failed to examine the differential class and gender positions men and women occupy in black communities."[9]

Various struggles over "racial" representation have been a politicized imperative, shaping the very nature of African American cultural identity since its inception. This cultural politics of representation can be seen in many areas. For one, the entire history of black music in the United States can be characterized as the inscription of the African American presence into America's representation of its cultural profile. But African American culture cannot be characterized solely in terms of a "liberation struggle." The diverse and sprawling processes we think of as "African American culture" did not develop simply as a response to hegemony, racism, and social oppression. Recent academic studies and populist discourses reveal a feisty intrablack dialogue about the representation of blackness in the public and scholarly arena: "Who," some of these debates seem to ask, "will be the representative, authentic Negro?" "Which of these voices will be privileged?"

The polyphonic articulation of postwar African American voices in the public and private spheres appeared within the context of a diverse and varied black urban culture-scape, one that had established itself firmly during the years of World War I. Literary and cultural critic Hazel Carby, for example, has shown how black urban histories have tended to privilege the narratives of the black middle class; such is the case with movements like the Harlem Renaissance. She has attempted to restore missing aspects of that history by focusing on working-class musical culture, characterizing the relationship between the Harlem Renaissance culture and the contemporaneous blues culture as contradictory—as "ideological, political, and cultural contestation between an emergent black bourgeoisie and an emerging urban black working class."[10] And Higginbotham has recently shown how, during the 1920s Negro Renaissance, the struggle over cultural authority occurred not only between the black literati and proponents of "oral" culture but also among the practitioners of vernacular music, namely, between secular and religious factions. This struggle or contest shows how black working-class culture itself comprised "multiple and conflicting subcultures."[11]

The metaphor of a representation "contest" *within* African American culture challenges the notion of a static sense of racial authenticity within African American communities. And it has implications for the interpretation of black vernacular music. One way to account for the concerns of representation, diversity, and meaning is to address a shortcoming that I perceive in much scholarship on black music. In a recent critique of resistance studies, anthropologist Sherry B. Ortner argues that insufficient focus on ethnography within these studies limits their usefulness. She calls this blind spot "ethnographic refusal."[12] Ethnographic refusal manifests itself, first, by limiting study of the "political" to the relationship between subordinate groups and those who hold power over them, not recognizing power conflicts and struggles *among* subalterns. Another form of ethnographic refusal fails to grant subalterns an "authentic" culture that is created out of their own systems of meaning and order and is not merely a response to the situation of social and cultural domination. As Ortner argues persuasively:

> If we are to recognize that resistors are doing more than simply opposing domination, more than simply producing a virtually mechanical *re*-action, then we must go the whole way. They have their *own* politics— not just between chiefs and commoners or landlords and peasants but within all the local categories of friction and tension: men and women, parents and children, seniors and juniors; inheritance conflicts among brothers; struggles of succession and wars of conquest between chiefs; struggles for primacy between religious sects; and on and on.[13]

Much of the research on African American music discusses "the black masses" or working-class folks without forwarding the specificity of the ethnographic stance of which Ortner speaks. More attention, for example, should be paid to the more "private" spaces of blackness—the "drylongso" ways in which black ethnicity is "performed" outside of the public discourses upon which scholarship usually relies to access and represent black ethnicity. I argue that interrogation of this arena of cultural memory and historical concerns will enable one to perceive more accurately connections that exist among community theaters, collective memory, and musical practice. For example, as I have noted above, for some African Americans, leaving the South during the migration was about more than racism and power relationships between blacks and whites. My relatives told stories that concentrated more on power relationships among family members. And the storytellers spoke of things other than "struggles": they told tales of the celebratory rituals of their southern and northern lives and of the social and material circumstances in which these rituals were played out.

If music is a coherent, signifying system or cultural transaction, then we need to understand more about various specific social settings in order to tease out what this system or transaction might mean. As I have stated above, meaning is always contingent and extremely fluid; it is never essential to a musical figuration. Real people negotiate and eventually agree on what cultural expressions such as a musical gesture mean. They collectively decide what associations are conjured by a well-placed blue note, a familiar harmonic pattern, the soulful, virtuoso sweep of a jazz solo run, a social dancer's imaginative twist on an old dance step, or the raspy grain of a church mother's vocal declamation on Sunday morning.[14]

The life stories or oral ethnohistories that appear throughout this book are undeniably specific to the families whose histories are told. I am convinced that these histories have not only shaped my worldview (a view that inevitably shapes the present text) but have also informed those of scores of other African Americans whose family histories, while distinctive and diverse, are intimately related to stories like these. To what degree do these personal experiences reflect, influence, or inform the musical styles that appeared in the late twentieth century; to what degree have they been shaped by these styles? Indeed, what is the relationship between musical practice and an audience of average African Americans?

The cultural practices that I recounted in the ethnomemoir took place in a northern context but were the result of an ongoing historical conversation among people, practices, and sensibilities from many locations. My own upbringing in a family culture that comprised the negotiations of the social deportment of the Rosses (southern first-generation migrants) and the Ramseys (northern second-generation migrants) illustrates such a discourse. Below I bring into high relief some of the social energies that characterized this North-South Afro-modernist conversation through the life experiences of my ancestors, whose stories, while singular, are also quite typical of other historical actors.

Farah Jasmine Griffin's important study, "Who Set You Flowin'?" The African-American Migration Narrative, provides a wonderful model for organizing the broader themes in some of the stories told in portions of this book. Griffin's framework consists of four important moments in the migration narratives she studied: (1) exploration of reasons or catalysts for leaving the South; (2) descriptions of initial confrontation with the urban North; (3) portrayals of the migrants' negotiation of the urban landscape; and (4) the migrants' consideration of the present and future consequences of migration and urban power.[15]

Griffin writes that "although there are different reasons for migrating, in all cases the South is portrayed as an immediate, identifiable, and oppressive power. Southern power is exercised by people known to its victims—bosses, landlords, sheriffs, and, in the case of black women, even family members."[16] This explanation of power relationships is confirmed in some of the stories in this book. We also see a very strong identification with the mother as the source of "Ancestral" strength. Of additional importance, Griffin has found the trope of Ancestor to be a powerful presence in the multimedia texts that she interprets. It is critical to mention here that I am not attempting to reify a singular negative experience of the South. In fact, the stories themselves bear this out. Although the northern city of Chicago had its obvious attractions for the interviewees, and they certainly found compelling reasons for migrating there, the South remained "home" in their imaginations for many years.

HISTORY, MEMORY, AND AFRICAN AMERICAN MUSIC

One of the challenges that I encountered in pursuing this particular line of thinking was reconciling what many perceive to be a great divide: the space between the subjective realm of "cultural memory" and the "truth claim" of objective scholarship. A book of collected essays titled *History and Memory in African American Culture* explains this chasm well, as a group of authors explore how we view the past through the twin modes of history and memory.[17] While both history and memory "involve the retrieval of felt experience from the mix and jumble of the past," they are perceived as quite different activities. History is science: a scholarly discipline, objective, based on empirical evidence and detached analysis. Memory, on the other hand, is personal, "subject to the biases, quirks, and rhythms of the individual mind." Describing a recent, "more expansive and yet critical attitude toward both history and memory," the collection addresses several broad questions: When is memory a part of history? In what sense are the things remembered a crucial part of what is passed on to future generations? What is the true relationship between art and history or between history and memory? Indeed, the meaning of music lies somewhere in the mix and jumble of the past: in the nexus of the biases, quirks, and individual rhythms of memory and the material evidence of history. As I explain below, this study orders the mix and jumble of the musical past through the twin lenses of history and memory.

AFRO-MODERNISM, BLACK CONSCIOUSNESS, AND POSTINDUSTRIALISM

The historical arc of the race music styles that I discuss comprises roughly fifty years, from the 1940s to the 1990s. For the purposes of this study, I identify three important points of arrival, the 1940s, the late 1960s to the early 1970s, and the 1990s. (I acknowledge, of course, that alternate models are plausible here.) They represent, I believe, anchor moments in the cultural, social, and political realms of twentieth-century African American history. Twentieth-century African American cultural history produced a grand narrative of "progress" that I call Afro-modernism, a loose system of thought that, in my view, came to a head in important ways around the 1940s. Although some scholars have warned that metanarratives are dead, I maintain that they can still help us to organize our thinking about the relationship between "the times" and cultural expression.

What exactly is Afro-modernism? In this study it is connected to the new urbanity of African American communities, the heady momentum of sociopolitical progress during the first half of the twentieth century, and the changing sense of what constituted African American culture (and even American culture generally speaking) at the postwar moment. The term helps us understand race musics appearing at this time as historically specific social discourses. This social energy circulating then shaped the formal procedures of race music and helped give it meaning and coherence for its audiences. The music, in turn, influenced the social setting of the Afro-modernist moment.[18]

In addition, I see Afro-modernism operating as a broad social imperative that has shaped culture, working as an aesthetic principle within individual musical expressions from this period. For my purposes, Afro-modernism is closely linked to a continuum with two rhetorical performance modalities represented by the North and the South. My discussion of the social energy created by the relationship between these musical rhetorics allows us to analyze important aspects of the cultural work being performed by various pieces of music. As I will discuss more thoroughly in later chapters, the idea of Afro-modernism brings into sharper relief the import of migration and urbanity for African American musical culture during the 1940s and thereafter.

The North-South cultural dialogue has larger consequences for the relationship between African and African American music. It helps us to understand the African past for what it is and what it is not. While it is obviously a historical-anthropological fact, it was continually manipulated as it emerged and reemerged with different kinds of signifying effect throughout the twentieth century. A host of historical actors has alternately valued the African past as either a rhetorical tool in African American cultural politics or as proof of black citizens' cultural inferiority. What is crucial here is how the troping, or repetitive use of various musical techniques, musicking activities, myths, canonical stories, cuisine, and so on, has signified for many not Africa per se but a southern-based cultural system.

As Hans A. Baer and Merrill Singer argue, "The current importance of these African elements derives not from their possible source but in the part they have played and continue to play in the crafting of special mechanisms for social survival, emotional comfort, and transcendent expression under the harshest of physical circumstances."[19] Throughout the twentieth century, particularly during the World War II years, the flow of black migrants to urban commercial centers such as Chicago supplied northern cultural spaces with "southernisms" that constantly interacted with urban modernity and with European and American cultural practices. The dynamic role that music played in these "cultural conversations" equaled, if not surpassed, that of literature.

During the 1960s, another sense of arrival occurred. The Black Power movement popularized a particular brand of black cultural nationalism within America. This new brand of nationalism or "Black Consciousness" found expression in a number of arenas, among them the religious, the social, and the cultural. This view was decidedly political; at times it was downright militant. It grew partly in response to the deteriorating so-called second ghettos, the northern urban spaces created by the large influx of African Americans during the Afro-modernist era. The cities that an earlier generation had considered full of promise were regarded quite differently by the late 1960s and early 1970s. Living in geographic spaces that resembled little "black nations" because of white flight to the suburbs, urban-dwelling African Americans developed a "nation within a nation" sensibility that, despite structural and institutional racism, spawned a flurry of dynamic postintegrationist responses in music and scholarship, among other domains.

The postindustrial moment, my third period of discussion, describes the late-twentieth-century condition of cities such as New York, Chicago, and Los Angeles. By this time, living in America's large cities had suffocated the life chances of many of the urban poor, especially that of the young and black. But it could not stifle the African American–based creativity that marked the earlier moments mentioned above. Thus, the period saw intense artistic expressions emanating from within the core of these urban spaces besieged by blight (the legacy of earlier riots), unemployment, crime, and hopelessness. Musicians, filmmakers, visual artists, and writers worked with two identifiable tactics in mind. Some wanted to depict (some might say glorify) the horrendous conditions of inner cities. Others attempted to re-fashion the image of the postindustrial city in more complimentary terms, portraying it as home—as a Safe Space, in the words of the critic Farah Jasmine Griffin.[20] In musical practice, we see an intense interest in revisiting and revising musical materials from the Afro-modernist and Black Consciousness past.

Other "points of arrival" can be identified in the last fifty years of

African American history. But I have found these three—the Afro-modernist, Black Consciousness, and postindustrial—particularly salient in the production of black musical styles. In my view, there seems to be a pre-occupation with these moments within and surrounding musical discourse. Along with my recognition of the social energies circulating at these moments, "history" in this study is also accounted for in my attention to historiography. By accounting for the historiographical dimension of black music history, I seek to bring a much-needed historical self-consciousness to its study.

CULTURAL MEMORY: "DON'T PLAY THAT SONG FOR ME, 'CAUSE IT BRINGS BACK MEMORIES"

Samuel Floyd has written that cultural memory drives music, and music often drives cultural memory. I concur with this statement and join a growing body of other black scholars, writers, and intellectuals who have used "the personal" as an important aspect of their work. In addition, many visual and literary artists have claimed to use various forms of black music as important rhetorical devices in their creative style, although this influence is not always obvious. Indeed, music and memory have been potent forces in black literary culture. Writer James Baldwin, for example, wrote these words about his time in Switzerland, during which he pondered his first novel, *Go Tell It on the Mountain*, a work that draws heavily on his coming-of-age in Harlem as a young minister in a Holiness sect. Music became a powerful medium to access important cultural memories:

> There, in that alabaster landscape, armed with two Bessie Smith records and a typewriter, I began to re-create the life that I had first known as a child and from which I had spent so many years in flight. . . . Bessie Smith, through her tone and her cadence . . . helped me dig back to the way I myself must have spoken when I was a pickaninny, and to remember the things I had heard and seen and felt. I had buried them deep.[21]

Poet Maya Angelou describes the "sweet oil" of music as a healing balm in one volume of her autobiographical series. The music of the black church helps her to "find herself" during a worship service that she attends against the will of her white and increasingly domineering husband. Angelou's attention to the cultural work of the music is riveting and poetic. In her mind, the kinetic imperative of black religious music issues forth into the ritual celebration and presses her to a zone somewhere between fear and pleasure, between volition and diminished defenses:

> The spirituals and gospel songs were sweeter than sugar. I wanted to keep my mouth full of them and the sounds of my people singing fell like sweet oil in my ears. When the polyrhythmic hand-clapping began and the feet started tapping, when one old lady in a corner raised her voice to scream "O Lord, Lordy Jesus," I could hardly keep my seat. The ceremony drove into my body, to my fingers, toes, neck and thighs. My extremities shook under the emotional possession. I imposed my will on their quivering and kept them fairly still. I was terrified that once loose, once I lifted or lost my control, I would rise from my seat and dance like a puppet, up and down the aisles. I would open my mouth, and screams, shouts and field hollers would tear out my tongue in their rush to be free.[22]

In her novel *Jazz*, set in the 1920s, Toni Morrison uses secular music to help her portray an inner-city world of fleshly pleasure and "nasty closeness," one in which dressed-to-kill bodies sometimes did kill: "And where there was violence wasn't there also vice? Gambling. Cursing. A terrible and nasty closeness. Red dresses. Yellow shoes. And, of course, race music to urge them on."[23] Morrison has commented elsewhere on her use of cultural memory. Writing in 1986 in an essay titled "The Site of Memory," she explained her method of "literary archeology" to create works of fiction. By combining her memory, imagination, and invention, Morrison tries to access the unlettered world of past black generations.[24] An artifact such as a photograph can inspire her imaginative reconstruction; a single memory or a historical fact can trigger the journey into her own or others' interior life. Her novel *Song of Solomon*, for example, represents her attempt to re-create some of the inner life of her own father following his death. The result is a "kind of truth" that is less concerned with "publicly verifiable facts" than it is with the exploration of two worlds: "the actual and the possible."[25]

Similarly, literary critic and professor Henry Louis Gates's memoir, *Colored People*, is a response to grief over his mother's passing.[26] He describes vividly the world that existed behind the veil of segregation. As the following passage indicates, "colored music" belonged to an intricate network of social relationships, institutions, political imperatives, and culinary habits:

> The soul of that world was colored. Its inhabitants went to colored schools, they went to colored churches, they lived in colored neighborhoods, they ate colored food, they listened to colored music, and when

all that fat and grease finally closed down their arteries or made their hearts explode, they slept in colored cemeteries, escorted there by colored preachers: old black-suited Southern preachers, with shiny black foreheads and an insatiable desire for fried chicken, men for whom preaching is a personal call from God, a direct line on His celestial cellular phone. They dated colored, married colored, divorced and cheated on colored. And when they could, they taught at colored colleges, preached to colored congregations, trimmed colored hair on nappy heads, and, after the fifties, even fought to keep alive the tradition of segregated all-colored schools.[27]

The list continues. The feminist literary critic Deborah E. McDowell has written *Leaving Pipe Shop: Memories of Kin*, a poignantly told memoir of her coming of age in post–World War II Alabama. McDowell paints a vivid portrait of the expressive culture in the South that includes oral recitations, gospel music, and moving sermons. Filmmaker Spike Lee used his film *Crooklyn* to explore his childhood in Brooklyn, New York, in the 1960s and 1970s. Lee's postindustrial era musical score for *Crooklyn* includes a slate of 1970s R&B hits, many of which were collected in a double-CD set that was released simultaneously with the film.[28] This attention to the autobiographical not-so-distant past by cultural producers is telling enough, but I am particularly interested in the intersection of scholarship and personal history. What, in other words, is the relationship between the studied and the one studying?

CULTURAL MEMORY AND COMMUNITY THEATERS: WINDOWS OF OPPORTUNITY IN INTERPRETATION

Musical texts, musicologist Lawrence Kramer argues, don't usually disclose themselves fully: audiences go through complex interpretive acts to understand them. "The text does not give itself to understanding; it must be made to yield to understanding. A hermeneutic [or interpretive] window must be opened on it through which the discourse of our understanding must pass."[29] Although Kramer's ideas are based on European art music, they have import for the interpretation of race music.

I want to say one more word about my use of family narrative as a "site of memory," a concept I am borrowing from the French historian Pierre Nora and the novelist Toni Morrison. While many studies exist on "the" African American family, few studies, if any, have used family narrative as part of a theoretical frame in scholarship on African American music and its attending cultural practices. Yet cultural forms such as tales, stories, and music (especially the *performative* aspects of such) function as reservoirs in which cultural memories reside. These memories allow social identities to be knowable, teachable, and learnable. And most important, the cultural, communal, and family memories associated with forms like music (the "musicking," as Christopher Small put it)[30] often become standards against which many explore and create alternative and highly personal identities for themselves. Looking at family or group consciousness in this light offers us one way to uncover some of the experiences through which individuals— and by extension ethnic groups—construct meaning in musical "acts." Moreover, family narrative expands our knowledge of musical practices into other realms of experience and musical activities. My strategy complements and complicates, for example, the "professional" realm in which many musical studies rest: the reflections of the musicians themselves, the popularity chart histories of a specific piece, and the written criticism that surrounds a musical style.

While African Americans certainly share a great many of the same attitudes and sensibilities as other Americans, their collective "American experience" has also been a specific one, producing subjective cultural memories that have reciprocal and powerful relationships with cultural forms such as black music. As Floyd argues, "All black music making is driven by and permeated with the memory of things from the cultural past and that recognition of the viability of such memory should play a role in the perception and criticism of works and performances of black music."[31]

I use narratives from oral history and ethnographic observations gathered from my own extended family of origin in order to tease out some of the meanings created by this interplay of music, memory, and history. As I explained earlier in this chapter, cultural memories of African American family and community life in the 1960s and 1970s influence my subjective understanding of black music as shaped continually by community sensibilities. My "informants," though I think the use of such a scientific term sounds trite here, are suggestive of a constituency forming an important part of postwar black music's audience base. Their stories are like those of many others: they tell of migration from the Deep South to the urban North, of building new lives within the context of a starkly new environment, and seeing their expressive cultural practices reproduced with differences by their offspring. As I stated above, the earlier narrative itself raises myriad issues, theories, and musical texts for exploration. Furthermore, by including the voices of one family and not "the" African American family, I can provide something of the complex habitus that comprises the private performance (and practice) of blackness. This strategy should not be seen as an attempt to authorize or authenticate my views about black music over those of others. I simply want to provide specific information from which more general or universal conclusions might be drawn.

Inasmuch as musicians' "professional" sites of memory have been privileged in traditional histories of African American music, my attention to family narrative (and other community theaters) brings a new dimension to the "folk-commerce-art" figuration into which many music studies are locked. This intervention does not sidestep the tension between these three domains but offers a new slant on their relationship. As I stated earlier, in my family, aficionados who were certainly invested in the "artiness" of jazz partied cheek to jowl with others whose primary musical tastes diverged from their own. I am thus arguing that family narrative offers my Afro-cultural poetics a kind of ethnographic perspective—a commitment to lived experience—that will, I hope, shed light on ethnicity's role in the production of musical meaning. But I also want to stress that the other community theaters play an equal role in getting at meaning, although my use of family here is certainly the most controversial community theater discussed in this scholarly study.

I should point out that my goal is not to exclude or devalue the dynamic reception histories of race music among other groups. Indeed, I want to offer a varied and nuanced explanation of the various meanings that race music generated for its audiences. As Susan McClary has observed about the Western art music tradition, research that considers first a cultural practice's historical and specific context carries the benefit of broader subsequent readings. She writes: "Understanding this repertory [Western art music] as the product of European males during a particular period of history helps to clear space for appreciating other repertories likewise as products of other groups in other times and places."[32]

Other studies on black musical history have relied on sources that privileged either the "discovery" of black music by white listeners or the musings of a select group of black intellectuals whose experiences were often distinguished from the masses they sought to represent. I want to explore this history from a different perspective. I forward here an interdisciplinary musicology of postwar black musical style written from "the bottom up," or so I would like to think, which does not suggest that my own subjectivity can necessarily position this book as such.[33] But I do believe that the oral histories and ethnographic material I use help me sketch the emotional, social, and cultural thrust—indeed the poetics—of a "drylongso," particularized blackness.[34]

"ISN'T IT ROMANTIC?":
PRACTICE THEORY AND THE PRACTICE OF BLACKNESS

In addition to the history and memory modes that I have discussed above, other premises and assumptions inform my interpretations. Because of the intense recent interest in black expressive culture in all the humanistic fields and social sciences, it is important for me to position my arguments within and against this virtual explosion of work. While I do not want to lead my readers into theoretical Never-Never Land, I believe the recent course of scholarship on black culture makes this "pause for the cause" necessary. One of the overarching theoretical frameworks governing my analysis is practice theory. A theory of practice comprises two kinds of analysis. On the one hand, it considers the ways in which historical subjects, cultural categories, and various aspects of subjectivity are shaped by structure or "the system." This aspect of practice theory seeks to understand what kinds of identities are made available or fashioned by cultural and historical discourses. On the other hand, practice theory tries to identify how real people in real time resist or engage a given system. This negotiation of the system may in the end produce the same phenomenon or "reproduction." Or it may produce something new. By using ethnographic work of some kind, this second impulse of practice theory looks at people doing things in the world at specific historical moments and tries to understand "how what they are doing or have done will or will not reconfigure the world they live in."[35]

Issues on both sides of the practice theory dyad have a direct influence on the central issue addressed in the present study: the issue of meaning and black music. Generally speaking, studies of African American music have always talked about the link between "the people" and the musical practice. Scholars, musicians, and audiences have made this link seem so indelible that recently, some observers have found it profitable to "deconstruct" this relationship, making claims that it has been overstated. In other words, instead of bringing into sharper relief the significance of black musical styles to African American identity, some believe that this constitutes "essentialism." Another criticism states that too much emphasis has been placed on the idea of a homogeneous racial or ethnic experience and that this represents a romantic view of group identity. Practice theory, in my view, helps us to pay careful attention to the ways in which in-group identity can be both "system" and structure—the thing to be negotiated or resisted—and the agent making meaning within the larger system of hegemony and power structures.

African Americans have continually (re)articulated, questioned, abandoned, played with, and reinforced their ethnic identities through vernacular musical practices and many other activities. Since "the black vernacular has assumed the singular role as the black person's ultimate sign of difference,"[36] then black vernacular music has emerged as a most conspicuous mode of signification in this realm of activity. Black vernacular musical styles and the various cultural practices surrounding them have existed as historically important modalities through which African Americans have expressed various conceptions of "ethnicity." This relationship does not simply represent, as some would argue, black folks' yearning for a transhistorical, romanticized, uncontested, or even fictive past. The process of repetition and revision that characterizes these musical styles shows how black musicians and audiences have continually established a unified and dynamic "present" through music.[37]

Thus, they have refashioned through music, and other cultural practices, the idea of blackness, with what poet, playwright, and jazz critic Amiri Baraka (a.k.a. LeRoi Jones) called a "changing same" at various historical junctures. My work argues, as Baraka's did, that black music "makes reference to a central body of cultural experience." At the same time, I should mention that I question several points made in Baraka's well-known essay "The Changing Same (R&B and New Black Music)." These points include Baraka's uneasiness about the various modalities through which African American ethnicity has been expressed, such as Christianity and commercialism; his belief in the existence of an unmediated, "pure" blackness; and the mystical language with which he portrays African American culture (not to mention his bent for overstating his case, as in the statement, "Black People move in almost absolute openness and strength").[38] Inasmuch as Baraka's essay articulates a historically specific ideology, we can appreciate what kind of cultural work it achieved in that historical moment. Some found such rhetoric empowering; others found the idea of pure blackness, for example, much too confining and exclusive. But such ideas have currency today and are thus open to a contemporary critique. I argue that such a critique generates a better understanding of "*blackness as practice*," or blackness as a dynamic process of cultural and ideological shape shifting. It can, in fact, operate as both structure and resistance in a theory of practice.[39]

Ethnic identities like African Americanness are, indeed, "socially constructed" yet powerful realities. They are the result of a multilayered cultural and historical dialogue. This dialogue involves two shifting forces: one that establishes and maintains a group's we-ness, and an external one that shapes its they-ness.[40] Moreover, ethnic identities represent thoroughly "modern" (as opposed to ancient) processes that employ cultural "mixing" and imaginative and quite selective uses of the past for present and future needs. The way that ethnicity passes itself off as ancient, natural, stable, and self-evident should be treated with a healthy dose of skepticism. What is generally thought of as "'folk' culture—especially during the past century—is actually *bricolage,* a cutting, pasting, and incorporating of various cultural forms the result of which becomes categorized into a racially or ethnically coded aesthetic hierarchy."[41]

Moreover, ethnicity is not a monolithic experience but one involving dynamic relationships among other aspects of one's identity: class status, gender, marital status, formal education, profession, religious beliefs, sexual orientation, age, geography, and other factors. Ethnicity, in other words, functions in much the same way as the musical practices do. Popular music (in actuality, all music) participates in a continual historical conversation, collecting important aspects of its meaning from dialogues between the present and the past.[42]

In fact, music provides an ideal site for exploration of the shifting terrain and process of black ethnicity. Or put another way: the aspects of identity mentioned above provide an excellent window into understanding what a musical style means to a specific audience and, in particular, how that meaning is conveyed. Americans' perceptions of their racial, ethnic, nationalistic, and religious identities, as well as their class statuses, have been unquestionably mediated by the various musical styles that have either appeared or been transplanted here since Africans and Europeans crossed the Atlantic.[43] These ideas about music and individual and group identities are passed along and transformed in both formal and informal ways, through history and memory, through institutions, and especially through cultural forms like music, literature, and mass media.[44]

My argument is that specific post–World War II musical "texts," as well as the discourses that surround them, do not simply reflect or symbolize the ethnicity process among African Americans; they are important sites within which the very process itself is worked out and negotiated. In other words, we need to understand something about how the musical forms under consideration "work." Music works not as a residual artifact of ethnic identity but as an important part of the materiality of ethnicity. And this function is not limited to ethnicity: it also involves how we experience our class status, our age, gender, sense of location and place, our daily activities, our rituals, rites of passage, and so on. This "invisible" function is part of what we as listeners find compelling, joyful, sad, off-putting, interesting, or boring about a particular piece or style of music.

As I have just stated, ethnic identity operates much the same way that musical practice does. First, each participates in a continuous historical conversation; they glean important traces of meaning from the dialogue occurring between the present and the past. Musical gestures, genres, and styles are performed; likewise, ethnicity and nearly every other aspect of identity should be considered performances. Blackness doesn't really exist until it is done, or "practiced," in the world. Musical styles and ethnicities are loaded signifiers, each doing important cultural work in the social world. Musical codes and ethnic markers are rather unstable: what they mean depends on many contingencies, such as historical context, geographic location, who is uttering them, and who is interpreting them. The perceived boundaries surrounding ethnicity and musical styles are rigorously policed. Sometimes we can't believe our eyes or our ears: Can white R&B singer Bonnie Raitt *really* sing the blues? Can white scholars *really* write about black music? Is biracial pop singer Mariah Carey *really* black? Can black scholars *really* achieve the "proper" objective distance from black subject matter? These questions are more than academic rhetoric: people struggle with them constantly in all sectors of American society.

Two prevalent attitudes make discussion of these questions contentious. First, "blackness" as a subcultural ethnic identity within the broader American one—and even in comparison to other, "white" ethnicities—has proven to be a volatile topic since the Emancipation and especially since the Civil Rights period of the 1950s and 1960s. Many, for example, have forwarded arguments that the idea of black cultural identity undermines cherished ideologies of American society, such as pluralism, thereby corroding the fabric of our social mosaic and even hindering the social progress and assimilation of African Americans themselves. Second, some scholars have rightly argued that all identities are socially constructed by a system or a structure. But some of this research underplays the "realness" of the lived experience of these identities. We must account for both structure and agency in the historical record.

All this talk about fluidity, indeed the idea of ethnicity as a process and not a static existence, does not prevent our understanding how people experience group identity from a reified, though contested, "center." And cultural practices like music are often perceived, interpreted, and evaluated from such a position. Furthermore, audiences *do* recognize some musicians as "authentic," as virtuosos of key musical codes, gestures, and practices. But it is important to remind ourselves that a significant number of these musicians' stars never rise above their local scenes. The crowning achievement of their careers might be an "appreciation service" held in their honor for decades of faithfulness stationed behind a church organ, for a steady gig that becomes a neighborhood institution at the corner pub, or perhaps for a low-budget recording that generates little interest beyond the musician's immediate community. In such cases, of course, connecting these musicians' work with a localized, ethnic identity seems like an easy fit.

But even musicians whose careers become internationally recognized may be linked to an ethnic "center." To cite one example, in his autobiography, jazz trumpeter Dizzy Gillespie tries to set the record straight on a few of the misconceptions about bebop in the 1940s. Many aspects of the bebop movement, including the musicians' dress and speech, have been treated as if they were dramatic breaks from tradition. But Gillespie, concentrating on the conception that beboppers wore "wild clothes," shows how dealing with "everyday" people can produce a different reading of the bebop phenomenon: "Watch the fashions of the forties on the late show, long coats, almost down your knees and full trousers. I wore drape suits like everyone else and dressed no differently from the average leading man of the day."[45] The same was true, Gillespie argues, about the "bebop" language. He remembered their slang as being part of cultural expressions already present in the broader postwar black culture. In other words, what observers portrayed as belonging solely to the insular world of bebop specifically, Gillespie saw within the specific context of the culture of his "folk" at a particular historical moment.

RECONSTRUCTING "THE FOLK" IN BLACK VERNACULAR MUSIC

Hitherto, I have spoken of "African Americans" and "African American or black vernacular musical culture" as though these terms were unproblematic and uncontested. Cultural critics such as Robin D. G. Kelley, among many others, have argued against the idea of an autonomous "folk" untainted by the mass media or popular culture. They have, indeed, "deconstructed the folk," as the title of one of Kelley's penetrating articles suggests.[46] In addition, some have pointed out the cultural hierarchies embedded in the use of labels such as "folk," "popular," "mass," and "traditional." The word *authenticity* seems to strike a nerve among some critics because of its association with "essentialism," or the suggestion that something like a particular brand of musical ability is innate or the result of one's biological makeup. In such critiques, terms like *the folk* carry pejorative connotations. It indexes a community supposedly trapped in a time warp. They are presumed to be preindustrial, agrarian, and untouched by the modern threat of mass-media culture. Scholars have rightly argued against such ideas, tracing their origins to both nineteenth-century folklore and pseudoscience.

"Vernacular," however, has emerged as a decidedly less controversial label. "The" vernacular has a more elastic quality to it than "folk." It can convey the sensibilities of a subculture or even those of an entire nation. Vernacular music can comprise folk, popular, or mass culture, as these terms are understood. Despite this elasticity, however, it still retains a sense of cultural hierarchy, and its implicit value is unquestionably implied. American vernacular music, for example, carries a sense of connection to the "common man," one born to a particular class, region, or racial group. Vernacular means "homegrown." It indexes a provincial outlook and not a cosmopolitan one. It can denote "American" and not the European "norm." It means "uncultivated" and approached "unselfconsciously." White ruling classes, it should be noted, are generally perceived to be devoid of a "vernacular" expression.[47]

While I am sympathetic to these critiques of the negative connotations of ideas like "the folk" and "the vernacular," I still find them useful up to a point. For one thing, I think that too much attention to the infrastructure of ideology (historical racism, pseudoscience) that determined the historical "they-ness" of the folk tends to gloss over, if not erase, the power of in-group identity, not to mention its pleasures. Moreover, to argue for a diversity of expression within black identity and to acknowledge various historical struggles for inclusion in its perceived center speak to its existence, in fact. As I will demonstrate below, attention to the specificity of context can diminish the totalizing quality of labels such as "folk." I believe that we can use these terms but at the same time convey their porous and flexible qualities in practice. One way to recognize the diversity of a culture's representation is to acknowledge that the scholar producing the representation has an identity, one that is involved in a dynamic relationship with "the studied" and with the final scholarly product.

THE MONOLITHIC BLUES MUSE?

As I have already mentioned, the idea of blues as African American cultural matrix has received a lion's share of attention together with some critical opposition among scholars. Objections to this idea are linked to the notion of a monolithic black folk, a notion I have already discussed. They argue instead for critical studies of African American culture to account for every dimension of human life such as gender, class, and sexuality. Certainly, we can achieve a more penetrating analysis of the music by factoring in other aspects of lived experience besides race and ethnicity. Attention to other dimensions of life will help us to build a vernacular theory but not one of romance.

I must reiterate here that while I recognize and share, to a large degree, the recent critical stance against a monolithic conception of black culture, I do want to rescue from the critical guillotine the idea of a collective black critique, a collective sensibility, however contested it may be. Together with the musical practices themselves, these critiques en masse not only keep venues of performance packed with paying customers; they continually fill churches and cause resilient musical techniques and tropes to circulate and recirculate across genres, historical periods, singers, and instrumentalists. Thus, for all of our academic enthusiasm to deconstruct monolithic impulses in the name of a diverse blackness, we must recognize that some cultural markers have remained remarkably stable in practice, albeit not in their precise meanings.

While my agenda may seem on the surface like a retro or reactionary move to reclaim some of the "mythic romance" of days gone by, I am, in fact, arguing for an understanding of the social and historical contingency of musical value. To this end, I discuss the formal logic of musical performances not simply to prove their "greatness" or universality. Rather, I want to explore their signifying potential *within* a specific social history at the nexus of musical pleasure, religious zeal, sensual stimulation, and counter-hegemonic resistance. To this end, I ask throughout this book, What modes of black subjectivity (namely, gender, class, and race) might have been explored, negotiated, or rejected by historical actors at a particular time?

The aesthetic realm is an excellent place to investigate this dialectic, because artistic expressions and even formal scholarship always tell us much about human agency. In midcentury African American literature, for example, there was a lively discourse about the struggles for an emerging African American sense of agency in modern American life. These struggles were played out and discussed vividly in novels such as Richard Wright's *Native Son*, Ann Petry's *The Street*, Dorothy West's *The Living Is Easy*, and James Baldwin's *Go Tell It on the Mountain*, and in documentary/social science–based studies such as Gunnar Myrdal's *An American Dilemma: The Negro Problem and Modern Democracy*, and Drake and Cayton's *Black Metropolis*.[48] These books paid close attention to everyday-life issues and to the various cultural and social institutions in which everyday life unfolded: family life, nightclubs, storefront churches, dance halls, and so on. Authors paid specific attention to gender relationships in courtship and marriage and among siblings, especially as they intersected with issues surrounding social class status. Migration and the dialectic between southern and northern "Negro" life emerged as key themes in this literature.[49]

In music these issues were also central. While black musicians participated in a number of stylistic idioms (such as Western art music), a strong case can be made about the primacy of the blues modality within African American culture at midcentury. The primacy of the twelve-bar blues pattern, the bluesy approach to melodic invention, and the troping elements identified by Murray and Floyd in African American music are much like the centrality of the sonata allegro form in eighteenth- and nineteenth-century music. The latter was, of course, the accepted paradigm for instrumental Western art music during that time. Within this form, composers could express their subjective, stylistic idiosyncrasies to knowing audiences. As Susan McClary has argued, they could reveal "depth, sensitivity, interiority."[50] In a similar way blues, R&B, jazz, and gospel artists expressed artistic authority and mastery, virtuosity, sensuality, and devotion—all within the blues-troping conventions.

SUBJECT POSITIONS AND POSITIONED SUBJECTS

I'd like to return to where I began and tie up the three strands of history, memory, and theory. I opened the first chapter with a series of selected experiences from my past that culminated (in the narrative, at least) with my father's second line, after which I outlined more theoretical issues. The use of this memoir mode and the interviews conducted among my direct ancestors and presented in subsequent chapters helps to make my own biases, quirks, and individual rhythms a self-conscious factor in my critical discourse. I believe that all critical writing reveals as much about the writer as it does about the object being studied. I am thus giving my readers an idea about the historical and material grounding of my own critical and musical biases. I hope to strike a "universal chord" about music and meaning among my readership through this methodology.

Most studies are conceived to understand the relationship between two arenas: the creation of the musical object on the one hand, and the lived experience of musicians and their audiences on the other. In addition to my own critical biases, I think about a third discourse in this book that is equally important: the relationship between the subject positions of the various scholars/critics and the subject(s) under consideration. While this kind of thinking runs the risk of "dating" this study, I choose to cut my losses for the benefit of situating my own thinking within the historical moment at which I am writing. In addition to the musical styles discussed, I want future readers to understand something about what it means to be writing black music research as an African American at this time.

As anthropologist Lila Abu-Lughod has argued, researchers who work on their own group of origin stand "on shifting ground," making "clear that every view is a view from somewhere and every act of speaking a speaking from somewhere."[51] I have resisted dressing in an objectifying "anthropological self" in the present study, choosing rather to work from the strength of my own subject position. Stomping the blues in Daddy's second line reminded me of the particularity of my own life experiences and thus my "particularized" critical outlook. All critics of culture, I should reiterate, seem to be traveling a similar road to self-discovery. And as Stevie Wonder's narrator in the tune "I Wish" seems to understand, history and memory may be our most powerful tools in building a contemporary black-music criticism.

3 "It's Just the Blues"

Race, Entertainment, and the Blues Muse

The blues is everywhere.
Auntie Totsie Ross, 1996

Certainly, if race is a construction, as some have argued, then in the twentieth century, the mass media is its primary building site.
Barbara Dianne Savage, *Broadcasting Freedom: Radio, War, and the Politics of Race, 1938–1948*

In July 1948, singer Dinah Washington recorded "Long John Blues," in which she boasted about her dentist, whose height topped seven feet.[1] Among other notable charms, Washington sings about the dentist's trusty "drill," which he pulls out and guarantees will fill his willing patient's cavity. She reports that Long John has entreated her to open wide, but not before he gives her a shot of Novocain. "Every woman just can't stand the pain," he explains. Washington delivers the song with classy, matter-of-fact understatement and reserve. She doesn't whoop, holler, or bray the lyrics but sings with a quiet sass, allowing the tension of sexual double-entendre running throughout the song to lend the performance its smoky sensuality.

The lyrics (written by Tommy George) fly in the face of the respectability and "proper" public deportment expected of women at midcentury. This is especially true since public activities like entertainment (especially musical performance) have historically constituted an arena of diligent moral surveillance. This has been particularly true of women's activities in music.[2] Historically, the black middle class has leveled the most sustained (but by no means exclusive) critique of black expressive culture in this regard. It sought for much of the twentieth century to shape and reshape the broader American public's images of African American people and their cultural practices.

The New Negro movement of the first decades of the twentieth century represents a well-known intervention of this type. Those involved in this movement purported to re-create the public image of African Americans, and through these activities they sought to shape favorable public opinion of them and other black people of the world. Wide circulation of stereotypes about African Americans in the broader society positioned the New Negro movement as major reconstructive surgery and not merely a facelift. This image makeover became a primary thrust of black twentieth-century intellectualism.[3] Thus, the most prominent New Negro intellectual would have cringed at the idea of a well-known female singer such as Washington celebrating her (presumably black lover's) sexual prowess and the size of his "drill." And the fact that she sings about so enjoying the dentist's services that she's requested weekly visits would only make matters worse in their eyes.

But in the 1940s, this kind of "blues-ing" became standard practice. "Long John Blues" is a twelve-bar blues, one of many being recorded at this time. The ascendancy and importance of the kinds of black vernacular music represented by Washington's recording constitute one of the most significant developments to occur in black cultural production after World War II. The numerous guises of the blues became for many almost synonymous with African American musical culture. As Samuel Floyd has argued persuasively, the blues stands as a supremely important musical system—its lyrical, harmonic, and melodic conventions served as a trope in much of twentieth-century black music history in America.[4] Floyd traces the history of bluesing from Africa, through activities like the ring shout from slave culture and into genres like country blues, urban blues, gospel, jazz, R&B, and even the classical music of black composers, showing the malleability and, indeed, the tenacity of the blues muse.

But some scholars have recently questioned the status of the blues as a key symbol of black vernacular authenticity on grounds that stem from larger critiques of "authenticity" and "essentialism." Music scholar Ronald Radano writes that the literary criticism of Houston Baker and Henry Louis Gates—work that these scholars claim is grounded in black vernacular music—embraces "romantic myths of music's super-structural capacities without acknowledging how these myths had developed out of the racialist language of folk authenticity." Radano argues that Baker, Gates, and others of their ilk perpetuate "an outmoded, nineteenth-century belief in music's ability to rise above the circumstances of political, cultural, and social change, to overcome, as an enduring continuity, the grand discursive web of racialist representations." Historian Evelyn Brooks Higginbotham has turned her critique inward, to the vernacular itself. She contests the idea that the blues stands as the sole signifier of black musical authenticity, of black ethnicity generally, or of black working-class status specifically. She argues that religious music and even recorded sermons are also important in this regard. And literary critic Ann du Cille writes that criticism that considers the blues as the primary sign for authentic blackness excludes the literary muse of the black middle class and devalues critical frameworks not based on black vernacular expressive culture.[5]

Certainly, the critical interventions represented by these scholars warn us against overemphasizing the blues muse in African American culture and criticism. At the same time, however, I think it is fruitful to recognize the importance of the blues modality in black culture. It is, indeed, true that the romance of folk authenticity has been extremely influential in shaping how we think about race. But we must ask, Is the romantic authenticity disparaged in scholarship identical to the in-group consciousness upon which Baker, Gates, and others have founded their vernacular-based criticism? Can we, somehow, acknowledge the influence of blues modality in black music history as singular and ever-present, yet not precluding other possibilities?

Historian Tera Hunter, examining the role of entertainment and nighttime leisure in the lives of the black working class in 1910s Atlanta, notes the emergence of the blues and its *dual* capacity as a reservoir of the historical consciousness of African Americans *and* their emerging modernist outlook. Subsequent musical refigurations of the blues tradition have also proved to be durable yet flexible sites for, as Hunter puts it, "African-American working-class self-understandings in the modern world."[6] Dinah Washington's open expression of sexuality in "Long John Blues" was, of course, not new to the blues tradition. Female singers of the classic blues style of the 1920s, for example, sang routinely and quite frankly of a range of erotic, domestic, and political sensibilities.[7] But the meanings of such expressions are always historically contingent and socially constituted, and thus, I want to explore in this chapter the specific context of the 1940s as a profound moment of African American culture building and identity formation, especially with regard to the blues muse.

Recordings such as "Long John Blues" and others helped to shape the social reality of many African Americans. Indeed, as the historian Barbara Savage points out in the second epigraph at the opening of this chapter, the mass media became an important space for this social energy. The blues muse from the "agrarian South" trekked northward at midcentury migration, and performers mixed and matched it with other styles from the "urban North." These activities created a field of new and varied rhetoric that laid the foundation for numerous developments of the next half century of cultural production in the United States and the world. Below I discuss several examples of recordings and musicians that muse the blues in various ways. These examples demonstrate that while blues musing existed across stylistic idioms, it also generated certain tensions in religious contexts, became a space for gender-specific expression, and provided a basis for what would be perceived by many as modernist, abstract innovation.

THE MIGRATING BLUES MUSE

I want to set the stage for what follows with a brief discussion about the ways in which the "urban North" and the "agrarian South" became mythic sites of cultural memory and cultural production. Music embodies this social energy. The North is signified by gestures and practices associated in the popular imagination with the urbane, sophisticated, and cosmopolitan. The South is referenced by musical gestures that evoke the southern, agrarian past of African Americans. These two rhetorical fields do not stand in direct opposition to each other (such as in the binary opposition represented in the classic dilemma of Du Boisian double-consciousness, in which two warring souls are viewed as irreconcilable). The relationship I am describing exists rather as a powerfully rich and complicated dialectic. Furthermore, this dialectic (and the continuum between these imaginary points) is inextricably linked to what I called the practice of blackness in the previous chapter or, as Manthia Diawara put it, the "compelling performance" of blackness.[8] The southern-based idiolect, for example, can be performed logocentrically, in oral discourse, or in musical gesture. My analysis of the recording "It's Just the Blues," for example, shows how the fusion of "southern codes" and the "suave" gestures of the urbane northern rhetoric constitutes an important principle in African American musical production at midcentury. Moreover, as we shall see, music became an important mode of expression for class and gender issues as well; but they were displaced within the blues-troping North-South dialogue.

I should make two important points here. First, I want to make clear that my use of the qualifier *rhetorical* when talking about the northern and southern codes seeks to center these ideas in the realm of performance. These musical gestures do not necessarily stand for one-to-one, airtight homologies with the North or South, urban or country, and so on. I am exploring, rather, the process through which musical styles and gestures were associated with such meanings. My second point concerns the southern past to which I have referred above. As I have stated, inasmuch as many of the conceptual approaches to music making embedded in these performance tropes (especially those that fall in the southern category) can be traced to similar ones in West and Central Africa, scholars have produced a large body of work theorizing this connection.

But since my work explores the *ethnographic* "truth" of musical meaning, we must reconsider the extent to which historical Africa really figured into the signifying effect of post–World War II black vernacular music. Rather than merely reveal the very real anthropological and historical relationship of Africa and African American musical practices, race musics signified for many of their musicians and audiences the free interplay of signs of the rhetorical North and South at the postwar moment. And other Afro-modernist modalities can be heard in many recordings from the period: in the new articulations of the virtuoso solo "voice" that appeared in bebop, jump blues, and gospel; in the developments in accompaniment styles that supported those solo voices; and in the abstracting, sanctifying, and jumping gestures that occurred in the blues idioms. As I shall demonstrate below, the "commercial" status of a recording did not frustrate the cultural work achieved by its formal conventions.

"IT'S JUST THE BLUES":
CODES, RHETORIC, AND MIGRATION

> Come here pretty baby, sit your fine, mellow body on my knee
> Good to me woman, sit your fine mellow body on my knee
> I wanna tell all these cats baby, how you been sending me.
>
> I got the blues baby, and I'm feeling mighty fine
> I got the blues baby, and I'm feeling mighty fine
> I'm full of my good whiskey, and I'm high as a Georgia pine.[9]

When the Four Jumps of Jive recorded "It's Just the Blues" in September 1945, they inaugurated Mercury Records, the first independent record label to appear following the end of World War II. The lyrical and musical content of "It's Just the Blues," its performance rhetoric, the backgrounds of the composers and performers, and its appearance in a specific historical moment and geographic setting have important implications for the criticism of black music of the 1940s. The Four Jumps of Jive consisted of vocalist and pianist Jimmy Gilmore; lead guitarist Bernardo Dennis; and rhythm guitarist Ellis Hunter. The bassist, Willie Dixon (1915–1992), became the band's most notable member. A native of Vicksburg, Mississippi, Dixon migrated to Chicago and, after a brief career as a prizefighter, began a musical career, singing in gospel quartets and playing bass in secular settings. Dixon's compositions and performance techniques, along with those of Muddy Waters, would help to define in the next decade not only the Chicago urban blues sound but early rock 'n' roll as well. "It's Just the

Blues" was composed by Gilmore and Richard M. Jones, the artists and repertory man for Mercury Records, who, like Dixon and many other black musicians in race musics, had experience in gospel music.[10]

The tune is a twelve-bar blues repeated over eleven choruses that alternate between two vocal strains followed by one instrumental. It opens with an entire instrumental chorus of musical codes and gestures drawn from black vernacular and popular sources. The most prominent of these features is a shuffle-boogie beat, created by Dixon's heavily accented chord outlines and Hunter's steady, rhythm-guitar strumming that interlocks with the bass line; they continue this pattern throughout the recording. Bernardo Dennis's sparse melodic figures and Gilmore's vocal declamations *(Well-we-e-e-e-ell-well!)* round out the introductory chorus. The absence of a drummer in this rhythm section leaves enough of the soundscape free to give the performance the characteristic lightness of many jump blues combos. Since this group was considered a "cocktail outfit" working in a Chicago nightclub at the time of this recording, it is likely that they opted out of having a drummer for economic, or perhaps even logistic, reasons. If Gilmore's declamatory style during the introduction brings a "country" or rural modality to this decidedly urban-sounding recording, the remainder of his performance highlights the tension between these two ideals. Gilmore sings in what might be called a "blues-croon" style, which, while capturing some of the immediate emotional impact of the "flat-footed" blues belters of the day, also signified a kind of urbane sophistication. Another gesture in Gilmore's blues-croon presentation is a warbling technique that he employs on various words, especially those falling on the lowered third, fifth, and seventh scale degrees. Gilmore securely mixes these rhetorical gestures. The lyrical content of the song continues this code-fusion aesthetic. In the first two vocal choruses appearing in the epigraphs above, we learn that, like many other blues lyrics, the narrative poetry of "It's Just the Blues" will be cast in the arena of the body, in sexual politics. The protagonist speaks directly to the object of his desire; he is feeling amorous, and his "good whiskey" is obviously helping his case of "blues," which in this case is not a bad thing, because he's "got the blues" and is "feeling mighty fine." Gilmore's use of Afro-urban argot—describing his female friend as "fine" and "mellow" and his male companions as "cats," her influence on him as "sending"—centers his rhetoric within the up-to-date field of contemporaneous African American dialect. Yet the simile "high as a Georgia pine" and Gilmore's exclamatory *He-e-e-e-e-y ya!* concluding the second chorus highlight the code-fusion between urban and rural (read southern) references.

These code-fusions continue in the third chorus. During the vocal choruses, guitarist Bernardo Dennis plays simple riff figures beneath Gilmore's melodic lines, adding to the sense of propulsion derived from Dixon's and Hunter's rhythmic foundation. In the fourth, seventh, and tenth choruses, Dennis plays pentatonic scale–based, electric guitar solos, none of which is necessarily highly technical in the Charlie Christian sense but draw attention to the instrumentalist as the central "voice" in the text. During all of these solo spotlights, Gilmore exclaims stock phrases that might well be heard in everyday conversation such as, "Rock on," "Well, well," "Knock me out," "He-e-e-y now," "If that's the way you feel, it's a good deal." One might interpret these solos in several ways: as the missing voice of Gilmore's love interest, as a gesture toward jazz solo virtuosity, or perhaps as musically contrasting statements in the narrative. We never hear what has gone wrong with the relationship portrayed here. But the progression of the song makes clear that it is not ideal, as Gilmore exclaims: "Come back here, pretty baby, talk some of that sweet jive to me. Come back here, pretty baby, talk some of that sweet jive to me. And I don't want you to hand me none of that stuff, talking about 'things ain't what they used to be.'" In fact, by the end of the piece, Gilmore decides to leave his love interest, because he doesn't want to be played for a fool. This reference to the song title, "Things Ain't What They Used to Be," indeed, even the name of this group, the Four Jumps of Jive, firmly positions the lyrical aspect of this recording within the social web of black urban culture. But as we have seen, other features referencing the "country" or the South are also present. In order to explore some of the meanings that these code-fusions may have generated, it helps to situate this text more firmly in its historical moment.

The subtle crisscrossing of stylistic borders in "It's Just the Blues" signified profoundly. *Billboard* reported in October 1945 that the Chicago-based Mercury label had signed only Negro artists, including two "cocktail units" such as the Four Jumps of Jive and Bill Samuels and His Cats 'N' Jammers; singers June Richmond, Sippie Wallace, and Karl Jones; and pianist Albert Ammons. Mercury would eventually cast a wide net for customers—a diverse range of American popular musics filled its catalog. But the company also deliberately courted a specific clientele: not the flood of southern black migrants who streamed into Chicago throughout the 1940s, but "the established South Side population which already prided itself in its urban sophistication."[11] Indeed, Mercury's producers appeared sensitive to the intrablack cultural dynamics caused in part by the migration and how elements of musical style could signify to them. The musicians responded to the diversity of musical tastes among the black communities created by geographic segregation. And they recognized Chicago's position as a commercial center, as an important site of black cultural production since the 1920s, and as home to a thriving network of churches, theaters, lounges, nightclubs, and dance halls, as well as a vibrant (and, for the most part, underdocumented) "house party" culture. Therefore Mercury executives' simple business decision to carve out a musical niche in this specific market rested on their understanding of some of the rapid, intense social and cultural shifts occurring in urban centers such as Chicago, New York, and Los Angeles and in the nation as a whole.

"It's Just the Blues" was drenched in Afro-modernist sensibilities. The recording codified a specific moment of urbanity for African Americans. Even the "commercialism" of the piece is suggestive of the aggressively new economic clout of African Americans, particularly those who lived in the urban North. A specific, and quite "modern," audience base interpreted the narrative codes of "It's Just the Blues." One of the important points here involves how bodies signified both in this piece and in others like it. The public celebration (some would say objectification) of the woman's "fine" and "mellow" body in the lyrics, the alcohol-induced "blues" in the protagonist's body, and even the black (and very likely white) bodies that without doubt danced to this recording marked a new beginning, a second Reconstruction, and a new cultural politics in African American history. If one of the legacies of nineteenth-century minstrelsy involved the public degradation of the black body in the American entertainment sphere, then one hundred years after minstrelsy's emergence, African Americans used this same signifier to upset a racist social order and to affirm in the public entertainment and the private spheres their culture and humanity. Although it has some precedent, the new attitude was so prevalent that it represents a huge departure from earlier modes of "racial uplift," especially the "politics of respectability" championed by the black professional and upper-class citizens, who sought to discipline black bodies into bourgeois submission.[12] A reliable measure of this new attitude in the realm of music can be found in the black newspaper the *Chicago Defender*. Coverage of African American music during the 1940s shifted significantly toward the entertainment–dance music field and away from the activities of blacks in classical music, who had at one time dominated the society pages of the *Defender*.

POLITICS, TWISTING, AND JAZZ IN THE CHURCH

Although gospel (or better, gospel-blues) has stood for many as the quintessential sign of the "vernacular," the oral, or folk impulses within the race music family of styles, it had gone "Afro-modern" well before midcentury. Gospel's success, on one level, provides yet another example of the emerging economic clout of African Americans as both artists and consumers. The career of composer Rev. William Brewster (ca. 1897–1987) shows how postwar economics converged with politics and musical style. Anthony Heilbut argues that "Brewster managed to insinuate themes of social progress and political struggle into his songs without turning them into watered-down propaganda, or gospel agitprop."[13] A good example of that sensibility resides in Mahalia Jackson's recording "I Will Move on Up a Little Higher," which Brewster composed.[14] Through the imagery of a "Christian climbing the ladder to heaven," the song encourages black upward mobility, hence reflecting the postwar Afro-modernist sentiments:

> The fight for rights here in Memphis was pretty rough on the Black church . . . and I wrote that song "Move on Up a Little Higher." . . . We'll have to move in the field of education. Move into the professions and move into politics. Move in anything that any other race has to have to survive. That was a protest idea and inspiration. I was trying to inspire Black people to move up higher. Don't be satisfied with the mediocre. . . . Before the freedom fights started, before the Martin Luther King days, I had to lead a lot of protest meetings. In order to get my message over, there were things that were almost dangerous to say, but you could sing it.[15]

Brewster's compositions enjoyed huge popularity over the years, providing gospel performers like Mahalia Jackson, Clara Ward, Marion Williams, and others with vehicles for some of their best-known recordings. Thus, despite the general view that gospel music has sprung unmediated from the authentic consciousness of the folk, its history is entangled in its commercial status, in its sociopolitical significance, and in its artistic component, such as the literary act of composing.

"I Will Move on Up a Little Higher" debuted in 1946 on a special program to honor Lucie Campbell, an important gospel composer and music director of the Baptist Training Union Congress. Mahalia Jackson sang on the program, which was held at Chicago's Olivet Baptist Church. It is culturally significant that Brewster's group, the Brewster Ensemble from Memphis, Tennessee, chose such a program to debut the song. Gospel performers, composers, and audiences have used this time-honored tradition to gauge a song's effectiveness since the urban gospel tradition appeared. In 1932, for example, Thomas Dorsey and his regular singer Theodore Frye introduced the important composition "Take My Hand, Precious Lord" at the Ebenezer Baptist Church in Chicago. Dorsey said of the performance: "The folk went wild. They broke up the church. Folk were shouting everywhere." Folklore and performance studies scholars characterize such events as important cultural interactions that can tell us much about the core values of a group.[16] And "Move on Up" (which became Mahalia Jackson's signature piece) was the kind of musical text that circulated postwar Afromodernist values throughout the black urban archipelago.

As Brewster noted above, he composed "Move on Up" to speak to African Americans in the specific social milieu of pre–Civil Rights Memphis. The entire country would some twenty years later see that southern city as a focal point in the Civil Rights movement when, in 1968, Dr. Martin Luther King Jr. was assassinated while lending support to a sanitation workers' strike. As early as the late 1920s Brewster had established himself as a progressive leader in the city, fighting the segregationists and providing educational opportunities for black ministers, missionaries, and other "Christian workers."[17] "Move on Up" was originally written for one of Brewster's religious pageants or passion plays. Brewster maintained that the entire piece— lyrics, melody, and harmony—came to him in one flow, and shortly thereafter he taught the song to his principal vocal soloist, Queen C. Anderson.[18] But it was the Queen of Gospel, Mahalia Jackson, who, according to Brewster, "knew what to do with it. She could throw the verse out there."[19]

Brewster set the piece with "a lot of bounce in it," a quality that he believed accounted for much of its popularity with contemporary audiences. The song is an unpretentious statement; much of it consists of a nonteleological vamp played by an organist and pianist. This convention features repetitive melodic, harmonic, and rhythmic materials but with spun-out lyrics that tend to "pile on one another." The singer provides her own call-and-response patterns: "I will move on up a little higher—meet Abraham and Isaac; move on up a little higher—meet the prophet Daniel; move on up a little higher—meet the Hebrew children." As Horace Clarence Boyer notes, "repetition is the strength of the performance" in this type of gospel song. But the improvisational skill of the vocalist is also crucial. That Jackson "knew what to do" with the song speaks to her mastery of gospel vocal techniques. Born in New Orleans and musically weaned in that city's black church culture and on blues race records, Jackson moved to Chicago as a teenager and brought a distinctively southern-style approach to gospel. Part of that southern sensibility involved the body in the vocals. For Jackson and other vocalists who cut their musical teeth in the South, "singing" and kinetic expression were one and the same act. Within northern, old-line churches in Chicago, however, such bodily demonstrations were not easily accepted. On the day of one of her first performances in one old-line church, Jackson fired the ire of its pastor, who rose and shouted: "Blasphemous! Get that twisting and that jazz out of his church!" Jackson countered, "This is the way we *sing* down South! I been singing this way all my life in church!"[20] Southern-born vocalist and preacher Theodore Frye also made his body an essential part of his personal gospel stylings when he teamed up with Thomas Dorsey. As Dorsey recalled,

> We teamed up and traveled through the South, East, and Midwest mak-ing the national meetings and winning the acclaim of every audience we sang and played to. He was doin' it [walking] in Mississippi, but he didn't have the right material to walk to 'til he found me. [He] was known as the "Walking Gospel Singer."
>
> They got to the place if Frye didn't walk, they'd holler at him, "Walk, Frye, walk!" Then Frye'd start struttin'. He would walk and sing; I would stand up at the piano and pound the beat out to his marching steps. Frye would strut; women would fall out—don't know whether he looked good or they were just happy. Frye could get over anywhere with anything.[21]

Much to the delight (and disdain) of many, what some northern church-goers no doubt experienced as southern sensuality was ultimately recon-textualized, revised, restyled, and refigured by the northern experience. During the 1930s Mahalia Jackson worked with Thomas Dorsey, who was at that time forging and spreading with evangelical zeal the new "gospel-blues" style, which itself blended Georgian and Chicagoan sensibilities. When "Move on Up" debuted in Chicago on Lucie Campbell's program, it was the hit of the evening; when Jackson recorded it on the New York–based Apollo label in 1947, the song provided the singer with her first huge commercial success. Jackson was soon widely recognized as gospel's first superstar; she toured Europe in 1952, appeared in films, and recorded a string of hits for Columbia Records.[22] Thus, the Memphis–New Orleans–Chicago–New York connection in the creation, dissemination, and reception of "Move on Up," the virtuoso vocal standards set by Jackson's performance, and the notion of black progress in the song make it a potent, Afro-modernist cultural text. Once again, the art–mass-culture–folk boundaries were troubled through African American performance.

The sacred-secular debate spurred by gospel's populist success has dis-tinguished black religious music's history in America. In an 1819 book titled *Methodist Error, or Friendly Advice to Those Methodists Who Indulge in Extravagant Religious Emotions and Bodily Exercises*, the Reverend John F.

Watson warned of a "growing evil" among black churchgoers in Philadelphia. Through a thinly veiled anger, Watson described vividly a typical
worship scene: He heard highly improvised, repetitive singing—he called
it "short scraps of disjointed affirmations, pledges, or prayers, lengthened
out with long repetition *choruses*."[23] Making matters worse, he saw ecstatic
religious dancing that looked very much like its African counterpart accompanying the singing. Today we understand that Watson experienced an
emerging body of black religious songs and practices that would later be
called the Negro spirituals. They constituted for Watson a threat to "sober
christianity" and "rational devotion." His "friendly advice" called for black
worshippers to abandon such activities.

Of course, they did not. African American Christians have cultivated
through the decades a dynamic tradition of music making, and each expression of it has attracted strident criticism. Much of the controversy has concerned the constant exchange of musical sensibilities between secular and
sacred by gospel, popular, and jazz performers, a busy intercourse that has
marked the history of African American music. A little over a hundred years
after Watson's *Methodist Error* appeared, the following candid testimony of
a gentleman hearing black gospel music for the first time expresses the
same indignation at gospel music's voracious muse:

> It is night. My errand brings me through a busy street of the Negro sec-
> tion in a city having a colored population of seven thousand. Suddenly, I
> am arrested by bedlam which proceeds from the open transom of a store
> front whose windows are smeared to intransparency. What issues forth
> is conglomeration itself—a syncopated rhythmic mess of tune accompa-
> nied by strumming guitars and jingling tambourines and frequently
> punctuated by wild shrieks and stamping feet. Above the din occasion-
> ally emerge such words as "Jesus," "God," "Hallelujah," "Glory,"
> and then I realize that this frenzy is being perpetrated in the name
> of religion. A young man of my own race who has stopped in amaze-
> ment turns to me half-quizzically and says, "What do you know about
> that? Jazzin' God."[24]

The "jazzin' God" frenzy described above, indeed "the syncopated rhythmic mess of tune" accompanied by guitars and tambourines, belongs to a
cluster of musical conventions identified with the blues. Dinah Washington's
frank, performed sexual discourse, the continued significance of "the
South," Jimmy Gilmore's blues-croon, William Brewster's gospel bounce,
Theodore Frye's gospel strut, Mahalia Jackson's riffing and riding are also
part of this blues system of music making. The prominence and influence of
black vernacular music and the blues muse at its foundation began to rise in

a definitive way at midcentury. One could argue, in fact, that the blues muse in all its figurations would, during the latter half of the twentieth century, play a crucial role in defining the "popular" realm of America's musical landscape. Three artists, Dinah Washington, Louis Jordan, and Cootie Williams, present exemplary case studies of the changing tone of American popular music and its relationship to the blues modality.

THE LIVING JUKEBOX:
DINAH MAKES HERSELF HEARD

The life and career of singer Dinah Washington (1924–1963) raise key issues with regard to female subjectivity in the blues at midcentury. Born Ruth Jones into a poor family in Tuscaloosa, Alabama, Washington moved with her family to Chicago during childhood. She was nurtured musically in the Baptist churches of that city's South Side. Washington's biographer, Jim Haskins, describes her early Depression-era Chicago life as filled with grinding poverty.[25] The family was so poor that Washington and her mother shared the same pair of stockings, which they washed and took turns wearing. The other children teased Washington; she was poor and overweight, and problems with her complexion earned her the nickname "Alligator." But Washington's mother, Alice Jones, sang and played the piano at St. Luke's Baptist Church and began to give young Ruth lessons. She blossomed musically and performed as a child soloist in the insular world of churches in black Chicago. She and her mother formed a duet for a time, trading duties singing and accompanying each other.

In 1939, Washington won an amateur contest at the Regal Theater, Chicago's counterpart of Harlem's Apollo Theater. After a brief stint as a nightclub singer—an activity she did without her strict mother's knowledge—Washington joined gospel music's matriarch, Sallie Martin, as her touring accompanist. Martin remembered the young pianist as being quite amorous with young men in the congregations, sometimes leaving with one before the end of services if he struck her fancy. Her travels with Martin also brought her in professional contact with gospel's elite circle: Mahalia Jackson, the Reverend C. L. Franklin (Aretha Franklin's father), and Roberta Martin (no relation to Sallie), the last of whom she credited as her greatest influence on the piano.[26] After leaving Sallie Martin, Washington returned to small nightclub jobs in Chicago. Sometime in the early 1940s, she saw Billie Holiday in a live show and thereafter adopted the singer as her primary role model for decorum and musical phrasing, according to Haskins.

Figure 1.   Crowned "Queen of the Blues," Dinah Washington was known for her striking fashion sense on- and offstage. Credit: Chuck Stewart.

Washington's big break in show business came in 1943 when bandleader Lionel Hampton discovered her one night working as a ladies' restroom attendant in a Chicago nightclub. (Washington would belt the lyrics of tunes from her station.) Hampton recalls of that time that Washington was "so poor she was raggedy."[27] The next day, she debuted successfully as "the girl singer" with Hampton's big band at the Regal Theater. Life was not easy for Washington in Hampton's band. She was not well received at first by the male musicians in the band; they thought she was homely and tousled. What is more, since the band's reputation rested on instrumental work, Washington did not record with Hampton until much later in her tenure. But she gained valuable experience on the tours and gradually earned the audiences' admiration and eventually the musicians' respect, although her becoming "one of the boys" offstage figured into this acceptance. Within this early musical and socioeconomic context, Washington laid the ground-work for her future musical activities, which would combine jazz, blues, gospel, and rhythm and blues. Hampton's description of Washington's musical assets are worth repeating: "She could make herself heard, even with my blazing band in the background, and she had that gutty style that they would later call rhythm and blues. . . . She had a background in gospel, and she put something new into the popular songs."[28]

Washington's vocal talents soon brought her to the attention of Leonard Feather, who produced her first known recordings in 1943 on Keynote, a small jazz label that produced recordings that made it to the Harlem Hit Parade.[29] Her releases—"Evil Gal Blues" and "Salty Papa Blues," both writ-ten by Feather—were both hits. She soon earned the title "Queen of the Blues."[30] In 1945, two years after joining Hampton's band, Washington embarked on a solo career. After a brief period with the Apollo label, in 1948 she signed with a larger company, Mercury, which had grown considerably since the years of "It's Just the Blues." Thereafter, Washington became "a liv-ing jukebox, recording what might be called reverse cover-versions: singing pop, jazz, country and R&B hits for the mainstream black audience."[31]

Washington's work, as Lionel Hampton pointed out above, did indeed put something new into popular song. I would argue that her work helped to establish a new paradigm for postwar pop singing and pop singers, especially female ones. While many black female singers cut their teeth performing in the church, few could claim to have influenced as many singers as Washington (Billie Holiday notwithstanding) before Aretha Franklin hit the scene during the soul era. Some of Washington's success can be attrib-uted to good timing. The development of her solo career coincided with some important shifts in the popular music industry. The hegemony of big bands was beginning to wane in the marketplace. Singers ascended to cen-ter stage in the popular imagination, replacing big band leaders as the focal point of popular music. Moreover, as I discuss in more detail in the next chapter, small record labels rushed to record race music. Eventually the major record labels also would recognize the commercial potential in record-ing black artists and record them. Washington's career is a case in point: she moved to larger and larger labels during her career. Her eclectic repertory—her blues pieces, jazz standards, novelty numbers, ballads, and pop-country covers—all bore her signature performance rhetoric: the acid timbre, the gospel-influenced shouting quality, the flawless diction, the "bluesy" interjections, and the precious understatement. Washington helped to codify these approaches in the pop-singing lexicon from the beginning of her recording career until her death. The analysis below discusses her vocal approach within a hard bop jazz setting, a 1958 recording of "Back Water Blues."[32] Washington's work here also provides an excellent instance of the centering of black female subjectivity within the logic of this piece's formal procedures.

Washington's version of "Back Water Blues" was recorded in the summer of 1958 at the Newport Jazz Festival. The rhythm section created a driving swing typical of hard bop recordings at that time. The song's composer is Bessie Smith, a woman to whom Dinah had been compared early in her career. It has been said that Washington did not enjoy the comparison; she thought that Billie Holiday, a woman she considered much more glamorous, was a more suitable model for her. Throughout the piece we hear Washington using some specific rhetorical strategies to "write" into the rendition her own performative subjectivity. Game rivalry and musical individuality within collectivity represent two of the most important elements in Washington's performance rhetoric here, although many others are also heard.

Washington opens the piece with show business patter, announcing homage to the composer of "Back Water Blues," blues singer Bessie Smith. Washington's clear diction and polished, cabaret-style intonation and cadence will be starkly contrasted with her subsequent singing performance, in which she strategically and ever so gradually moves into the "gutbucket" zone. During this introduction, however, we meet another protagonist: jazz pianist Wynton Kelley, joined here by Paul West on bass and drummer Max Roach. (It is not unimportant to the present discussion that Kelley and Washington had an on-again, off-again affair in the 1950s.) Together, and over the course of this recording, these performers will deliver some cultural pay dirt on at least two levels. First, Washington and Kelley seem to be involved in game rivalry. The musical and metaphorical struggle we hear is closely related to Floyd's notion of musical individuality within collectivity, in which musicians strive for *personal* "vocality" even as they contribute to the *common* goal of the overall performance. This trope is a prevalent feature of the R&B, jazz, and gospel genres.

The second cultural imperative involves what I call the troping cycle.

Musical troping cycles grow out of harmonic repetition and can be found in many forms: the twelve-bar blues; the spoken emphatic repetitions in black sermons as well as the dramatic call-and-response patterns at their climaxes; the emotional four-bar vamps of gospel songs; the two-bar "shoutin' music" cycles that accompany religious dancing in the black church; and in a more abstract sense, the thirty-two-bar forms that constitute the basis for improvisation in the jazz tradition. All of these display the troping-cycle sensibility. I use the somewhat arid term *troping cycle* to describe these events because (1) the word *vamp* seems to denote only the harmonic successions and melodic patterns typical of the section; and (2) the term *troping cycle* seems to refer not only to the section's function but also to the aesthetic demands and requirements placed on the singers or instrumentalists. In order for the troping cycle to succeed, the performers must use as many of Floyd's call-and-response tropes as they can successfully execute.

"Back Water Blues" is a twelve-bar blues played in the key of F. Seven choruses (or troping cycles) compose the performance. Through the lyrics, Washington portrays herself as a "poor girl" besieged by something she refers to as trouble that results from a violent five-day rainstorm, a tempest from which she needed to be rescued. Narrative references to her standing "on a high, old lonesome hill" in order to survey the damage could easily, however, refer to problems of a more personal kind as well. Yet this portrayal of helplessness is rather unconvincing. The subjective presence that Washington invents through her rhetorical troping, her almost nasal timbre, the tightly wound, intense melismas, her constant elisions into open musical spaces, and her precise interjections serve notice that this woman can and will stand in the face of whatever this "trouble" may be. Moreover, Washington's defiant straddling of the crossroads linking gospel, blues, and jazz stylings in "Back Water Blues" adds to the listeners' understanding of her resolve as well as to their pleasure.

Throughout this performance, pianist Wynton Kelley demonstrates why he was considered in his lifetime an extraordinary jazz accompanist. Like Washington, he also takes many opportunities to occupy the open spaces created by the natural pauses in Washington's phrases: he contrasts and taunts Washington's rhetoric but, at the same time, fulfills his role as her harmonic support. As the cycles repeat, Kelley's cultural work becomes more and more animated, sometimes spilling over into the singer's phrases with melodic filigree, supplying moans and groans with tremolo chords (chorus 3), joining forces with the bass and drums with rhythmic accents, becoming the thunder and lightning beneath the lyrics, and creating his own call-and-response phrases. During the final troping cycle, however, Washington ultimately blows the top off this rendition as she pleads—no, as she demands through the forceful timbre in her vocals —that somebody, *somebody* please tell her where's a poor, poor girl like her supposed to go.

We learn a lot in a remarkable moment at the end of the piece in a line that calls attention to itself because it is situated at the end of a chorus that interrupts the *aab* formal pattern set up by the previous six troping cycles or choruses. Despite the challenges of her troubles as well as the pesky intrusions of her pianist's virtuosic tropes, our female protagonist threatens everyone in earshot that she is more than an equal match for a flood, the blues, or, for that matter, any disciplining authority that might appear in the future.

Washington's performance rhetoric and Smith's lyrics give the narrative voice in the song an almost heroic presence. While performances like this are artistic inventions and not homologous with real lived experience, audiences invest powerful meaning in them. They are real in this sense and circulate many different kinds of social energy, such as ideas about a performer's agency, on the one hand, and broader notions about race, gender, class, and sexuality, on the other.

By the time of this recording, some of the details of Washington's rocky personal life and salty demeanor were well known to her public. She obsessed about her personal appearance, overcompensating for feelings of insecurity about her fluctuating weight (and probably memories of childhood poverty) by spending lots of money on fashionable clothing. Washington was on a perpetual diet. A female friend, quoted in her biography, stated, "I always told her how gorgeous she was and how good she looked. But she didn't like her body. She would look at me sometimes and say, 'If I had your body and my voice, I'd be a bitch, wouldn't I?'"[33] Washington married seven times in her life, which was cut short with an accidental overdose of diet pills. However, throughout her career, she established a reputation as a staunch professional, despite the adversities facing female vocalists in a difficult business. She demanded control over the musicians that accompanied her; she had marvelous musical instincts and a good ear. One can't help but hear these struggles within the context of this blues performance, as in this last chorus of "Back Water Blues":

> Somebody, somebody please tell me, where's a poor, poor girl like me
> to go,
> Can't you see I'm tired and I don't feel like moving no more,
> But if I ever get my nerves settled down, I'll be a mean so and so.

"KEEP IT SIMPLE":
LOUIS JORDAN, KING OF THE JUKEBOX

Louis Jordan's (1908–1975) early career sheds light on other musical and social factors in midcentury African American music. Like Washington, Jordan was born in the South, in Brinkley, Arkansas. His father was a talented professional musician who toured with minstrel troupes in the South. The elder Jordan trained young Louis to succeed musically, supporting his son's activities enthusiastically. Interestingly, Dinah Washington's mother strongly discouraged her secular career in its early years. Her objections were mostly on religious grounds, although one cannot help but speculate that they also had to do with her gender. Jordan, however, received lessons in music theory, learned the importance of a practice regimen, and moved with ease between the musical activities of his family's church and his work in the secular world. The musical influences on Jordan were multifaceted: the traveling medicine and minstrel shows of his youth and the Baptist church were several of them. But most of all, Jordan credited the great actor Bert Williams as his primary influence, although the more theatrical jazz stars such as Cab Calloway and Fats Waller were also important to his entertainer's approach.

After migrating to Philadelphia in 1932 in search of work, Jordan spent a few years paying dues in various musical outfits. He joined Chick Webb's band in 1936, staying for about two years. Jordan formed his own group, the Tympany Five, in 1938 and put into practice all of the discipline and showmanship that he learned during his years on the minstrel circuit. Much of this showmanship comprised time-proven performance conventions for black male entertainers—animated bodies and a comical bearing. Jordan saw his plan for success in these terms:

> I worked with Chick Webb and Ella Fitzgerald, and I played jazz. And then I switched over. I didn't think I could handle a big band. But with my little band, I did everything they did with a big band. *I made the blues jump.* After I got into the public, they said I should straddle the fence . . . that I shouldn't play just for Negroes, but for the world. Then I decided that when you come to hear Louis Jordan, you'd hear things to make you forget what you'd had to do the day before and just have a good time, a great time.[34]

It is important that Jordan's outline for success was expressed in terms of the musical genre, the economics and politics of leading a big band (which was, of course, the industry's standard at that time), the blues modality, race, and a specific attitude toward entertainment. Jordan's plan

Figure 2.   Louis Jordan cultivated his stage skills early in life on the minstrel circuit in the South. His mannerisms became the hallmark of his performance style throughout his career. Credit: Chuck Stewart.

worked. He enjoyed huge commercial success and popularity among blacks and whites, especially during his peak years, 1938–1946. He made five million-selling 78-rpm recordings in part because of his popularity on Nickelodeons, which "perfectly captured the fun of his live shows, and sold records."[35] This presentation antedating music videos makes Jordan a pioneer in this arena.

According to Nelson George, Jordan's popularity was also due to the way he combined progressive musicianship and an entertainer's stance—he "leaped over the walls of segregation."[36] Clearly, Jordan's diverse talents offered something for everyone on both sides of the racial divide. His shows consisted of a "skillfully paced assortment of humorous patter, searing saxophone solos, and remarkably sly and witty blues lyrics."[37] The time was ripe for his brand of entertainment. The Afro-modernist narratives—the rhetorical North and South—embedded in his music painted a composite portrait of "big-city blacks often not one generation removed from life in the rural South."[38] These themes dovetailed with the experiences and memories of black *and* white working-class migrants. "The songs' titles 'Beans and Cornbread,' 'Saturday Night Fish Fry,' and 'Ain't Nobody Here but Us Chickens,'" George writes, "suggest country life, yet the subject of each is really a city scene."[39] Jordan's postwar rhythm and blues cast a long shadow of influence. It set the stage for a watershed rock 'n' roll movement that would dominate popular music in the following decades.

Jordan's success drew some negative reactions, too, mostly concerning responses to aspects of his public image. A "split image" characterized black representation in twentieth-century mass media. Since the advent of minstrelsy in the nineteenth century and the film industry in the twentieth, American popular culture has continually perpetuated negative stereotypes of African Americans. Some of these have included the mammy, Uncle Remus, the "crazed mulatto brute," or some variations of these. African Americans have responded by creating their own images but also by repackaging these images for popular consumption. As Jannette L. Dates and William Barlow argue, "The definition and control of black images in the mass media have been contested from the outset along racial lines, with cultural domination provoking African American cultural resistance."[40] Such resistance was prevalent among entertainers; and the intense debates surrounding the appropriateness or the political expediency of many African American performers' public bearing highlight these tensions.

Jordan's brash show business antics, polished (some have said overrehearsed) stage show, and stern business approach occasionally evoked resentment from his sidemen. Tenor saxophonist Paul Quinichette called

Jordan "a dictator with Uncle Tom qualities. . . . I didn't like the type of thing he was doing, it wasn't swing. . . . I got sick of wearing those sequined, Christmas-tree-type uniforms, red pants, vivid green coats, sequined ties and boots, and we had to stand up there and dance and play those tunes."[41] On the other hand, many jazz modernists, such as Art Pepper, Sonny Rollins, Dizzy Gillespie, and Charlie Parker, were counted among Louis Jordan's admirers.[42] Furthermore, Jordan himself liked and respected bebop and other idioms of jazz. He shared a big band background with Parker and Gillespie, but he had a different vision for his own group. Jordan's motto, Quinichette notes, was "Keep it simple. . . . He wanted music that a working man could relax to." The irony in the Uncle Tom accusations is that Jordan had learned his showmanship from black culture itself: "All of his tricks of the trade [were] mastered," his biographer John Chilton notes, "while he was playing to black audiences. If later, white audiences also found them funny this was not, in his eyes, a disgrace."[43]

One can see many of the performance attributes for which Jordan was famous in excerpts of the short film *Caledonia*, which appeared in 1945 and is considered one of the first music videos. Named for the title of one of Jordan's most popular recordings, the brief film was seen in "soundie" machines and in movie theaters before the main features. This visibility catapulted Jordan's popularity and helped him to sell many recordings. Beginning in the living room of a home, the film is a kind of "video within a video," telling the story of Jordan's band making a short film. Ultimately, the feature is an excuse for the performances of some of the band's recordings, "Caledonia," "Honey Chile," "Tillie," and "Buzz Me, Baby." Taken together, they provide a thumbnail view of the emerging style that would become known as rhythm and blues.

"Caledonia" is a classic twelve-bar jump blues piece. It features the shuffle-boogie rhythmic approach of the style. Jordan's vocal delivery comprises a subtle blend of crooning, blues shouting, and preacherly rap. Although other musicians are featured in short riff-based solos, Jordan as both singer and instrumentalist is the focal point of each performance. The lyrics tell the story of a love affair between a male protagonist and a female named Caledonia. In a typical love song, the words would celebrate physical or emotional attraction to an object of desire. In "Caledonia," however, the song describes the female in humorous but repugnant terms such as long, lean, and lanky with great big feet. Clearly, this kind of gesture pokes fun at the love song tradition of Tin Pan Alley.

The poetic structure of "Caledonia" is also a slight revision of the typical *aab* blues framework. Instead, the song compresses narrative information by not repeating the second line of the blues that would normally be heard in bars 5 through 8 of the twelve-bar pattern.

Bars 1–4
Walking with my baby she got great big feet, she's long, lean, and lanky
 and she ain't had nothing to eat

Bars 5–8
But she's my baby and I love her just the same

Bars 9–12
Crazy 'bout that woman cause Caledonia is her name

Jordan and the rest of the cast cut striking figures in the video. Although his acting seems a little stiff and contrived, we do get a clear sense of Jordan's "entertainer's" approach to music making. His subtle yet noticeable eyeball bulging, wide grin, animated body gestures, and even the comical gesture on the word *Caledonia*, on which he flips into a falsetto yelp on the last sylla-ble, seem to recall Jordan's beginnings in minstrel shows. In the first scene in which the band performs "Caledonia" in the living room, the musicians are dressed dapperly and perform the title song, complete with an anony-mous dancing girl in the corner and a slim, fair-skinned, beautiful African American actress playing Caledonia. Throughout the performance, the young actress is perched on the piano, making a series of provocative poses during the lip-synced performance.

"Honey Chile" is set on the imaginary sound stage of a business associ-ate's film company. The song begins with a brief rubato verse and then moves into a snappy jump rhythm as Jordan describes another love interest: a woman with "arms like a blacksmith, feet like a beam, the ugliest woman you ever seen." During the solos in the performance a huge silhouette of a shapely dancing female looms behind the band. The band performs "Tillie" in the kind of outlandish getups that would have inspired the disdain of side-men like Paul Quinichette, who was quoted above. Some of the band mem-bers wear clown outfits; the others, including Jordan, are dressed like big city sporting dandies. The resurrection of these stereotypes seems designed to be sensational, since the lyrics of these songs have nothing to do with these por-trayals. Included in the performance are four dancing girls who shimmy in front of the band and a cameo appearance of two dancers, a man and a woman, executing some contemporaneous moves during the instrumental solos. "Buzz Me, Baby," a down-home, medium tempo, heavily riffed, twelve-bar blues piece, again features Jordan's blues vocals, tenor saxophone solo, and, of course, a reclined female model fiddling with a telephone.

Jordan's popularity may be viewed both as a source of black pride and inspiration on the one hand and, on the other, as a point of tension between what the black masses enjoyed as entertainment and what image they could risk presenting to white America. The growing presence of African Americans in the mass media during the postwar years—a visibility emblematic in Jordan's success—made black "representation" a central issue in black cultural politics. It remains so today.

HAPPY FEET OR FUTURISTIC?:
COOTIE WILLIAMS—CAUGHT BETWEEN STYLES

In the world of instrumental jazz, we also find issues of Afro-modernist blues musing in the case of Charles Melvin "Cootie" Williams (1911–1985). Like Dinah Washington and Louis Jordan, Williams paid his professional dues in the big bands, including those of Chick Webb, Fletcher Henderson, and, most prominently, Duke Ellington. Born in Mobile, Alabama, Williams, a largely self-taught musician, moved to New York in 1928. He joined Ellington in 1929 as the replacement for the well-respected trumpeter Bubba Miley, one of Ellington's star soloists. Williams left Ellington in 1940 and joined Benny Goodman, staying with him for one year. When Williams formed his own band, he was an already famous instrumental soloist in jazz, but he elected to play an eclectic repertory that resists the usual categories.

Despite Williams's contributions to Duke Ellington's Orchestra in the 1930s, ones that set a benchmark in the history of jazz, his own band has received scant mention in jazz or rhythm and blues histories. Gunther Schuller, one of the few scholars to comment (albeit briefly) on Williams's band, describes it as "a transitional ensemble halfway between swing and bop, and a haven for many of the younger up-and-coming black players who were unable to find a place in the older well-established orchestras." Williams, Schuller writes, "fell prey to the risks and flaws inherent in being caught between two styles. Not fully committed to the incoming bop, and at the same time not quite able to relinquish the safe ground of swing, Cootie, both in his choice of personnel and in the performances of his players, seemed to waver, unable to assume a clear direction."[44]

As a prolific and important critic of jazz styles and as a writer with an obvious investment in the perseverance of the implicit boundaries among the modernist narratives, Schuller seemed to believe that R&B represented "superficial" excitement. Schuller recognized the importance of playing successfully at venues like the Savoy Ballroom, "Home of the Happy Feet" (apparently the entire "Afro-modern body" enjoyed jitterbuggin' the night away). But I also get the feeling that Schuller wanted to separate the musical

Figure 3. Cootie Williams became one of the important virtuosos of the Swing Era and one of the early architects of rhythm and blues instrumental conventions. Credit: Chuck Stewart.

wheat (jazz) from the tare (R&B), the elitist jazz from the working-class rhythm and blues, in his discussion of Williams's big band. One might say that with regard to his anti-R&B stance, Schuller fell prey to the risks and flaws inherent in being caught between two modernist narratives. In fact, the group in compositional repertory, personnel, and soloing techniques embraced a number of styles, and these were all requirements for sustaining a commercially successful dance ensemble. But the band's eclectic style should not be counted against it. Rather than demonstrating a lack of direction, Williams's music provides a clear example of the stylistic flux in black popular music during the war years. In fact, I view this group as a progressive, early R&B band.

While some believe that Williams's eclectic repertory and stylistic thrust limited his popularity, other factors certainly played a role; the most significant may have been simply a matter of timing. An Office of Defense Transportation edict banning the private use of buses in June 1942 was devastating to black dance bands, further exacerbating already dismal travel conditions. Chartered buses provided bands with the safest and most economic mode of transportation, especially in the South, where Jim Crow practices often made extended tours degrading and even dangerous.[45] Two months later, a recording ban called by the American Federation of Musicians (AFM) stalled recording opportunities for Williams, forcing him and his men to rely on local jobs in the New York area for their livelihood. Williams's group did not record again until January 1944. By that time, key personnel changes had taken place. Recording as the Cootie Williams Sextet and Cootie Williams and His Orchestra, the group now included, among others, a talented nineteen-year-old pianist called Buddy Powell, a musician who would become a key figure in modern jazz.

Like many black bands, Cootie Williams's group found work where it could and cast a very wide net for an audience. Eddie "Lockjaw" Davis, a popular saxophonist, recalls that the group went on a six-month tour of the RKO theater circuit sometime in early 1944. The tour featured a mixed bill typical of many shows presented in black theaters: singers, large dance bands, and dancers. The show included Williams's group, Ella Fitzgerald, the Ink Spots, a dancer (Ralph Brown), and a comedian.[46] During the West Coast leg of the tour (or possibly in New York shortly prior to the tour), the band made a short movie titled *Cootie Williams, His Hot Trumpet and Orchestra*. Unlike Louis Jordan's *Caledonia*, the film had no plot, consisting of a nonthematic string of tunes, each announced by an attractive young woman.[47] The soundtrack of the performance reflects the general makeup of the band's repertory: Ellington's "Things Ain't What They Used to Be," sung by Eddie Vinson, and other blues-based selections.

On August 22, the band recorded "Is You Is or Is You Ain't My Baby?" "Somebody's Got to Go," "'Round Midnight," and "Royal Garden Blues." The presence of Louis Jordan's tune "Is You Is or Is You Ain't My Baby?" and Monk's "'Round Midnight" on the same recording date provides further evidence not only of the band's diverse repertory but also of the consolidated world of black musicians. Jordan, as noted earlier, represents one of the first rhythm and blues performers. He had performed "Is You Is or Is You Ain't My Baby?" in the 1943 film *Follow the Boys*. Although Williams and his band take the song at a more bluesy, slower tempo than Jordan's popular version, the big band arrangement here places the piece clearly within the jazz domain.

As Francis Paudras quotes him, Earl "Bud" Powell, the young pianist and future bebopper, claimed to be the impetus behind the addition of Monk's composition "'Round Midnight" to the band's repertory. While the following version of the composition's early history easily fits into a braggadocio, individualist mode, it also portrays the collaborative compositional process one expects in the "folk" realm of cultural production:

> I did most of the arrangements for the orchestra since I was the only one who could write music. I worked a lot with Thelonious in those days, and I suggested one day to Cootie to include "Midnite" in the orchestra's repertoire. He refused immediately bu [*sic*], since I insisted, he accepted on the condition that he himself add a second part to the piece, which at the time had only the principal theme. It was afterwards that Dizzy wrote the beginning and the end when we played the composition in his orchestra.[48]

(Paudras also states that Williams later recalled that young Powell threatened to resign if the piece was not added to the band's repertory.) The big band arrangement of "'Round Midnight" features Williams and a composed verse section (totally out of character with the otherwise sultry mood of the rest of the composition), transforming it more in line with a typical dance number. The new verse was not used in later recordings, including Gillespie's 1946 big band arrangement.

I want to explore the possibility that in true Afro-modernist fashion, this "marginal" or "transitional" ensemble of Cootie Williams's may have intended to straddle the stylistic fences when in April 1942 it recorded the Thelonious Monk–Kenny Clarke composition "Epistrophy," a piece that is recognized today as a classic modern jazz composition.[49] Schuller criticizes pianist Ken Kersey's solo because it "didn't at all fit Monk's new language," but Joe Guy's trumpet solo reflects "a totally futuristic musical world."[50]

Let's concentrate first on Monk's new language in the compositional aspect of the recording. Its melodic, harmonic, and rhythmic qualities seem to satirize popular song, common-practice classical music, and the jazz tradition itself.

The rifflike melody of "Epistrophy," a typical blueslike practice, sets up an antecedent-consequent phrase in the first four measures. The major sixth in the first two measures moves up; the same pitch in the last two measures— now a minor sixth—of a D7 chord is pulled down to E, which not only creates a tritone but is itself a dissonance in the D chord, emphasized by its relatively long duration. The harmonic construction of the piece also pushes the boundaries of tradition. First, the harmonic syntax is original and consists almost entirely of seventh chords. And second, Monk finds a staunchly unorthodox way to use standard thirty-two-bar song form (A A¹ B A¹). The first eight bars (A) consist of four dominant-seventh chords—C-sharp 7, D7, D-sharp 7, and E7—and Monk's treatment of these is idiosyncratic. After the first four bars he sequences everything up a whole step to complete the last four measures of A. Next, Monk exchanges the first and second four bars (A¹) to end where he began. The bridge section (B) provides some tonal (and rhythmic) contrast with the first and only minor chord of the piece, an F-sharp minor that is followed by a B7 chord. (The bridge's melody also provides contrast but retains some of the rifflike character of the A sections.) The final two bars of the bridge make a transition into the last eight measures by suggesting the rhythms of the A section melody. Monk repeats the A¹ section, which weakly confirms C-sharp as a tonic.[51] Finally, "Epistrophy" 's somewhat uniform rhythmic construction and the seamless, "looping around" quality of its harmonic syntax combine to make it an eccentric composition.

For all of the unusual compositional features present in "Epistrophy," Williams's version makes no attempt to present the tune as a bebop composition of the kind that came to be common five years hence. The band's arrangement treats Monk's piece instead as a big band dance number. After a two-bar introduction on the high hat by drummer George "Butch" Ballard, the band plays four choruses of the tune. In the first, Williams plays the melody while the brass and woodwinds create a simple call-and-response pattern behind him. Kersey takes a piano solo in the second chorus, accompanied by the same trumpet pattern played in the first chorus. Next, as Guy solos in the third chorus, he is accompanied by the saxes repeating the same background figures they played in chorus 1. Ballard "opens up" the third chorus with a heavy backbeat on beats 2 and 4, giving the section the character of a shout chorus.

In performance practice, too, Williams's recording emphasizes swing

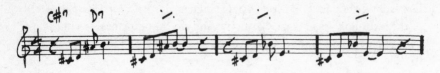

Music example 1. "Epistrophy," measures 1–4.

band techniques. Ballard maintains predictable rhythmic patterns throughout the recording; even in the third chorus described above, he does not push
far beyond the "timekeeping" one expects from standard swing drumming.
Improvisation is restricted to the solos: The rhythm section in general
closely follows the prescribed chord changes and the rhythmic accents of the
ensemble's arrangement. As Schuller explains, only Guy's solo reaches outside the standard conventions of swing. When Kersey plays single-note
lines during his solo, he ignores for much of the chorus the chromatic
neighbor harmonies of Monk's progression. Williams's open and muted
performance of the melody of "Epistrophy" is solid and expressive, and he
does not solo on the tune. Thus, this performance amounts to a fascinating
and telling hybrid: one of jazz's premier stars giving a swing performance of
a composition by one of the most eccentric and, at that time, marginalized
jazz musicians.

Cootie Williams drew on many resources as a bandleader: the repertory
of his Ellington years, the jazz and swing tradition of his youth, the diverse
talents of new instrumentalists and vocalists such as Powell, Vinson, and
Davis, the innovations of new composers such as Monk, and the novel
sounds of two emerging styles, bebop and rhythm and blues. Obviously,
Williams knew the importance of playing "the familiar" and that his group's
commercial success depended on his ability to do so. The Williams group
never lost touch with its audience: Eddie Vinson's unrivaled vocals were a
popular drawing card, and the group was always enthusiastically received at
the Savoy Ballroom, the perennial "Home of the Happy Feet," as well as at
other, similar venues throughout the country. Throughout the early to mid-
1940s Williams remained popular, especially in New York. One article heralded his group as "the current standout attraction . . . where they have
been held over twice due to popular demand." The engagement also featured
"a coast-to-coast hook-up twice weekly over the Mutual network."[52]
Furthermore, the band's records sold well. "Somebody's Gotta Go" and
"'Round Midnight" of the August 22 session were both issued in December
1944; they hit the Harlem Hit Parade on January 6, 1945, and rose to number one on February 10.[53] Within the context of Williams's early-1940s

Music example 2.   "Epistrophy," measures 17–20.

recordings, the bebop style (and compositions) apparently did not represent anything approaching a "futuristic" or esoteric musical world. Like rhythm and blues, it was simply another black vernacular resource that various artists used to fashion individual styles. The Williams group conformed to a core value in African music: "Within the African context the aesthetic ideal is integrated with the utilitarian ideal . . . but the quality of 'intrinsic perceptual interest' is seen as an integral aspect of the utilitarian function."[54] In other words, the Savoy crowd could appreciate the band's musicianship and celebrate that appreciation with their bodies in dance.

EDUCATING THE BODY IN AFRO-MODERNIST DISCOURSE

While the traditional modernist narratives have worked as important paradigms for African American musical production, in Afro-modernist practice these ideals were also revised and rearranged through cultural expressions. This revisionism has been a hallmark of Afro-modernism. It shows how the consciousness, sensibilities, and values of African Americans were not contained by boundaries set either by commercial marketing strategies or by the arbiters of tastes within and outside black culture. When Dizzy Gillespie joked, bumped, and ground during his performances in the 1940s, for example, journalists reprimanded him for demeaning the bebop aesthetic. Yet Gillespie has cautioned us about leaving the body out of the Afro-modernist aesthetic: "Jazz was invented for people to dance. So when you play jazz and people don't feel like dancing or moving the feet, you're getting away from the idea of music. Never lose that feeling of somebody wanting to dance; that's one of the characteristics of our music."[55] When singer Sarah Vaughan recalled her apprenticeship in early bebop ensembles, she deconstructed one of the earmarks of the modernist mind-body split by collapsing (in classic Afro-modernist fashion) the divide separating mental "education" and bodily celebration:

> Oh listen, I was going to school. I really didn't have to go to Juilliard, I was right there in it. . . . I just learned a lot. Lots and lots, a whole lots. I used to stare at them in amazement. But I used to feel it; you know,

both of us used to sit on the stand and we'd get to swinging so much, Dizzy would come down and grab me and start jitterbugging all over the place. It was swinging.[56]

We tried to educate the people. We used to play dances, and there were just a very few who understood who would be in a corner, jitterbugging forever, while the rest just stood staring at us.[57]

As the "race" category of popular music was gradually dismantled into several separate ones in the years after the war, for example, some black performers moved with relative ease among them. Thus, strong currents of stylistic cross-fertilization continually revitalized each genre even as marketing practices divided them into manageable, yet related, parts. Sharing and borrowing among musicians took place on many levels. Various groups toured the black theater circuit together; they mixed socially—usually after or between jobs; they played for the same record labels; they visited each other's rehearsals; they lived in the same neighborhoods; many had attended the same schools; and the constant shuffling of personnel among bands kept musical techniques circulating, together with some of the lore and gossip that community members share. Allowing for differences and nuances, a consensus image of the black professional musician emerged, rooted in a core set of performance practices and a code of values. (This last point is especially important in understanding the world of bebop, for it was against that consensus image that modern jazz performers were first measured by the public and thereafter perceived as something radically different.) On the other hand, the ideal of artistic autonomy began to grant bebop a kind of critical distance from other postwar styles of black music. A vibrant art discourse formed around modern jazz that was distinguished from the popular-commercial and folk discourses through which many understood music like gospel, blues, and jump blues.

The blues modality provided midcentury artists with an artistic framework in which to build personal styles and new musical idioms that spoke powerfully to various constituencies. Indeed, the blues were everywhere. It became a musical system through which women such as Dinah Washington could articulate a subjective presence into a male-centered musical discourse like jazz. It was molded and "jumped" by Louis Jordan into a personalized style that influenced subsequent innovators such as Chuck Berry. Indeed, Jordan fashioned a stage presence and musical legacy "for the working class" that became the basis for numerous developments in American popular music, most prominently rock 'n' roll and rhythm and blues. Cootie

Williams's work reminds us of the power of the artistic narratives that grew around jazz in the 1940s. Its tenets made it difficult to satisfy the requirements of happy feet and the tastes of the critics no matter how hard the musicians tried. Taken together, our brief looks at these artists give us a sense of the varied and certainly dynamic kinds of social energies that circulated within and around the blues muse in African American culture.

4 "It Just Stays with Me All of the Time"

Collective Memory, Community Theater, and the Ethnographic Truth

For various reasons, the average, struggling, nonmorbid Negro is the best-kept secret in America.
> Zora Neale Hurston, "What White Publishers Won't Print"

Since I don't see myself or most people I know in most things I see or read about black people, I can't be bothered with that. I wish you could read something or see a movie that would show the people just, well, as my grandmother would say, drylongso. You know, like most of us really are most of the time—together enough to do what we have to do to be decent people.
> Harriet Jones, quoted in John Langston Gwaltney, *Drylongso*

In the previous chapters, I outlined what I believe to be important considerations for the study of or, rather, the disciplining of African American music. I began in chapter 1 with an ethnomemoir, recalling specific events in my life in which music was central or played an important role. The themes raised in those passages provided a springboard into some of the intellectual issues explored in chapter 2 and throughout this book. They also grounded some of my observations and interpretations within a specific web of culture, a relationship that I believe exists in all humanistic scholarship, despite the reluctance among scholars to recognize and explore this dialectic.

Chapter 3 examined some of the formal parameters of the blues muse—a system of music making enjoyed by and influential among many Americans but linked historically and socially to specific communities of African American innovators and audiences. In each example discussed, the blues sensibility informed musical structures and gestures that expressed various kinds of social energies for historical actors at the postwar moment. Indeed, the world of entertainment and mass media, which were the settings for these expressions, provided an accessible space for the forwarding of many kinds of "performed" identities through the musical rhetoric of the blues writ large. Thus, far from being a monolithic enterprise, in the hands of capable practitioners, the blues muse helped performers to express a diversity of identities at specific historical moments. And undoubtedly, these expressions meant different things to different audiences.

One of the key points that I stressed earlier is that meaning in music is, in large part, generated in what I call community theaters. These public and private spaces provide audiences with a place to negotiate with others—in a highly social way—what cultural expressions such as music mean. In this chapter, I want to explore the possible impact of a particular community theater on the notion of musical meaning. The basic idea here is to make more explicit the relationship among cultural memories, historical moments, and musical discourse.

Anthropologist Arjun Appadurai has identified migration and the mass media as two important factors shaping what he calls "the work of the imagination." Through the process of the work of the imagination, groups of individuals begin to imagine themselves and feel as one group, connecting their past, present, and future. This idea is very similar to how I use the term *collective memory*, a contested space that represents "a property of collectives, and not merely as a faculty of the gifted individual." In Appadurai's work, the imagination has become a collective and social fact of modern life that transcends the will of the individual and helps to make sense of or, perhaps better, to create social realities. The imagination or collective memory is crucial, in my view, to any interpretation, because it provides "the conditions of collective reading, criticism, and pleasure."[1]

There exists a cyclic relationship between the mass media and collective or cultural memory. Again, Appadurai's work is useful in illustrating this point. He argues that the media "offer new resources and new disciplines for the construction of imagined selves and imagined worlds." The mass media transform everyday discourse, providing "resources for experiments with self-making [or self-imagining] in all sorts of societies, for all sorts of persons." As Appadurai points out, migration also figures into this cyclic relationship. The dynamic movement of social energies involved in mass migration of any kind works together with the flow of mass mediated information, sensations, and images to create "a new order of instability in the production of modern subjectivities."[2]

I want to explore the connections among midcentury mass-media music, migration, and the self-imaginings or collective cultural memories of a specific group of people. As I have already stated, I am dealing with my own family of origin's "work of imagination" for several reasons. These stories form the foundation for my own sense of history and self-imagination, and therefore they inform my critical voice and perceptions as a scholar. While the stories represented below underscore the specific circumstance of a particular family, they are simply one representative imagining of a larger story of migration, one that many similar families shared. Thus, they are unique but at the same time somewhat typical.

The experiences shared in this narrative—indeed, a veritable community theater of ideas—depict real people making sense of the world and, in fact, making a world as they went along. But a question is begged: What connections exist between musical discourse and the real-life experiences represented below? I should make clear that I am not interested in drawing one-to-one homologies between a certain recording and the stories told in the interviews I conducted. Such connections are extremely problematic to prove definitively. However, I am suggesting that the *sensibilities* endowing these cultural memories and musical works possess a tangible coherence and are drawn from the same social and cultural well. In other words, the social energies that circulate in the memories are the same as those that make the music make sense to historically situated actors. At the very least, by putting these discourses into play with one another, we can perhaps speculate an answer to Christopher Small's provocative query: Why are these people listening to this music at this time in this place?

The Rosses of Valdosta, Georgia, were one of many southern black families that migrated to the North in the years following World War II. One by one, they would leave Georgia's red clay for Chicago's paved streets in order to build new lives, shedding various aspects of their southern rural past. Peter Mallie Ross (1895–1975) and Martha Bynum Ross (1907–1991) married and bore five children: Celia, Marjorie, Peter Mallie, Jr., Dorothy, and Bobby Lester.[3]

The scenario that opened chapter 1 depicted a specific example of musicking in family life, one in which the Rosses were an important element, and represented a blend of southern and northern cultural sensibilities. Through the recounting and analysis of the selected stories told below, I hope to tease out some of the historical grounding of the ethnomemoir of the first chapter. Moreover, I want to provide some idea about how the lived experience of historical actors might figure into our understanding of musical discourse. In the first epigraph to this chapter, Zora Neale Hurston's lament about the missing "nonmorbid Negro" is very much a response to social science literature on American blacks that has emphasized pathology, nihilism, and hopelessness in African American culture. The narratives below serve as a counterweight to such depictions, even while the challenges facing blacks in the Depression-era South are quite clear.

Several patterns and themes emerge from this family migration narrative, and I have tried to respond to them in appropriate ways. Migrants' perceptions of themselves in the South were not those of backward country bumpkins; instead, they possessed a rather refined sense of who they were in the world, despite the hardships present in the South and those that became apparent when they arrived in Chicago. They talked about having impeccable taste in clothes and music, although their financial circumstances sometimes lessened their enjoyment of these areas. Musical entertainment was an important factor in their lives in the South and provided one of the ways in which they were socialized into aspects of northern living. On this last point, it is important to note that when these family members arrived in Chicago, they brought with them a definable worldview and culture that eventually became blended with northern sensibilities. The formal qualities of African American music produced during this period display this same social energy.

Finally, I should point out that a pattern related to gender issues became prominent throughout the interview process. Women positioned themselves as important culture bearers and the storytellers of history. Their imaginings of family histories dominated, making it difficult for any man present even to get a word in edgewise. I interpret these women's role in this process as a stringent critique of patriarchy in African American culture. The blues muse, especially, has been primarily (but with some notable exceptions) associated with male performance culture. But the forwardness with which female perspectives became part of this study reminds us that the creation, performance, and interpretation of any aspect of African American culture should not proceed without balancing masculinist perspectives with other ones. As we shall see, the contrasting ways that the migrants frame their mother's and father's roles in their early lives bring this point home succinctly.

IMAGINING THE SOUTH

The elder Peter was born in a tiny hamlet called Waucissa, Florida, which lies outside the city of Tallahassee. The lifestyle in Waucissa was rural, with few of the city's amenities, and life there changed little throughout the first half of the century. Celia and Marjorie both recalled that during their visits there in the 1930s and 1940s, the extended Ross family comprised a fairly large number of the town's population. Peter's adult children explained that "in this particular area, there wasn't anybody around that wasn't a Ross. It was sort of like the Kennedy compound," they recalled with sarcastic and signifying delight, "only southern-style—in the woods, without street-lights and stuff. . . . It was black, dark at night. You had to know where you were walking. And those people knew where they was going at night because they didn't have streetlights." The pitch-black darkness in Waucissa informed social custom, as evidenced by the strict codes of conduct between the sexes during "the after-church courtship walk":

> If he was courting someone, they went to church on Sunday night— everybody went back to church. And if there was a particular girl that you liked, the mother would walk ahead with a lantern; the young man and the young lady would be somewhere in the middle with the father coming up in the back. When the mother got home first, which she usu-ally did, she would take her lantern in and light the lamps. When the couple got to the gate, the young man would have said all he needed to say to that young lady, because when the father got to the gate, the young suitor was already on his way back where he came from—with-out light. The girl just walked right on in the house ahead of her father. There was nothing else said. You just walk right on in.

The older Ross siblings recalled a huge celebration held every May 20— a "great picnic day." While none could recall the reason for the holiday, it was important enough to seem national or at least statewide in scope. "It was a holiday for everybody," they recalled, a time for families to come together "pretty much like we have family reunion picnics now. . . . Everyone in the local area participated with each family doing their thing the way you wanted to do." Celia and Marjorie could remember wearing fancy dresses made from many yards of material and eating lots of good food—huge seven-layer chocolate cakes, and "lemonade tasting like it never tasted before, because it was made in nice, big No. 8–sized tin tubs." The tubs were not the same ones used for baths on Saturday night, they stressed; these tubs were new, purchased especially for the lemonade.

The men in the clan would fish in a nearby river, cleaning their catch for the women, who prepared elaborate dishes. The fish would be deep-fried in wash pots that were used during the week for washing clothes in the yard, a process that included boiling them until they were whistle-clean. And there was lots of music: "Wherever there was black people, there was music," they recalled. The music was recorded and, as they recalled, it was always the gutbucket blues.

Peter held two occupations in his lifetime, one legitimate, the other not. Being born and raised in the country, Peter learned to survive off the land, hunting and fishing for some of the food his family ate, and working as a woodcutter. He would go to the pine forests and make a little cut on the trees from which the rosin would drop down into a cup and later be collected as an important ingredient in turpentine. Peter also cut the wooden planks from which cross ties for railroad tracks were made. His children remember Peter in his young adult years as a cowboylike figure—bow-legged in denim jeans with a long knife tucked quite conspicuously into each cowboy boot. Peter also gambled.

Martha was born in Clyattsville, Georgia, the child of an African American man and a Native American woman, Daniel and Julia Bynum. When Peter met Martha she was a slim, copper-skinned woman with long slender legs, long jet-black hair, and a beautiful figure. She was "one of the better dressers" at that time, according to her children. Martha loved pretty clothes, making many herself with skills that she learned during her informal training as a seamstress. Her taste in clothes drew so much attention, in fact, that one of her daughters reaped some of the benefits indirectly:

> I remember when we were in school that I got all of the leading ladies' parts in our productions because my mother had beautiful clothes. It wasn't because they thought I was beautiful, even though I *was* beautiful, they just didn't think that. They would give me these parts because they knew I could wear my mother's clothes. One time, however, they told me that they wanted to give another young lady a chance at the leading lady's role, and wanted to know if I would ask my mom to let them use her clothes. My mother said right away, "Hell, no." So, of course, guess who got the leading lady's part again. I did, because they wanted to see my mother's beautiful clothes.

According to her children, along with her elegant taste in clothing Martha possessed other admirable qualities, including a gutsy, will-to-survive attitude. She could and would do anything to get her family through the Depression years, working numerous jobs from sewing to factory work. As her children tell the story, Martha's emotional and physical strength, abilities, and sensitivity kept the family together during hard times—and there were many. Ultimately, this same resolve would influence the entire family to migrate to Chicago. Her ability to care for her family still made her offspring shudder when they recounted some of her heroics.

Woodcutting could be a dangerous way to earn a living. Once, Peter, Sr., was cutting railroad planks with a huge broad ax and with a miscalculated powerful swing he delivered a slicing swipe to his knee, splitting wide open the flesh surrounding the joint. Empathy was one of Martha's gifts. She could "look at anyone and tell when something was wrong with them."

"What's wrong with you?" she asked. He replied, "Nothin'." "Then why don't you sit down?" she said. He did—just to please her, favoring the injured leg. Martha noticed immediately, and with her bare hands ripped Peter's denim jeans open, revealing the open wound. Without hesitating, she looked in her sewing box and retrieved a large needle. There was no alcohol in the house, so she boiled the needle and some thread and sewed his knee up in front of the family members present.

And Martha didn't "play," as they put it. She was a strict disciplinarian, commanding respect from every living creature that crossed her path. When the family lived in Valdosta, she held a job that released her from her duties at 5:00 P.M. Her children would time her arrival by a theme song from a radio broadcast that began at 4:45 sharp. Each day they would clean up after themselves furiously, knowing that at 5:05 Martha would be coming up the walk. So predictable was this pattern that, on its own, the dog that had been in the house against Martha's wishes got up and went outside. Even the chickens that had wandered outside their appointed area in the fenced yard would, as Marjorie put it, "come walking right back on in there—everything that had sense started moving."

Martha's presence could also heal, according to her children. During her teen years, Marjorie worked in the Walgreen's in Valdosta, a thankless position for a young black woman to hold in segregated Georgia. Once she was so sick, she thought she would faint, but her boss didn't release her, because it was rush hour.

> I called my mom and I told her. She said, "What I want you to do is take off your apron, your uniform, put your clothes on, walk out of that door, and I'll be walking down Patterson Street to meet you." I was really, really sick. And when I saw my mom, she reached her hand out to just take my hand. It was gone, the hurting, the feeling, and just everything. She was just that kind of person, a person you could adore, just love. I just reached out to her; when she touched me, it was gone.

Before moving ahead I want to highlight some issues raised in the narrative up to this point. The early history of the Ross clan as presented in this context constituted my representation of the interviewees' collective creation. Their collaborative "imagined" past depicted a southern ethos during the early decades of the twentieth century. They portrayed a world in which celebrations were extremely important and elaborate affairs in which food, dance, dress, and music were central. Gender roles also became an important theme. Strict courtship rituals defined relationships between the sexes. Men were primarily judged for their breadwinning capabilities, especially as they related to their relationship with living off the land. Women, however, were not only celebrated for how they helped to support their families financially; they were also valued for how they dressed, for their ability to keep house, and for their resourcefulness and overall toughness in the face of adversity. In fact, as the narrative above suggests, the interviewees revered their mother. Finally, no matter what the topic—difficult times or good times—the interviewees' ironic sense of humor about their history and memories permeated the interviews and their perspectives.

REPRESENTING "THE SOUTHERN MASSES"

The following passages continue this story of the Rosses' Depression-era life in the South. But now I want to direct your attention to my mode of representing this narrative. The discipline of folklore has taught us the difficulties—some would say the impossibilities—of conveying in prose all of the performative parameters of the kinds of storytelling from which I fashioned the family narrative thus far. As a music scholar, this problematic reminds me very much of the act and, especially, the limits of musical transcription. So many elements are missing from my prose representation: the timbres and tones of citified, southern-flavored dialects of these transplanted Georgians; the rhythmic cadence in their speech patterns; the expressive body language punctuating the stories; and the playfulness marking the cultural space. Much of this has been lost in my story thus far. However, my experimentation with the representational mode below tries to capture something of the performative dimensions of the storytelling.

Below I provide a more or less verbatim representation of their words. Several factors are important. I continue to take note of various themes and concerns raised by their stories. But I am also interested in the somewhat musical and quite collaborative manner in which these stories are recounted. I should also point out that the Rosses lived a life of Depression-era itinerancy in the South. One of them recalled that it was like "running from the rent man." They attributed much of this bustling lifestyle to their father's inability to assume the stereotypical male role as provider because of the racism of the South. The siblings were careful not to upbraid their father unmercifully when talking to me. But clearly, in their minds, Martha led the family.

The interviewees told stories involving difficult familial relationships and the financial challenges of growing up poor in the South. They spoke knowledgeably about the music in various southern cultural spaces, such as the jook joints, about their socialization into northern life, including their adapting to new cuisine and house parties, and about being introduced to "the jazz" by in-laws who had been raised in Chicago. Music constituted a central space for both solace and historically specific "culture making" in the interviewees' memories.

Again, it is important to remember that throughout these interviews the women situated themselves as the true culture bearers. They told the stories primarily from their perspectives and were often the central characters in the narratives, although, according to one woman, the blues (the music that they heard most in the South) relates what "the man" has gone through. I should admit that I was caught somewhat by surprise by the intersection that emerged in this study among female life perspectives, the mass media, and the migration issues I wanted to analyze. While it is now clear to me, upon reflection, that so many of my aesthetic choices and critical perspectives had been shaped by the worldviews of the women in my family, I had not until now considered enough how crucially their knowledge and sensibilities needed to be inscribed into African American critical discourse. Clearly, their primarily unwritten histories, ideas, and voices represent a "subjugated knowledge," of which the black feminist critic Patricia Hill Collins writes.[4] Collins argues that while black women's ideas have been suppressed in traditional scholarship, they have nevertheless developed ways to order and evaluate their experiences, even in the face of race, gender, and class oppression. Their words in this chapter bear this out.

In the section above I crafted the narrative in a way that smoothes out some of the rough edges of conversational speech and the sometimes uneven, rambling flow of long-forgotten stories and thoughts. Yet I am reminded here again of Patricia Hill Collins's work, which states that "oppressed groups are frequently placed in the situation of being listened to only if we frame our ideas in the language that is familiar to and comfortable for a dominant group."[5] This requirement can change what words and ideas mean. As a response to this critique, I will adjust in the remainder of the chapter how I represent the narrative: the words of the interviewees are presented roughly in the way that they said them. One important feature of this mode of representation (still mediated somewhat by my editorial decisions) is that the collective work of imagining the past reveals itself in an almost call-and-response format.

Below, I present episodes that I have selectively gleaned from the interviews. In this series of vignettes, the interviewees reveal details of their life of southern itinerancy during the Depression and of the role that music played within it. Peter's difficulties in providing for his family and Martha's heroics in spite of their hardships emerged as key themes in their memories.

This particular tension between the sexes became an important theme in some of the lyrics of 1940s World War II–era bluesing.

"A Lot of Times We Moved Away"

In this passage, the interviewees remember surviving the Depression. What is striking is how music was considered not a luxury but a necessity; it could not be sacrificed. We learn that their access to recorded music was shared with whites, an idea that calls attention to how some boundaries between blacks and whites were permeable despite segregation. The importance of music in their lifestyle provided a paradigm for how they would be socialized into northern living in Chicago through music and other expressive practices. Apparently, it was more than a matter of just "liking music." Music seemed to be as crucial to their lives as the food they ate. Again, in their depictions of hard times we see the ever-present trope of the thoroughly efficient and equipped mother making the most of the harshest of circumstances.

CELIA: Let me tell something else about my mother. My father was a gambler, you might say. And so one time we had to move away. He had got in some trouble.

    A lot of times we moved away. :MARJORIE

CELIA: So we moved to this place. I really don't remember the name of the place. But there were only nine houses there, and the rolling store, which was a store on wheels, would come around once a week. Right? And we would buy everything we need off of this—they called it a rolling store because it was [a] truck that had groceries and all the supplies that a household would need. And it would come.

    Bob was born then, was he? No, he wasn't. :MARJORIE

    No, he wasn't born. :CELIA

        That's why you don't know about this. Sweetheart, it's all right. :MARJORIE [patting Bob's back facetiously]

CELIA: But we were in this place. And we did have the little [she makes a winding motion with her hands]—

    That's when we had the grasaphone. :MARJORIE

CELIA: —the little grasaphone. The music box with the little symbol on it that you had to wind up with the horn, thing like. We had one of those. And nobody else had any music but us [Marjorie echoes the last two words]. And because our family liked music. And so my father did have this piece of machinery for the music. And even the whites in that area would come on Sunday evening to listen to the music. They just sat there and listened to the music, you know. We moved a truck full of furniture, but my father owed the people for the furniture. They finally came and got the furniture, took the furniture back. So what my mother did—there was [a] fireplace just like that one there, and she took a piece of tin and spread it out and bent it on the side and put it on the fireplace, and this is how she prepared our meal. She put the coals under the tin to cook food on top of the stove. And if she wanted to make bread, she put the coals on top of the tin and it became a oven. And this is how we would eat. Because we didn't have no furniture. They had taken all the furniture away.

And when we didn't have food, there was a CC camp. All of you all are too young to know about CC camp. But there was a CC in this area, and they would leave food. And this man know that we were there and knew that we didn't have a lot of food. He talked to the head man of the CC camp and told him instead of dumping the food into the garbage can when they were finished, that he would kind of put it aside so we would have this food. 'Cause he said there's a man and woman, he doesn't really have a job and there are small kids there. So they would leave the food separate, not dumped all together. And my father would go along and they would say, just let him think that he is stealing food—which my dad thought that he was doing, you know. When they put the food aside, then they would just move and go back to work. And my father thought that he was stealing the food, but they was actually putting the food out there for him, okay, so that we would have food to eat.

"That's One Reason Why I Beat 'Em, Too"

On the surface this next passage seems to be solely about how Marjorie had inherited aspects of her mother's indomitable spirit. Predictably, in each scenario we see how Martha's quick heroic actions saved the day while Peter remained somewhat on the sidelines. Despite the gloss of a "Calamity Jane" persona painted into these scenarios, other issues in African American culture can be teased out. Just below the jokes, for example, we learn through Marjorie's decisive and physical reactions to the perception that she didn't measure up to specific standards of beauty such as hair length and texture that these were touchy and, hence, important subjects indeed.

CELIA: One of these particular times when all of these people was sitting around and was listening at the music and everything, we had wandered off—it had nine houses in this place. It also had nine deep wells. The wells were this big around, like the same area as this living room. And most of them was deep. But one of those wells, we had been throwing dirt and sand and all kinds of junk in there with it, until it was beginning to fill up. But we still liked to go there and throw at the snakes and the frogs and whatnot.

MARJORIE: There couldn't have been snakes in there when I fell in there.

CELIA: And guess who fell in?

There couldn't have been a snake when I fell in the well. :MARJORIE

CELIA: Guess who fell in this well? [She points to Marjorie.]

BOB: You fell in a well?

CELIA: She fell in the well. She fell in this well and we had to run home and tell my mother. And my daddy was still sitting there, wondering what happened. And we said, "Totsie, Totsie, Totsie [Marjorie's nickname]!!!"And all we were saying was "Totsie." And my mother just ran. She didn't . . . she never stopped. She just start running from the way we had come, 'cause she would always be watching where we were. And she just start running in the direction we came from, and my daddy was still standing trying to get together what we were saying and everything. And my mother went straight there, to this well. Looked down in there. Saw this little short, nappy-head child. She always wore a wool cap on her head [laughing].

Because my hair was short and Celia's and Dorothy's was long. :MARJORIE

Hers wasn't that short. It was just about that [makes a gesture with her fingers] long. It was about that long. :CELIA

And you couldn't braid my hair. They couldn't braid my hair and whatever. They had long hair . . . that's one reason why I beat 'em, too. I did fall in a well. :MARJORIE

CELIA: She had a skullcap on. And she also kept a jawbone-breaker in her jaw all the time. Like Popeye the Sailor Man. And my mother just got down [she gets up and bends down], she just went straight to that well. I guess she was going to jump in. But she laid down on her stomach, reached way down into that well, and pulled her child out that well.

MARJORIE: And I guess I went on home and fell on out the window on the car motor.

BOB: Oh, boy. You . . .

CELIA: And then another time, she just climbed out up in the window, fell out the window—there was a car motor right under the window—she just fell over, then split her head and my mother had to doctor on her.

MARJORIE: And I'm fine.

CELIA: Well, that's a matter of opinion [and everyone falls out laughing].

"That's Where You Get That From"

Peter's hobo days spark warm, if conflicted, memories about his long trips away from the family in the passage below. His shortcomings provide, in the context of this storytelling, yet another opportunity to praise Martha's interventions to keep the family together. In one of the few male-centered stories that emerged in the interviews, we learn of Peter's brush with the criminal justice system and the costs he paid in trying to provide for the family, a toll that sometimes included his pride. Again, one of the reasons that I present this information here is to understand the historical and material grounding of the dynamic "South in the City" culture of the mid-1940s. These migrants brought culture with them when they arrived in Chicago. To that end we see that hard times in the South and particularly Peter's response to them had a specific and long-lasting effect on one of his children once she moved North. In the next section, titled "This Really Hurts," which recounts one of the few stories that they told about discrimination directly, Celia relates a memory of a very specific kind of emasculating, blatant racism. The story demonstrates for her the difficulty that many black men in the South faced as they tried to provide for their families.

CELIA: But anyway, these were the things that my mother did [Marjorie nods in assent]. She just made, like Marjorie say, she was able to survive—[to Bob] you didn't know, did you, about the stove that she made out of tin?

MARJORIE: —in the fireplace. For us to cook. And making our socks and everything.

CELIA: When my daddy got in jail—

What? :BOB [perplexed]

—and they told us we could come to see him, we didn't have nothing to wear. My mother had took the flour sacks that it came in and she bleached them, and made us little dresses so we could go see our daddy. And she even took pieces of it and made socks so we would have nice little pretty socks when we went to the jail to see our daddy. :CELIA

GUTHRIE RAMSEY: What was he jailed for?

CELIA: Gambling and for stealing money.

MARJORIE: Gambling and when he . . .

He must have been a rogue. Goodness. :BOB

CELIA: Yes.

MARJORIE: When my father'd come home, all our food would be all mixed together. Like the rice, he might hobo the freight train and when he'd get home, he'd throw the sack off first, but he would always have five moon pies in there.

For his kids. :CELIA

For all of us. :MARJORIE

CELIA: He did this when he finally got out of jail, he couldn't work anywhere.

He would have five moon pies. :MARJORIE

He had to go out of town— :CELIA

MARJORIE: So he was thinking about us. But then the rice and maybe the meal or whatever would all be mixed together. But then he would have those five [splays her hand] moon pies.

—'cause he had to hobo. :CELIA

MARJORIE: 'Cause he worked in the woods and he might didn't come home 'til maybe every two weeks or something like that.

CELIA: So when the train comes by, when he get near the destination, near our house, he would throw his croaker sack full of groceries and the goodies that he had bought—he would throw them off the train and then he had to get himself off. See, because the train didn't slow down because he was going to get off it. They didn't know he was on it.

MARJORIE: [chimes in, laughing] They didn't know he was on it.

CELIA: So they didn't slow down.

MARJORIE: And he was a sweet man, but Daddy has instilled something within me that I have said that I would never want any of my kids to have to go through with, and that is writing notes to grocery stores—and asking us—for food. Every week, he'll write and say somebody had died. Or his sister had died and he'll have this list of the foods that—they want to have on credit. He didn't have the money. And he would send one of us. And this stayed with me all of my life.

BOB: I remember some of those.

MARJORIE: Do you remember too?

BOB: I carried a few. I remember that.

MARJORIE: Aha. I mean every week, it was somebody that had died in our family, in Daddy's family. And these people would say, well, dag, "Who dead this time?" You know? That would just hurt me to know that, hey, these people are looking down on me and stuff. And I had said, whenever I get grown, this I would never do. I would never do.

CELIA: And she, honestly, she has always kept her a freezer and has always saw that it was full of food. Because she remember those times.

BOB: Hmm. That's where you get that from.

CELIA: That's where she get it from.

MARJORIE: I used to hoard food. Like if stuff be on sale.

She don't eat it, but she'll get it. :CELIA

MARJORIE: I would go and get all the flour and I would put it in the freezer. The meal and put it in the freezer and whatever. Although the kids are gone now, and everything. But I would just get stuff that I didn't need because of this . . .

'Cause of what happened with her then. :CELIA

"This Really Hurts"

CELIA: One time my father needed some money, which his word was not reliable and everything. He went to this loan company to borrow some money. And he told them what he wanted and everything. They took the application on him. And what they did, so then they looked at it . . . I guess it was either fifty or seventy-five dollars, or something like that. And in front of his face . . . This really hurts. This man got on the phone and called my mother and said, [Peter] Mallie is up here to borrow some money and if you say it's okay, I'll give it to him. And my mother said [it] was okay and they gave

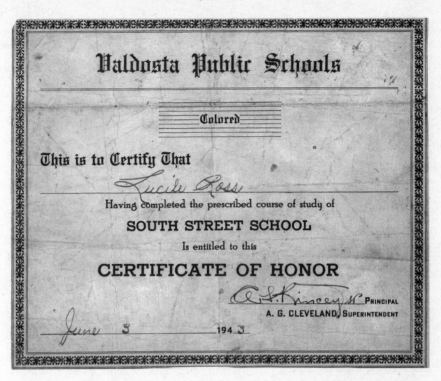

Figure 4. "Certificate of Honor." Growing up poor and black in the Deep South didn't deter the Ross children from striving for educational excellence, despite the separate and unequal ways of segregation. Credit: Marjorie Jones.

my dad the money. I just . . . it was the way that . . . because he was a black man. You know what I'm saying? And his word was no good. But his wife's word was good and all she had to say it over the phone. To me, if he had went in another room and called my mother, it would have been fine. But he called her right there in front of my dad. That hurt me to this day, that they called my mother right in front of my dad's face and say if it's all right. . . . And say if it's all right, I'll give him the money.

"I Knew I Could Dance"

As the interviewees mused about their memories of expressive practices in the South, their stories eventually led to the country jook joints of which they painted elaborate descriptions and explanations of bluesing culture in a specific context. Key ideas about southern culture of this kind are revealed in this passage. They believed that music was a central factor in their lives

as African Americans. Dancing well to recorded music represented an important form of cultural capital and a mode in which individual attention could be attracted even as one participated in the collective. Although the setting of this passage is the South, it is clear that some of the cultural and geographic spaces were considered more "country" than others. An underground economy existed in the jook culture, in which various kinds of spirits and food were sold at a marked-up price. This particular observation demonstrates that even within the "folk" setting of the country jook, which supposedly existed outside the realm of commercial and mass culture, financial considerations were central.

CELIA: We really did like music. Okay, so there are certain . . .
Whatever you want, or whatever you like, people, black people have always found a way to have that one thing that would satisfy them out of all the other things that they wanted. And music, I don't know whether it was from my mother's side or from my father's side, but we had to have some music in the house.

MARJORIE: Music was just the thing. I never shall forget that when I was in . . . I was the only one that really could dance. [Snaps her fingers and sways.] I mean I could get it. I wasn't shy. We were like in Valdosta and when we'd go out to Clyattsville

Figures 5a–c.   Styling and profiling "southern style." Martha's sewing skills kept her children immaculately dressed in the current fashions of the mid-1940s. Far from being the stereotypical "unkempt country bumpkins" of social-science lore, they brought this sensibility with them when they migrated north to Chicago. Credit: Marjorie Jones and Celia Ramsey Wynn.

where my mom was born but we had moved in the city, like. But we . . . I would go back out there and on Saturday nights when they . . . Friday, Saturday, and Sunday. That was jook night. That was jook night. And I would love to go out in the country, because I knew I could dance. And I knew everybody was going be standing around looking at the city girl coming and dancing. And we would be in, just a wood frame [drawing the parameters with her hands], you know. And we would just . . . that was the best time of my life. I really enjoyed those times. It wasn't nothing but the blues. You know. Blues. Jook music and everything. Those times were really, really . . . it just stays with me all of the time.

CELIA: [The blues] is the story of what the man had gone through, the whole week. And so this was his way of letting it out. You know. You go to this jook joint and get the fried fish sandwich—

    And the beer. :MARJORIE

        —and the beer and just listen to the music. :CELIA

MARJORIE: And the sealed whiskey that would be up in under the mattress that we weren't supposed to sell. But they called it sealed whiskey. It was just like . . .

    It wasn't moonshine. :CELIA

MARJORIE: You'd get a half a pint of vodka or something. They called that sealed whiskey because it had a seal around the top. But they had it up under the mattress or wherever, because you aren't supposed . . .

CELIA: So the person in the jook joint—you'd just tell them—if you didn't want the moonshine, which was illegal, too, you'd tell them you wanted a half a pint of sealed whiskey, and they'd say, "Okay. It'll take me a little while." So maybe they had to go somewhere and get the whiskey. And they'd bring it back to you and they would charge you their price, because they may have spent one price for it, but since you want it, you pay whatever their price is for it.

In the community theater of family life presented in this chapter, I have tried to give voice to a representative constituency whose modern subjectivities are often flattened and washed out under the rubric "the black masses." The subjugated knowledge that I am attempting to theorize into this study's interpretive framework represents a particular work of the imagination or collective memory of a specific family. These memories embody a cultural sensibility that should be a factor in the interpretation of African American music from this particular period and beyond. These collective memories (and certainly others like them) provide the historical grounding of my own cultural priorities and, thus, my critical and interpretive perspectives, although this relationship is often transparent and seemingly "natural." It, however, is not natural but the result of the intergenerational sharing of cultural and social knowledge. More important, since the experiences recounted by the interviewees mirror those of many others born into similar social stations—and these include black musicians at this time—we can consider these interviewees' worldviews as dependable indexes of the historical social energies shaping African American identity at this moment.

If cultural critics before me have dismissed the idea that African American culture should be gendered as essentially male, then the ideas presented here further this critique. The serendipitous female-centricity of the interview process has added a dimension of complexity to my representation of "average, struggling Negroes." The Rosses' migration to the big city of Chicago represents to many an important step in their becoming more modern subjectivities. But before I discuss this move in detail, let us once more move away from the private spaces of culture and focus on structure; in this case, the larger forces at work in the sociopolitical and economic setting and in the culture industry. Within the public sphere of the 1940s, we find dynamic changes in musical production occurring on all levels. These shifts, as we shall see, brought to the surface new ideas about the modernist profile of African American culture and, by extension, about that of African Americans such as the ones whom we have learned about in this chapter. Before we continue (in chapter 6) the story of the Rosses' move to Chicago, let's consider the larger sociocultural context in which this migration took place.

5 "We Called Ourselves Modern"

Race Music and the Politics and Practice of Afro-Modernism at Midcentury

To be modern is to live a life of paradox and contradiction. It is to be overpowered by the immense bureaucratic organizations that have the power to control and often to destroy all communities, values, lives; and yet to be undeterred in our determination to face these forces, to fight to change their world and make it our own.

Marshall Berman, *All That Is Solid Melts into Air*

The music wasn't called bop at Minton's. In fact, we had no name for the music. We called ourselves modern. That bop label started during the war. . . . That label did a lot of harm.

Kenny Clarke, *Hear Me Talkin' to Ya*

In music, I don't see too much difference between head arrangements and written arrangements. The jazz musician, though he practically never receives credit for it, is constantly composing during his improvisations, and most of the melodies he creates are never set down on paper, nor on record. . . . If they had those midget tape recorders on the market back in 1942, I could've written a song a week without taking off time from what I believe is the essence of jazz composition, playing and improvisations.

Dizzy Gillespie, *To Be or Not to Bop*

In the last of the epigraphs above, modern jazz musician Dizzy Gillespie conflates what is considered different modes of musical creation in jazz: the improviser's oral-based head arrangements and the composer's written arrangements. By privileging improvisation as the source of jazz composition, he turns on its ear one of the "truths" of the Western music tradition and of modernism. Moreover, when he talks about the potential role of the tape recorder, Gillespie points to the place of technology in establishing "modern" cultural forms. As drummer Kenny Clarke points out in the second epigraph, the processes described by Gillespie were thought to be expressions of modernism by some of the musicians creating them. Moreover, Clarke's use of the term *modern* and his rejection of the market-ready label "bebop" reveal strong feelings about where he (and many others) thought the music fit into America's cultural hierarchy. The label "bebop" tainted his music with a commercial veneer unworthy of its artistic contribution. But as we shall see, the perceived chasms between so-called modernist artistic expressions, commercial expressions, and those of "the people" are not so clear in the context of African American culture in the 1940s.

African American music, as I will argue in this chapter, became in the 1940s a site for expressing some of the paradoxes, contradictions, tensions, and, of course, the joys and pleasures of African American life in those years. The musical expressions that circulated these social energies articulated what I'm calling here Afro-modernism, a concept whose genesis belongs to previous decades but which ripened in the 1940s. In the broadest sense, I use the concept Afro-modernism to identify African American responses to the experience of modernity. In chapter 3, I discussed the North-South cultural dialogue as a particular manifestation of the expression of Afro-modernism. In chapter 4 I provided the historical and personal dimensions of the southern side of this cultural equation. But I need to flesh out the Afro-modernism idea more fully, because in many ways all roads in this book lead to it.

The term *modernity* (a historical moment) is associated with other "modernization" processes and concepts such as industrialization, the "City," bureaucracy, and secularization. Modernism has historical, socioeconomic, political, and, as important, aesthetic or expressive dimensions. From its emergence in Western culture in the fifth century A.D. to the late-twentieth-century notion of the postmodern, the idea of the modern has articulated something about historical actors' self-conscious attitudes about and their responses to the relationship among the past, the present, and the future. As Marshall Berman puts it, modernism is "any attempt by modern men and women to become subjects as well as objects of modernization, to get a grip on the modern world and make themselves at home in it."[1] For African Americans, part of this making themselves at home consisted of the creation and, certainly, the reception (the political and pleasurable uses) of musical expressions that articulated attitudes about their place in the modern world. Thus, Afro-modernism asks: What was modernity to African Americans at the historical moment under consideration? How were their attitudes about it worked out artistically and critically?

To cite one example, Dizzy Gillespie saw the formal qualities of his composition "A Night in Tunisia" as representing artistic innovation in modern jazz and as a way to situate himself and his artistic contributions in history and in the African Diaspora. "A Night in Tunisia" expanded on the idea of a North-South cultural dialogue in Afro-modernist jazz by musically commenting on the past and the future of the musical style. Gillespie believed, for example, that the repetitive ostinato bass pattern that begins the composition linked this sonic experiment to an African past, to his South Carolinian not-so-distant past, and to an Afro-Cuban future for jazz music. Gillespie recognized the communal process that created "A Night in Tunisia" as participating in a new transatlantic cultural dialogue. Gillespie fashioned a world that sought to situate African American experiences of modernity within the large African Diaspora.

There were many other Afro-modernist moves in the 1940s, and as I explain below, they were created within a complex of specific socioeconomic and historical developments that I consider part of the modernization of African American culture. But the modernist expressions that resulted in this process articulated a hybrid modernism that answered to the political imperatives of the moment. In this chapter I discuss examples of these processes and their contradictions and paradoxes. Mass migration, the use and misuse of the black body, a new urban profile, a swelling sense of black political, economic, and social efficacy, and conflicting discourses on art's role in social change provided the context for new cultural expressions in the 1940s.

Specifically, music and the critical discourses it inspired became conspicuous public activities within which these issues were sorted out, expressed, and debated. Tera Hunter has noted the ability of blues music to participate in important cultural work: "The centrality of the singer's individual persona, the highly personalized subject matter of songs, the thematic shifts toward the material world and the pursuit of pleasure were all characteristic of an emergent modern ethos."[2] The project of the modern ethos, while having deep roots in previous decades and manifestations in vocal and instrumental music, was continued into the 1940s, as we shall see.

"THINGS AIN'T WHAT THEY USED TO BE": MIGRATION, MODERNIZATION, AND SOCIETY

The decade of the 1940s saw a number of remarkable shifts within the nation's intellectual, political, cultural, economic, and artistic life. American intellectuals began to rethink how they perceived American culture and heritage, a new sense of nationalism emerged, a "baby boom" and a new prosperity shaped American family life, a modernist sensibility swept through the arts, and a new efficacy among working-class citizens transformed

Figure 6.   Dizzy Gillespie was not only an innovator of the bebop style of jazz in the 1940s; he also set fashion standards for other musicians and even for fans around the world. Credit: Chuck Stewart.

economic relationships and popular culture. Indeed, as historian George Lipsitz notes, mobilizing for World War II and the reconversion process after the war shook American culture to its core, sending waves of change through almost every realm of the American experience. Music of this period cannot be divorced from these developments. Dizzy Gillespie, for example, reminds us in his autobiography that even the performance rhetoric of modern jazz was linked to the specific tenor of the postwar moment: "My music emerged from the war years . . . and it reflected those times in the music. Fast and furious, with the chord changes going this way and that way, it might've looked and sounded like bedlam, but it really wasn't."[3]

For many African Americans, however, these times were bedlam. In the interlocking realms of politics, economics, and culture, the 1940s saw many developments that touched the lives of all Americans but held specific consequences for African Americans, especially within their expressive cultural practices. Chief among these developments, and in many ways causing them, was the dramatic demographic shift created by thousands of black citizens leaving southern states for urban communities like New York, Chicago, and Los Angeles, among other destinations. The force of this migration would carry long-term effects for the country's social policies and, as we shall see, especially for its artistic and cultural profile. The 1940s were marked by contradiction. On the one hand, the Jim Crow system that appeared after Reconstruction seemed to be drawing its last breath because of political, legal, and economic pressure mounted by African Americans in grassroots protests. On the other hand, the shifting maze of discriminatory practices constantly undermined these various struggles for equality. These cultural dynamics played themselves out in postwar African American expressive culture such as literature, visual arts, and music.[4] One notable shift occurred in the "Race" division of popular music, where fragmentation took place, separating genres into different marketing categories.[5]

A booming wartime economy, a huge migration of rural citizens to urban centers, and technological advances in the recording industry also promoted change. The postwar period's strong economy had a profound impact on the American entertainment industry, most notably in the area of record sales. In 1945, for example, the recording industry anticipated a sales boom of 600 million records because of postwar consumers' appetite for new artists. New technology emerging from military efforts during World War II improved sound reproduction, further encouraging American interest in purchasing recordings. Among the new advances to appear were wire and tape-recording and reproducing machines and a Russian-captured German Magnetaphon, which gave superior fidelity to American commercial recordings. In 1948

Columbia Records introduced the long-playing disk (LP), allowing about twenty-five minutes of uninterrupted music on each side. This technological advance was well-suited for the inspired freedom of modern jazz solos.[6]

The atmosphere ripened with new possibilities, experimentation, and innovation. Musicians (such as the ones discussed in chapter 2) and entrepreneurs alike exploited the situation, seizing opportunities to establish careers. Fledgling record companies such as Mercury sought out new artists and attempted to find a market niche for themselves by satisfying the public's growing appetite for new talent. As a result, the postwar years spawned hybrid styles that proliferated in the popular music industry. An impressive array of new artists appeared, and many of them were recent migrants to northern cities.

The shifting profile of urban America throughout this decade changed American musical life. George Lipsitz has noted the importance of black *and* white migration to America's cities, contending that "the new urban realities of the 1940s . . . allowed for new cultural exchanges that would have been impossible in prewar America." Industrial labor created by defense production for World War II, for example, provided unprecedented interaction among diverse ethnic groups and their musical sensibilities.[7] These new cultural exchanges produced a variety of musics that were popular among urban blacks and whites. Accelerated by advances in communication and transportation technologies that were "making the world an ever-shrinking globe,"[8] these musical developments encouraged changes within the popular music industry. As we shall see below, the 1940s also saw new technologies and attitudes toward black bodies as a major force in the new Afro-modernism.

Integration and the Second Reconstruction

Manning Marable has characterized the postwar era as the beginning of black America's "Second Reconstruction," primarily because African Americans made huge strides in their struggle for social equality. African Americans mounted a series of national confrontations to elevate their collective social status during Gillespie's "war years." During the war, a defiant optimism swelled as African Americans rallied around the "Double V" campaign (victory at home and abroad) that was widely hailed by the Negro press. Double V represented an important benchmark for the national political efficacy and the international vision of African American voters. The idea behind the campaign originated during an NAACP-led conference held in November 1943; the meeting produced the slogan "Victory must crush Hitlerism both at home and abroad." If the first Reconstruction witnessed black bodies freed from chattel slavery, then the second one saw African Americans using their collective bodies as a threat to de facto and de jure racism in American society.[9]

The black body has represented an enduring, contested sign of difference in Western thought. It has become symbolic for conflicting ideas that have inspired both fear and fascination in the popular imagination. As an instrument of free labor in chattel slavery systems, as a tool for forced human reproduction in these systems, as a site for mockery in nineteenth-century minstrelsy, and as "the" image of criminality (such as in the infamous Willie Horton television ads of the 1988 presidential campaign), the black body has remained an important, yet enigmatic, presence in the Western world. African Americans have participated in and resisted these representations. Through mass migrations, labor, dance, and protest, they have used the body, as British cultural critic Stuart Hall has noted, "as if it was, and it often was, the only cultural capital we had." By midcentury, African Americans clearly believed that if they sacrificed their bodies in war, they would no longer accept the segregation of these same bodies in American society.[10]

But challenging physical segregation meant putting black bodies in the line of fire. After the April 1945 death of the New Deal's architect, Franklin Delano Roosevelt, white workers mounted a series of "hate strikes" that were aimed at preventing the unpoliced presence of black bodies in the industrial workplace. Lerone Bennett wrote that "blowtorch killing and eye-gouging of Negro veterans freshly returned from . . . war," among other atrocities, prompted the National Association for the Advancement of Colored People to designate the year 1946 as "one of the grimmest" in the thirty-six-year history of the organization. Racially motivated violence was commonplace during and after the war. Detroit, Harlem, and twenty-five other cities exploded with black bodies taking to the streets in the race riots of 1943. These civil eruptions underscored the tensions created by the mass exodus of thousands of southern blacks to the North in search of defense jobs.[11]

African Americans achieved modest gains in education, labor, and politics during the 1940s. The establishment of the United Negro College Fund in 1943 symbolically represented the increased quality and accessibility of educational opportunities for African Americans. Black teachers throughout the nation mounted successful legal campaigns to equalize their pay scales with those of their white counterparts. But black parents were less successful in increasing state allocations for black—and, for the most part, segregated—public schools. The decision to ban segregation in public schools in the mid-1950s and the violent public reaction to heavily escorted black schoolchildren entering white school buildings show the importance of black bodies, even small ones, crossing the color lines at this time. In industry, for example, the gradual desegregation of the nation's work force, spawned primarily by the increased need for laboring black bodies during wartime, provided African Americans a measure of economic muscle and political clout. The United States experienced a period of unprecedented economic growth as a result of World War II, and this new prosperity was shared by African Americans, who, as Mary Frances Berry and John Blassingame observe, experienced great economic gains between 1940 and 1950.[12]

Under the leadership of A. Philip Randolph, the influential black trade unionist and leading proponent of desegregation, black membership in labor unions such as the American Federation of Labor and the Steelworkers of America increased dramatically. The growing political influence of African Americans was shown by the government's response to Randolph's threat to stage a huge march on Washington, D.C., in July 1941, protesting unfair employment practices. President Roosevelt's Executive Order 8802 prevented the march. The order, decried or ignored by many white employers throughout the country, banned "discrimination in employment by companies filling defense contracts."[13] Enthusiastic black support for the proposed march arguably announced the beginning of a new era in African American politics. Jacqueline Jones portrays the rise of this kind of grassroots protest, which energized the Civil Rights movement, by quoting a woman she identifies simply as "a black female delegate to a civil rights convention in Chicago" in 1941: "We ought to throw fifty thousand Negroes around the White House, bring them from all over the country, in jalopies, in trains and any way they can get there . . . until we get some action."[14] Such words seem to confirm what the ever astute George Lipsitz observes—that at this moment, the black working class began to understand how to produce "political and social change out of the crucible of economic struggle."[15]

Migration and the New Black Archipelago

The grassroots politics behind the proposition of the female delegate to the Civil Rights convention confirm how the 1940s saw intensified and, in some cases, entirely new figurations in the political economies of the African American body. The threat of throwing fifty thousand Negro bodies around the White House in organized protest can be seen as connected to the mass movement of five million to six and a half million black southerners to the North between the years 1910 and 1970. This massive displacement of black bodies, called the Great Migration, marks a crucial event in America's social and cultural history. The specific migration that took place during the 1940s announced the end of the cotton industry's hegemony over laboring African

American bodies, especially in the South. Nicholas Lemman argues that, with the appearance of the mechanical cotton picker in the mid-1940s, the post-Emancipation sharecropping system, which locked many African Americans into a substandard lifestyle, sputtered to an end and set the stage for segregation's demise as well. African Americans, betting on the promise of decent wages and enhanced mobility in the North, flooded its cities and then transformed the urban spaces they now occupied. Indeed, the "decoupling of race from cotton" and the migration that followed left an indelible mark on a variety of areas in American life, including popular culture, politics, urban history, educational policy, and the social welfare system. That influence is prevalent in the musical, literary, and visual arts; indeed, the discourse of migration has worked its way into the fabric of black expressive culture. Cultural critic Farah J. Griffin argues that the migration narrative was one of the twentieth century's primary modes of African American cultural production.[16]

We need to keep in mind several important points about black migration. During and after the 1940s, new arrivals were initiated into an African American urban culture whose foundation and framework had been established during the early years of the twentieth century. The peak years of the earlier migration during the 1920s witnessed a contestation between two emerging groups: a black bourgeoisie and a new black urbanized working class, each striving for upward mobility. This tension was inscribed with gender and intraclass issues among African Americans, many of which have only gradually come into high relief in recent studies. By the end of the 1950s a new demographic figuration among African American communities was clearly established. Black America now existed, in Nicholas Lemann's words, as "an urban black archipelago" with a stratified social-class structure. For the first time, America began to think about African American issues as essentially urban, rather than as primarily rural, because of migration. In addition, the migration caused these urban communities to acquire a more heterogeneous demography, and this provided new political, economic, and cultural possibilities.[17]

The specific processes of modernization that I have outlined above—migration, integration, social and economic progress, urbanization—contributed to a dramatic shift in the mass consciousness of African Americans. While one must always make allowances for difference among African Americans, this transformation was widespread enough to impact every segment of African American communities. On many levels they sought to make their own world in the context of a social structure designed to keep them subordinate and without real power over their circumstances. But gradually the system was being eroded, and gains toward equality were achieved. As part of this broad development, black musicians achieved unprecedented exposure in the 1940s and beyond, enhancing their profile in the American popular imagination. The role of mass media in these processes was central. For one, a new discourse of art began to form around jazz, partly as a result of the new cultural possibilities that presented themselves in the 1940s. Below I discuss some of the historical and social grounding of the "jazz as art" idea while giving some attention to some of the quite different perceptions surrounding the other race musics.

MAPPING NEW MODERNISMS:
RACE, ART, AND RECORDINGS (1920S–1940S)

Thelonious Monk, a musician credited with playing a key role in the creation of modern jazz, offers a view of bebop's origin that seems to compete with the standard narrative.

> I was just playing a gig, trying to play music. While I was at Minton's anybody sat in if he could play. I never bothered anybody. I had no particular feeling that anything new was being built. It's true modern jazz probably began to get popular there, but some of these histories and articles put what happened over the course of ten years into one year. They put people all together in one time in one place. I've seen practically everybody at Minton's, but they were just there playing. They weren't giving any lectures.[18]

Monk "just" wanted to play satisfactorily on the gig and presumably earn wages for that service. Monk states that anybody could participate at Minton's if they possessed the skills and recalls a distinct lack of a self-conscious attitude—"we are collectively trying to build something new here"—that has often been connected to the bebop project of the early 1940s. But Kenny Clarke's sentiments about the modern profile of the music (quoted in the second epigraph to this chapter) mesh better with the idea of "new cultural possibilities" during the postwar era. Indeed, contradiction and paradox marked the modernist project.

Contemporary evidence shows that the stylistic conventions of bebop sounded wildly avant-garde to some listeners. And as I have stated, when scholars and musicians talk about that period, they draw homologies with the avant-garde qualities of bebop and the sociopolitical shifts I have outlined above. There are numerous accounts of bebop musicians rejecting their entertainer's stance for that of modern artists.[19] These accounts argue that the creators of bebop worked in a self-conscious way to dispel the stereotypical image of shuffling, smiling Negro entertainers, who provided danceable beats and recognizable melodies for segregated audiences. Bebop musicians seemed to symbolize a new order. Unwilling to accept the limits placed on black jazz musicians by the white-dominated music business, they took a stance that helped give their music a sharp and, to many, an uncomfortable edge. These portrayals also stress that bebop was not dance music, not conceived for mass consumption, but at the same time not designed for traditional "high brow" concert audiences. This narrative of jazz self-consciously dressing itself up in the trappings of modernism and being a singular sociopolitical statement has several underlying assumptions: that this idea was new in black musical culture, that it was new to jazz specifically, and that it was not true of the other postwar race musics.

But to focus on bebop musicians as the quintessential "race men" of their hour does not account for how Afro-modernism resonated in the so-called popular and folk realms. For African Americans, the thrust of Afro-modernism has *always* been, in my view, defined primarily within the sociopolitical arena: as the quest for liberation, freedom, and literacy as well as the seeking of upward mobility and enlarged possibilities within the American capitalist system. Literary critic Houston Baker has talked about the Afro-modernist project as "renaissancism"—a "productive set of tactics" and not simply the "success" and influence of black literary and black "classical" music such as those from movements like the Harlem Renaissance. When Baker describes Afro-modernism in this way—as cultural work and as a political strategy—he can then identify elements of the Afro-modernist project in a cluster of activities. These include important speeches and entrepreneurial efforts—any "productive competence" that counters the legacies of black people's arrested historical relationship with American capitalism and its cultural hierarchy.[20]

I should stress here, however, that Afro-modernism has similarities to classic (or canonical) modernism, the other experimental developments in music, literature, and art that emerged in European and American metropolitan centers during the late nineteenth and early twentieth centuries. These artistic expressions articulated how the culture of modernity—the transformed character of economic, social, and cultural life associated with the rise of capitalism, industrialization, and urbanization—was experienced by many. A few of the discourses that emerged from the state of modernity include an antagonistic relationship between "high art" and mass culture, rejection of the norms and values of bourgeois culture, and, in some cases, an alignment with progressive cultural politics.

But along with this "mainstream" modernist impulse, one can identify and trace various African American responses to modernity as well—an Afro-modernism that was articulated within African American letters, art, and music.[21] The idea, for example, that bebop ushered jazz out of the realms of popular and folk music gets its logic from some very traditional and modern ideas about musical culture.

In a groundbreaking essay, musicologist Charles Hamm has argued that a set of metanarratives emerged during the modern era that have shaped scholarly and populist discussions of popular music. These narratives have served the project of modernism well, legitimating one of its tenets such as cultural hierarchies and, by extension, power relationships within the social domain. The modernist narratives, according to Hamm, address notions of musical autonomy, mass culture, authenticity, classic or classical style, and youth culture. An important piece of modernist work that these narratives perform in the musical world is the partitioning off of the three main musical categories: art, popular, and folk. David Brackett has clearly summarized the logic behind these ideas:

- "Art" music revolves around providing a transcendent experience; however, only those with the right training can experience the real meaning of "great" music.

- "Popular" music values are created by and organized around the music industry—musical value and monetary value are therefore equated, and the sales charts become the measure of "good" pop music.

- "Folk" music revolves around providing an authentic experience of community.

These narratives provide a lens to better see some of the transparent boundaries surrounding musical styles. They also show how black musical texts have critiqued, teased, and taunted these boundaries and the logic of "modernist" aesthetics outlined above. In fact, bebop displays a specific kind of hybrid modernism when viewed within the framework of the modernist narratives.[22]

Indeed, the cluster of stylistic conventions that defined the bebop sound has proven remarkably ripe for competing interpretations. Virtuoso solo improvisations, elaborate harmonic and melodic revisions of Tin Pan Alley songs, and dramatic, irregular, and unpredictable rhythmic accents called bombs from the drummer marked a departure from the conventions of earlier styles. For many, these innovations signaled complexity and abstractness, making jazz's emergence as "art" logical. William Austin's description of

Charlie Parker's solo rhetoric, for example, is suggestive of a modern artist: "Passages of flowing motion with frequent changes of direction and no obvious sequences; in contrast, abrupt beginnings and endings, with a feeling of impatience, self-consciousness, wry humor; brief emphasis on an occasional burst of dissonant, chromatic harmony, and no pausing to enjoy its resolution." Austin concludes that Parker's music "required for discriminating appreciation as thorough a specialized preparation as any 'classical' style. . . . [Parker] stood for jazz as a fine art, knowing that this meant exclusiveness."[23]

For Austin and many others, bebop's stylistic "incomprehensibility" rendered the music a political tool. Thus its complexity and the mental challenge it required became "signs of reason," signs of mental and creative prowess, in much the same way as Henry Louis Gates has shown how, in racist discourse, literacy became a sign of humanity for African Americans.[24] Thus the political import of bebop could not be (and was not) ignored. And although many argued for its artistic profile, bebop resisted claims of autonomy—ideals that would have considered its works to be self-contained artifacts shaped according to abstract principles. No, these were signifying texts, indeed.

The tension between autonomous-creative-artistic-modern virtuosity and the *political* work that bebop achieved on behalf of "the folk" can be seen in the following examples. Eric Lott writes that "bebop was about making *disciplined* imagination come alive and answerable to the social change of its time"; it "pitted *mind* against the perversity of circumstance," and it represented a sensibility that chose "blinding *virtuosity*" as a weapon in political struggle. Furthermore, he argues, "bebop was intimately if indirectly related to the militancy of its moment. Militancy and music were under girded by the same social facts; the music attempted to resolve at the level of style what the militancy combated in the streets." Cornel West writes that bebop was "a *creative* musical response to the major shifts in sensibilities and moods in Afro-America after World War II . . . [it expressed] the heightened tensions, frustrated aspirations, and repressed emotions of an aggressive yet apprehensive Afro-America." For Amiri Baraka, bebop's artistry was "the exact registration of the social and cultural thinking of a whole generation of black Americans."[25] Thus, bebop's "artistic autonomy" was certainly overtly political. But this Afro-modernist sensibility had precedence in black music history.

Although the Western art music tradition has been studied in large measure according to the principle of artistic autonomy, recent work in the field of musicology has sought to understand the ideological, social, and political functions of musical categories such as serious, popular, and folk. Some of this research is known as the new musicology, a name that has been as coolly received as the word *bebop* was in the 1940s. The new musicology calls for, among many other goals, what Richard Leppert and Susan McClary call a "crossover" methodology: It reveals the social and political functions of serious music, and it discusses the aesthetic qualities of popular music.[26] Such inquiry dismantles the perceived gaps among the modernist narratives of art, mass culture, and the folk. But African American musical studies had troubled these modernist waters long before the new musicology appeared.

As I have written elsewhere, the cultural politics of African American music has developed within powerful ideologies surrounding race.[27] For that reason, the principle of artistic autonomy could not develop within black culture in the same way as it had with regard to the Western art music tradition. This is not to say, however, that inquiries of African American music have not fought for the traditional social advantages that attend the notion of autonomy—prestige, "greatness," genius status, and transcendence of the social world, among other related ideals.[28] The same tension existed within attitudes about the category of literature among the critics of the Black Cultural Nationalist school of the 1960s and 1970s. They sought to deconstruct the notion of literature and at the same time claim its prestige for political purposes.[29] Writers on black music have pushed for this kind of recognition. But this prestige was not bestowed easily by the society at large. In fact, an argument can be made that throughout the twentieth century, many considered African American musical production in opposition to the ideology of autonomy. Thus, any argument that music from black practitioners could exist within the autonomous realm should be considered a politically charged statement that invested in the music itself a specific kind of *social* signification.

Consider for a moment the work of James Monroe Trotter (1842–1892), a nineteenth-century writer considered America's first African American music historian. Trotter's book *Music and Some Highly Musical People* (1878) was written, in his words, "to perform . . . a much needed service, not so much, perhaps, to the cause of music itself, as to some of its noblest devotees and the race to which the latter belong." Trotter's attention to black musicians involved in Western art music confirms his modernist cultural values; furthermore, his statement of purpose for including in his book a 152-page collection of compositions from the pens of black composers underscores the political and social thrust of his activities: "The collection is given in order to complete the author's purpose, which is not only to show the proficiency of the subjects of the foregoing sketches as interpreters of the music of others, but, further, to illustrate the ability of quite a number of them (and, relatively, that of their race) to originate and scientifically arrange good music."[30] As the assumption of autonomy gathered steam during the nineteenth century—an ideology that would inform the repertories and methods of music theory and musicology—Trotter was showing how participation in the same music could serve political ends. In other words, if music theory and musicology have traditionally kept "separate considerations of biography, patronage, place and dates from those of musical syntax and structure,"[31] the ideology of race grounded people like Trotter in the cultural, social, and political work that their activities performed. That ideological pattern would persist well into the twentieth century among those who wrote about African American music. A voluminous body of journalism as well as the musical writings of James Weldon Johnson, Alain Locke, and Maude Cuney Hare, who used what I have called elsewhere "the rhetoric of the New Negro," continued Trotter's line of thinking, though with some differences.[32] Patterns in the literature on bebop suggest this struggle. Jazz writers who have written about bebop as "art" have depended heavily on the narrative of autonomy for prestige, but their arguments have always had a political edge. This observation includes the work of other writers such as Gunther Schuller, Leonard Feather, and Martin Williams, whose collective writings are usually thought to be anything but overtly "political" in this sense.[33]

To better understand some of the historical grounding of what I mean by the "political edge" of this cultural work, I take a detour below to discuss a specific Afro-modernist moment known as the Harlem Renaissance. This "movement," if you will, clearly had an indirect impact on the contour of cultural formations in the 1940s, especially in jazz. I use literary scholar Houston Baker's notion of "renaissancism" to illustrate several connections between the 1920s and other decades, between Harlem and other locations, between books such as Alain Locke's *The New Negro* and Leonard Feather's *Inside Jazz*, and among the discourses of art surrounding both literature and musical forms. I make these connections with qualifications, however. I do not believe that an idea such as renaissancism (or any other cultural theory, for that matter) can explain indiscriminately the motivations of people from different historical moments. There are simply too many contingencies and subjects to account for. Nevertheless, there have also been some constants in African American life in general, and one of them has been social oppression. With that fact in mind, we can assume that resistance to this oppression over the years has also taken a certain degree of historical consistency. Thus, an idea like renaissancism can serve a useful purpose, albeit a limited one.

ON NEW NEGRO PRACTICE:
MODERNISM, BOOKS, AND AFRO-ART DISCOURSE

The term Negro or Harlem Renaissance refers to a period in American history that witnessed a dramatic rise in African American literary, artistic, and musical activities. While Harlem became the hub of this so-called cultural awakening, similar flowerings occurred in other metropolitan centers such as Chicago and Philadelphia.[34] Black intellectuals believed that the idea of black arts and letters "coming of age" would provide a tool to end racism and social inequality. The success of the movement has been hotly debated. These arguments divide into two broad camps.

On the one hand, critics have returned "repeatedly to this textual field as if to embrace a heralded center, familiar and stable."[35] The Renaissance provided late-twentieth-century scholars of black culture a way to consolidate a canon of varied African American works and a body of criticism to explain them. On the other hand, "skepticism regarding presentations of the era as a coherent whole has inspired redefinitions of the period's demarcations, classic works as well as national and transnational intertextualities."[36] Some writers have even argued that the Renaissance was somewhat of a "historical fiction, a contrivance of imaginations steeped in resurrections and similar rites of spring,"[37] and that it was "an abstract concept based on personal commitments and loyalties rather than on a single identifiable person or institution."[38]

Imagined or real, most accounts confirm the 1920s as the Renaissance's strongest years, with its earliest works appearing in the previous decade. The Great Depression of the early 1930s is traditionally thought to mark its end.[39] Debates about these demarcations will probably continue. But if we for the moment accept both the dates and the notion of renaissance as an accurate portrayal of this period, then how should we characterize the production of the black literature, art, and, especially, music that followed it? Or put differently and more specifically, can the cultural issues raised by the Renaissance serve as an interpretive framework for subsequent black musical activity? Did the Renaissance continue? And if it did, was it somehow changed after the "high years" of the 1920s?

Queen Harlem, Inc.: Symbol of Black Urbanity, Black Modernity

The growth of black Harlem and the prolific volume of arts and letters that it inspired are linked to several interrelated developments. With the rise of the industrial revolution and World War I, southern blacks seeking better economic and social conditions first trickled and then flooded into the nation's urban centers, including New York City, which doubled its black population between the years 1900 and 1920.[40] The majority of these new migrants who chose Harlem came from the southeastern seaboard states. Their class status varied. Harlem attracted, for example, many black educators, writers, musicians, politicians, and businesspeople of the so-called talented tenth. For this constituency, "Harlem meant proximity to Broadway, to the little magazines and the big publishing houses, to Greenwich Village and its white intellectuals, to avant-garde literary groups and established, successful writers." For the most part, however, these migrants were like many migrant groups: young, unskilled, and unmarried.[41] The dynamics between these stratified groups infused the Renaissance movement with class-related themes, energy, and tensions.

Together, both groups helped to make Harlem a "fresh urbane black community" that symbolized for each "a new age of urbanity and sophistication for blacks in America."[42] This ideal was achieved by the sheer size of Harlem's black population and especially through the "aggressive black businessmen [and women] who snatched Harlem's newly developed real estate from white middle-class hands," making it "the biggest and most elegant black community in the Western World." For African Americans, Harlem represented political, economic, and cultural opportunity. That collective optimism and "sense of place" were shared by intellectuals and artists as well as the proletariat. The cultural elitism of the black intellectuals, for example, provided the masses with pride and ammunition against racial discrimination,[43] even as they held tenaciously to their preferences for black vernacular culture expression, such as the blues and jazz.

Harlem's intrigue also existed as an important symbol in literature. While a "Euro-American vision of the living-dead megalopolis" that offered "no home to the human body, social spirit, or soul" thrived in American literature, black writers of the Renaissance presented an "alternative stream of urban imagery." Their vision portrayed Harlem, New York, as a "symbolic home" in the same spirit as previous American literature had depicted "the sentimental, rural-cottage." These black writers collectively viewed Harlem's neighborhoods as a "promised land, . . . birthright community, and a cultural aspiration."[44]

The potency of this literary vision and the reality of Harlem's energy spilled over into and received energy from the musical world. Indeed, the music of black Harlem seemed to fuel the artistic landscape of the Renaissance, although the movement is, perhaps, best understood as a literary movement. Black music in Harlem and the larger New York musical scene enjoyed a mutual relationship in some ways. During the 1920s, for example, recording and performance opportunities for black musicians helped New York become the recognized commercial hub of jazz activity. By the end of the decade, Harlem itself was a fashionable entertainment center, home to several successful jazz venues, among them the Savoy Ballroom, the Cotton Club, Small's Paradise, and Connie's Inn. Furthermore, beyond Harlem and the world of black jazz, New York's musical life was vibrant. The world premiere of George Gershwin's jazz-inspired *Rhapsody in Blue* appeared in what Charters and Kunstadt refer to as the "First American Jazz Concert" on February 12, 1924. Earlier that month, Igor Stravinsky's *Sacre du Printemps* made its New York debut and caused a sensation.[45] African American concert artists Roland Hayes and Marian Anderson began high-profile careers in the decade's early years. (Anderson made her debut in Town Hall.) Both "became racial symbols, whose successes were shared vicariously by the great mass of blacks that could never hope to attain similar distinction."[46] In 1920, a recording by blues singer Mamie Smith helped to establish the race records institution in American popular culture. These events, among many others, stood as evidence of New York's position as the nation's center of music culture. As Gunther Schuller noted, "Sooner or later everyone in the music field, regardless of where his [or her] successes were scored, had to come to New York for ultimate recognition."[47] And Harlem's musical energy benefited from and contributed to the city's overall musical reputation and profile. Its growth during these years as a "black megalopolis" and the "queen of all black belts" continued to inspire and impact the musical and artistic consciousness of African Americans.[48]

Making and "Smoothening" a New Negro Modernism

Alain Locke's important anthology *The New Negro* (1925) provides a central text to outline some important aspects of the Renaissance movement. According to Locke, his book had been "culled from the first fruits of the Negro Renaissance."[49] Many soon recognized the book as a definitive statement. *The New Negro* set two primary and interrelated goals. First, it sought to elevate the social position of African Americans in the eyes of white Americans. Second, and most important to the present discussion, *The New Negro* urged America toward a new artistic maturity, shaped in part by a national literature, art, and music influenced by black artists, according to Arnold Rampersad's introduction to the 1992 edition.[50]

The New Negro indeed served as a challenge to the idea of white supremacy. So despite the self-consciously genteel ring of the term *renaissance*, the movement struck right at the heart of a stubborn discourse in

Western culture, namely, "the prevailing notion among whites of blacks as not only physically and culturally inferior but without much hope of improvement." To achieve the goal of elevating the social position of African Americans, Locke had to exercise considerable editorial "smoothening" in order to make all of his artists and intellectuals represented in the book conform to his own idea "of a new breed of Negroes in a brave new world of Negro-ness."[51] Moreover, Locke seemed to concede to some of the tenets of white supremacy in order to prove his larger and more urgent point: that America's black citizens had culturally "grown up" despite a history in the West that included chattel slavery and illiteracy brutally enforced by the laws of the land. He viewed, for example, African American culture as *evolving* over time: progressing from infancy to "cultural adolescence," and only by the 1920s had it "approached maturity." Locke writes: "Liberal minds today cannot be asked to peer with sympathetic curiosity into the darkened Ghetto of a segregated race life. That was yesterday. Nor must they expect to find a mind and soul bizarre and alien as the mind of a savage, or even as naive and refreshing as the mind of the peasant or the child. That too was yesterday, and the day before."[52] Despite Locke's promotion of black artistic achievement on Eurocentric grounds, however, *The New Negro* "remains a reliable index to the black American sensibility at that point where art and politics meet, as well as to the events in Harlem and elsewhere among blacks in the 1920s."[53]

Locke's tapered vision of what constitutes "Culture" left little room to appreciate the intermusical landscape of his time or the impact of black vernacular music on it.[54] He excluded extended discussion of the blues in *The New Negro*, recommended that composers transform the spiritual more fully into symphonic dress, included an essay by black historian J. A. Rogers that depicted jazz's origins as vulgar and crude,[55] and ignored Garveyism, in Rampersad's view, "the most important mass movement in black America of the 1920s."[56] These writer's reasons for snubbing black vernacular music are obvious. As Samuel Floyd has noted, while "the pre-Renaissance activities of black music had created a climate in which the movement could take root," some of the intelligentsia viewed black music of the cabarets, theaters, and speakeasies with ambivalence.

> Renaissance leaders aspired to create a "New Negro," one who would attend concerts and operas and would be economically and socially prepared to enter an ideally integrated American society. . . . [S]he would not frequent musical dens of iniquity, for [s]he would then tarnish the image that was to be presented to the world as evidence of [African

Americans'] preparedness. So, at first, the "lower forms" of black music were frowned upon by those of this outlook.[57]

The following discussion shows that attitudes toward Locke's "lower forms" continually changed both within and outside African American culture. These shifts in attitude occurred even though key aspects of the black vernacular musical aesthetic remained more or less consistent over the years. Jazz, for example, grew to become "America's classical music" (or this country's indigenous equivalent of the Western art music tradition). And other blues-based musical forms soared in popularity and importance. Despite a large number of African American musicians who built successful careers within the Western art music tradition, the black masses, for many reasons, have chosen with each generation to "reinvent" the cultural spaces in which jazz, blues, and gospel musicians have created some of the nation's most exciting music.

Sounding Modern in the New Ghetto Archipelago

Houston Baker has suggested a critique of the Harlem Renaissance that I believe can be successfully extended into analysis of a range of black musical activities following the 1920s. Many accounts of the Renaissance have described it solely through a discussion of its artistic, social, and political accomplishments. Baker, however, theorizes the movement as a discursive strategy he describes as "renaissancism":

> By this term, I want to suggest a *spirit* of nationalistic engagement that begins with intellectuals, artists, and spokespersons at the turn of the century and receives extensive definition and expression during the 1920s. This spirit is one that prompts the black artist's awareness that his or her only possible foundation for authentic and modern expressivity resides in a discursive field marked by formal mastery and sounding deformation. Further, I want to suggest that "renaissancism" connotes something quite removed from a single, exotic set of "failed high jinks" confined to less than a decade. It signals in fact a resonantly and continuously productive set of tactics, strategies, and syllables that takes form at the turn of the century and extends to our own day.[58]

Baker's rereading convincingly debunks the notion that the movement "failed." In fact, two of the discourses he identifies as constituting renaissancism and cultural nationalism support the idea that the renaissance spirit continued into the 1930s, 1940s, and 1950s.

I am dangerously close to an ahistorical acceptance of Baker's renaissancism here and need to take a moment to clarify my position once again. My use of this term in the present context is not meant to convey a homogeneous, essentialist African American worldview. All cultural expressions need to be explained as historically and geographically specific activities. What I am responding to with the term *renaissancism* is the very real and collective impulse in African American culture to combat a relentless system of ideologies, laws, and practices designed to keep its people socially subservient. Although we can identify various kinds of historically specific resistances, the "combat" has often taken place in the realm of expressive culture. Indeed, the work of the imagination that has constituted this nation building has produced a body of art, literature, and music that has posed through the years a consistent challenge to America's social hierarchies based on race, class, and gender. The important cultural work of imagining these efforts as having a unified thrust has been one of the primary defensive and offensive moves of African American subjects and institutions, linking them through time, space, and place. My use of Baker's term *renaissancism* seeks to portray the political impulse of these acts of resistance without discounting their historical contingencies.

The idea of sound has played an important role in renaissancism. "A nation's emergence," Baker argues, "is always predicated on the construction of a field of meaningful sounds" that help "human beings seeking national identity . . . achieve a vocabulary of *national* possibilities." Baker reads, for example, Locke's *New Negro* as a broadening "and enlargement of the field of traditional Afro-American discursive possibilities," for in the book Locke depicts "a newly emergent 'race' or 'nation'—a national culture." In other words, Locke "sounded out" a new nation in his writings. This argument, of course, has dramatic import when black music styles are brought into the discussion, for no other medium has sounded nation for African Americans more poignantly than their music.[59]

Like many black urban neighborhoods between the years 1935 and 1955, Harlem declined as a residential and commercial community. In fact, like its counterparts in other locations around the country, it became a segregated community, "a city within a city." Catastrophic social, economic, and political events always had a greater negative impact in black communities. The two decades spanning the years from 1935 to 1955, for example, saw historical changes that would shape the experiences of African Americans profoundly. Recuperation from the Depression, World War II, the cold war, and the start of a domestic legal battle over civil rights, to name a few, all occurred during this period. These struggles affected Harlem and other urban spaces profoundly. What was considered a place of refuge in earlier decades became, with the passage of time, a system of urban ghettos ravaged by poverty, a transformation that intellectuals of the Harlem Renaissance would have thought impossible.

Yet the indisputable successes of black musicians during this period served as a counterweight to this plight. For within these urban contexts and in Afro-modernist style, black musicians continually produced influential musical genres and styles. They were especially prolific in the realm of popular culture, and it is into this realm that I want to extend the idea of renaissancism and modernism. The idea that maroons possessed skills and knowledge in both the "master's" culture and in "African modes of existence" certainly applies to these capable musicians. With professional and musical savvy and with the cooperation of an interracial array of audiences, producers, critics, and entrepreneurs, black musicians "mastered" the American music business and at the same time continued to "trope the blues," by using their African musical legacy (with historically specific differences) to their advantage. They resolved at the level of musical style a central tension in Locke's *New Negro* by cultivating vernacular forms such as bebop and the other race music styles, achieving the cultural equity (one might say dominance) that Locke and his contemporaries desired.

THE NEW RECORD MEN:
PRESSING VINYL, SELLING ART, AND WRITING RACE

Although Locke and the other New Negroes stressed the political potential of autonomous art in the struggle for racial equity, it was in the domains of popular music and jazz that the most visible gains were achieved in this regard. This progress, however, was by no means a cohesive project. The discussion below of various approaches to marketing the race musics in the "real" commercial world of the cultural industry—the recording, the live showcasing, and the written criticism about each of these activities—shows both the variety of attitudes that developed around each musical style and the many ways these attitudes converged.

Bebop shared some of the same venues and recording labels with other race music genres, particularly in the years following the war. In the late 1940s, gospel played many of the same arenas, venues, and halls that jazz and R&B stars played.[60] In addition, the Apollo and Savoy companies both recorded gospel as well as early bebop and rhythm and blues. But perceptions about postwar jazz began gradually to veer away from the other genres within the culture industry. It was in those years, for example, that nightclubs catering to small group jazz rose in popularity and soon replaced ballrooms and theaters like the Savoy and the Apollo as jazz's primary performance venues. This process was gradual; it began in the early years of the decade with the waning popularity of big band jazz. Eventually, small nightclubs like those found on 52nd Street discovered that featuring small jazz combos was a smarter choice both economically and aesthetically than big floor shows. Thus, music business practicalities figured prominently in musical decisions. This view differs from the discourse on small group postwar jazz, which usually portrays that ascendancy as the exclusive artistic imperative of the musicians rather than their clever response to economic realities. As bebop musicians began to leave their jobs in established swing bands for jobs on the street, they found it possible to make a living doing what they had done in Harlem jam sessions. Furthermore, since bebop players were for the most part younger than their employers, they were more inclined to experiment with new ideas, having far less to lose in terms of an established following and everything to gain with respect to reputation and wider recognition. And the audiences enjoyed and sought out the small group format because it was a more spontaneous setting for the musicians.[61]

For similar reasons, small groups became attractive to the smaller record companies that proliferated after the war. Although profit was always an important aspect of the record business, the philosophies of small companies specializing in jazz and those concentrating on other genres differed in important ways. Jerry Wexler, a former reporter for *Billboard* who became an executive at Atlantic, an "indie" formed in 1947, reveals the philosophy of making rhythm and blues records during the postwar period while describing his idea of the ideal "record man." His blunt scenario, though perhaps not universal, provides a candid glimpse of the rhythm and blues market:

> First, he had the brass to imagine that he could do it, that he could find somebody who would spend a dollar, a good hard-earned American dollar, for his phonograph record. Then he had to find an artist, find a song, con the artist into coming into his studio, coax him into singing the song, pull the record out of him, press the record; then take that record and go to the disc jockeys and con them into putting it on the radio, then go to the distributors and beg them to take a box of twenty-five and try it out.[62]

Not all promoters took such a brute approach, however. Record companies dedicated to jazz prospered in the postwar period, and one such company was Blue Note, formed in 1938 by Alfred Lion, a former German citizen who had settled in the United States earlier that year. (He was joined later by his childhood friend Francis "Frank" Wolff as co-owner.) It is no small point that this migration became important to the formation of Afro-modernism in the mass media. From the beginning, Blue Note positioned itself as a promoter of a discriminating, specialized taste in jazz. Its first releases, recordings by Albert Ammons and Meade Lux Lewis, were pressed on twelve-inch disks at $1.50 each, the same format and price as classical music at that time. In 1939, a brochure issued by Lion carried a statement of purpose outlining his belief that the marketplace was not the sole measure of success for jazz. The words essentially collapse the language of the "art" and "folk" music discourses, promising both transcendence and authenticity:

> Blue Note Records are designed simply to serve the uncompromising expressions of hot jazz or swing, in general. Any particular style of playing which represents an authentic way of musical feeling is genuine expression. By virtue of its significance in place, time and circumstance, it possesses its own tradition, artistic standards and audience that keeps it alive. Hot jazz, therefore, is expression and communication, a musical and social manifestation, and Blue Note records are concerned with identifying its impulse, not its sensational and commercial adornments.

During the late 1940s, with the guidance of musician and talent scout Ike Quebec, Blue Note began recording small group sessions with bebop musicians such as Tadd Dameron, Art Blakey, James Moody, Bud Powell, and Thelonious Monk. Lion and Wolff were noted for following their own instincts with regard to artists. They recorded Monk frequently, for example, "despite critical resistance and poor sales."[63]

Other small companies also aggressively recorded small group jazz of all kinds: Commodore, Keynote, American Music, and "bebop" labels such as Guild, Manor, and Dial were among them. Savoy, formed in 1942 by Herman Lubinsky, found small group jazz profitable but also recorded a variety of music, including gospel and jump blues. If Lubinsky was mercenary, this characteristic was balanced by the visionary talents of his artists and repertory staff, which included Ozzie Cadena, Buck Ram, and Teddy Reig: "One would never characterize Lubinsky as a patron of the arts," as Dan Morgenstern points out, "but he had hip people working for him."[64]

It was Blue Note, however, that gained "cult status" among its listeners. Lion and Wolff worked out an artistic formula for achieving recordings of lasting artistic merit: good music "with feeling"—products of "carefully planned sessions, always preceded by sufficient [paid] rehearsal time . . . [allowing] challenging material to be played with the greatest creativity."[65] Atmospheric candid photos, advanced graphics for their LP cover designs, and excellent engineering also set Blue Note apart. Rudy Van Gelder, Blue

Note's engineer, said recently that Lion "knew exactly what he wanted to hear. He communicated it to me and I got it for him technically. He was amazing in what he heard and how he would patiently draw it out of me."[66] Contrarily, Atlantic's executive vice-president Jerry Wexler recalls of the same period: "We didn't have any specialized knowledge. We didn't know how good it was. All we needed was to sell 6000 singles in a month to cover everything. Our release schedule was three singles every two weeks. . . . We couldn't miss. We were all driving Cadillacs. We didn't know shit about making records, but we were really having fun!"[67]

Despite Blue Note's example, many postwar jazz labels operated with substandard conditions and were run simply to make a profit with as little effort as possible. At the same time, that flexibility allowed a certain kind of artistic freedom within the restraints of these conditions. As a general rule, for example, record companies allowed the musicians to choose their own personnel and to record original compositions.[68] That relative freedom allowed bebop musicians to create many of the tunes in the jazz canon today, and it allowed them unprecedented control over the final product. The spontaneous quality exemplified in the informal jam session format became a vital force in the tradition of jazz recordings and in the "jazz concert." Finally, Blue Note's "artistic approach"—the belief that they were creating something of lasting value beyond the fashion of the marketplace—served as a model for future labels such as Prestige and Riverside in their approach to recording jazz. That philosophy arguably provided an important basis for jazz's acceptance as art and as something distinctly different from other race music genres.

AFRO-MODERNISM, JAZZ, AND THE POLITICS OF INTEGRATION

Jazz's primary mode of dissemination, particularly its improvisational aspect, has been through recordings and not written scores, and that feature is one that distinguishes it from the classical tradition. According to Ben Sidran's analysis, the "orality" of black music has hindered its acceptance into the academy and as a full partner in "the Western tradition." Many have recognized the importance of literacy in its broadest sense to African Americans throughout their history in the United States. Jannette Dates and William Barlow observe, for example, that literacy acted as a catalyst for liberation. "Former slaves were recognized as speaking subjects in the dominant culture only to the extent that they could inscribe their voices in the written word."[69] Because of the importance of writing in Western culture, jazz criticism (and later scholarship) has no doubt contributed to jazz's gradually increasing cultural pedigree. Through criticism jazz became somewhat "legitimate."

It is important to remember, however, that institutionalized writing has supported other genres of black music. Gospel music pioneer Thomas A. Dorsey's publishing activities and those of his contemporaries have been well documented. For Dorsey's *written* scores—no matter how sketchy—provided gospel with its first wide-scale avenue of dissemination. In that respect, gospel was just as "progressive" as jazz, in which notation became an important means of dissemination, especially during the Swing Era (e.g., in sheet music, stocks, and written arrangements). The institutionalization of gospel was also seen in the formation of the National Convention of Gospel Choirs and Choruses in 1933 and in the incorporation of written gospel music in official hymnals of numerous black denominations. But these activities did little to raise the prestige of gospel outside the black community.[70]

The growth of formal criticism—*writing* about jazz—supplied a crucial impetus for the elevation of the music's status. Moreover, at the same time that jazz criticism increased in the 1950s, rhythm and blues and rock 'n' roll were commercially dominating the American music business, enhancing the perception that jazz was a quite different enterprise from the others. During the 1960s, that changing status began to take cogent form. By the 1960s, jazz began to attract "support of the kind that classical music had been receiving for years: public and private patronage, university positions for jazz musicians, and academic programs to train jazz performers and certify them with diplomas and college degrees."[71]

But anyone aware of the musical challenges presented by extemporaneous accompaniment in the gospel tradition or the skillful virtuosity present in gospel performances of the best gospel singers would have good cause to challenge the notion that these endeavors should remain locked in a less "prestigious" sphere of folk music. Gospel music, however, has yet to receive the criticism necessary to support a claim of "art" music status. Written criticism, as much as musical criteria, clearly determines the pedigree of a genre.

Jazz criticism written during the 1940s, with its unique representation of the race trope, represents another significant break with other black music genres. As the boundaries that had long separated black and white citizens by law were successfully challenged during the 1940s, expressive culture emerged as a site of contestation for people invested in keeping those boundaries intact. As a conspicuous public activity, jazz emerged as an important arena in which racial ideology was articulated and contested. As I stated earlier, black classical musicians such as Roland Hayes, Jules Bledsoe, and Marian Anderson built successful concert careers and emerged as important symbols of progress for African Americans. But jazz musicians raised the stakes in racial progress. Contemporary reviews of Hayes's, Bledsoe's, and Anderson's concerts often hailed their unique talents but at the same time marveled at their *lack* of black musical idiosyncrasies. Jazz musicians, on the other hand, featured and even flaunted these idiosyncrasies as a fundamental aspect of their music and threatened the status quo on many levels: they asserted "racial" aspects of their performances as the strength of the whole enterprise. Thus, heightened interest in jazz as an "artistic" pursuit posed a serious challenge to one of the central tenets of America's caste system: "racial" inferiority. In fact, the politics of race has continually mediated jazz's advance toward international prestige. A few examples will show how the trope of race has shaped jazz writings.

When *Esquire* magazine began its regular jazz features in late 1943 under the direction of Leonard Feather and Robert Goffin, a "critics jazz poll" was promptly organized. In a move unusual for the time, the panel of critics included several African Americans, among them *Esquire* cartoonist E. Simms Campbell, Associated Negro Press writer Dan Burley, and writer and singer Inez Cavanaugh, who had contributed to both the *Crisis* and *Metronome*.[72] The winners of the first poll included black stars such as Louis Armstrong, Coleman Hawkins, Art Tatum, Billie Holiday, Lionel Hampton, and Cootie Williams. In addition, the critics also extolled the accomplishments of white musicians such as Benny Goodman, Jack Teagarden, Artie Shaw, and Dave Tough. The Negro press, noted for its sustained call for integration, celebrated the results: the *New York Amsterdam News* and the *Pittsburgh Courier* carried complete coverage of the poll. But as Feather points out, the poll's winners roster raised more than a few eyebrows. One publication, *Jazz Record,* accused *Esquire* of practicing "inverted Jim Crow" and stated emphatically that the "top men for small hot-jazz band work today are predominantly white men!"[73] The question, Which *race* plays the best jazz? represents a problematic and recurring theme in jazz criticism. Stan Kenton, for example, after reading the results of the 1956 *Downbeat* critics' poll, accused Feather and other editors of creating "a new minority group, white jazz musicians."

An important contribution to jazz literature that grew out of *Esquire's* new commitment to jazz was Robert Goffin's *Esquire's 1944 Jazz Year Book.* The volume's introduction reveals much about the goals of jazz criticism of the time, especially the way in which writers manipulated the "art," "folk," and "popular" discourses in order to exert influence on jazz's reception. Arnold Gingrich (*Esquire*'s editor and cofounder), Feather, and Goffin sought to direct and "elevate" the tastes of listeners in the name of edification, and at the same time, they eagerly pursued new converts to *true* jazz and promoted informed listening habits. As Gingrich writes, "The most important thing to do about hot jazz is—not to write about it, not to argue about it, not (even) to dance to it—but, of all things, to *listen* to it."[74]

Bernard Gendron argues that jazz criticism of the mid-1940s—especially those writings that constituted the war of words between the "moldy figs" and the "modernists"—helped bring about a revolution, "a new mapping of the jazz discursive terrain—a new construction of the aesthetic discourse of jazz."[75] The debate, Gendron explains, set the stage for the bebop revolution and ultimately legitimated jazz's crossing the chasm separating mass culture and art. As we shall see below, the enterprise of jazz criticism, as expressed by the British expatriate Leonard Feather, participated in Afro-modernism's aesthetic of integration and further facilitated jazz's march toward becoming America's so-called classical music.

TO RACE OR NOT TO RACE:
INSIDE JAZZ AND MAKING THE NEWEST NEGROES

Leonard Feather's book *Inside Jazz* is a particularly telling document of postwar jazz literature. *Inside Jazz* appeared in 1949, and its publication represents a landmark in bebop and jazz historiography because it was the first book on modern jazz. Feather's cultural politics—he migrated from England and was staunchly integrationist—and ideologies pervade *Inside Jazz*, and in many ways the book set the tone for subsequent criticism. As a journalist, record producer, and musician, Feather claims and asserts his "insider's" stance with the bebop movement. He describes *Inside Jazz* in the book's introduction as the first book on jazz complete with technical data written by an author with "empirical experience as a jazz musician and composer." Feather's status in the modern jazz scene is confirmed when Dizzy Gillespie recognizes him on the book's dedication page as "one of the few people who have been in our corner for years, trying to make people understand and appreciate the kind of music we believe in." While disparaging keen interest in bebop personalities, goatees, and berets by the popular press, Feather tackles what he calls "the more serious aspects of the music."[76]

The lack of racial references in *Inside Jazz* could be read as a political statement in itself: no race theories here, just vivid historical accounts, technical analysis, discographies, and the first biographical dictionary of bebop musicians. In fact, *Inside Jazz* was originally titled *Inside Bebop*. The term *bebop* probably was seen in the popular American imagination as racially coded. Feather writes in his introduction of the book's new edition that the name was changed a couple of years after the book appeared because the publisher was "scared by the supposedly pejorative significance of this much maligned term."[77] Feather's occasional reference to race does evoke black and white worlds that were separate but gradually converging within bebop: "By 1939, a few scattered attempts at real mixed bands began along 52nd Street. The important thing was that musicians were getting to know each other; there was no longer a fence that kept white culture on one side and a Negro culture on the other." Feather also makes a distinction between the expectations of Savoy ballroom audiences and the 52nd Street audience. The uptown Savoy audience was eclectic: "Savoy audiences consisted of local jitterbugs, who wanted music that jumped, and jazz hunters downtown, who were concerned more with the esthetic qualities of the performances."[78] Apparently, at the time of this writing Feather believed that bebop was directed toward the latter.

At the same time, Feather makes a point to assure his readers that beboppers' musical tastes extended to the classical world. Through association one gets the impression that the work of Parker, Monk, Gillespie, and Dameron was comparable—whether formally or just "in spirit" is difficult to determine—to that of other harmonic innovations of the Western art music tradition: "Like so many modern jazz musicians, Charlie [Parker] has listened intently to music outside the world of jazz; he has studied Schoenberg, admired Debussy's *Children's Corner*, Stravinsky and Shostakovitch. He credits Thelonious Monk with many of the harmonic ideas that were incorporated into bebop." Trumpeter Joe Guy, while commenting on Gillespie's ferocious appetite for music, comments, "I've spent whole evenings listening to his [Gillespie's] collection of records—classical and jazz."[79]

Feather makes no mention of Gillespie's or other beboppers' interest in the blues, rhythm and blues, or gospel. In one account, Feather recalls that in late 1941 while supervising a blues session for the Decca label, he was reluctant to use Gillespie, finding his style "alternately fascinating and nerve-wracking." As the arranger and contractor, it was Feather's prerogative not only to choose the musicians but also to use them at his own discretion. Since Feather "could hardly see [Gillespie] as a blues man," he assigned him no solos, a decision he ultimately regretted. "He read the music excellently, but if I'd thrown away my arrangements and let him loose, *Unlucky Woman Blues* and *Mound Bayou* could have become Gillespie collectors' items."[80] Thus, Feather's restraining of Gillespie demonstrates both an early attempt to isolate the bebop style from other genres—perhaps Gillespie would have chosen to play a bebop-style solo on the tunes—and how the perceptions of those in decision-making positions could control the packaging, dissemination, and, ultimately, the public reception of music.

Inside Jazz shares the integrationist tone of postwar literature by African American authors. As pressure for racial integration increased throughout American society after the war, those sentiments were reflected in African American letters. Abby Arthur Johnson and Ronald Maberry Johnson assert that the integration theme was dramatically illustrated in many publications by African Americans: in novels, in journals associated with historically black colleges such as the journal *Phylon*, and especially in poems, short stories, and editorials published in the short-lived yet important magazines such as *Negro Quarterly*, *Negro Story*, and *Harlem Quarterly*. These magazines provided both younger and older black writers a space to articulate in theory and practice a "literary aesthetic of integration." Moreover, when more widely circulated publications such as the *Atlantic*, *Collier's*, *Fortune*, *Harper's*, *Life*, and the *Saturday Evening Post* began featuring articles by and about African Americans, integration was a central motive and theme.

White authors also participated. In the foreword of *Inside Jazz*, Feather thanks Richard O. Boyer for his "excellent profile of Dizzy" that appeared in 1947 in the *New Yorker*. Black writers sought "non-racial outlets for their works" and began to consider themselves, as Johnson and Johnson have observed, "first as American authors and then as universal writers involved in subjects common to all persons regardless of background or origin."[81]

This aesthetic of integration trend was by no means uncontested. Black leftist writers often condemned a "raceless" aesthetic and advanced these views in leftist publications such as *Masses & Mainstream*. Lloyd Brown, black associate editor, published an essay stating that the integrationist movement threatened "the very *existence* of *Negro* literature."[82] The aesthetic of postwar integration had roots in the philosophy of Alain Locke and other black intellectuals who rose to prominence in the 1920s. Locke, writing in 1950, praised postwar black writers for what he described as "the rise of the universalized theme supplementing but not completely displacing the poetry of racial mood and substance." He believed that "universalized particularity" had always marked the world's great arts. In an article titled "Self Criticism: The Third Dimension in Culture," Locke declared emphatically: "Give us Negro life and experience in all the arts but with a third dimension of universalized common-denominator humanity."[83]

Locke's "third dimension" is reflected throughout Feather's writings in *Inside Jazz*, and, in fact, his integrationist tone may have influenced the route that jazz criticism took throughout the 1950s and 1960s. Feather was certainly aware of postwar racial politics. His memoirs demonstrate both his impatience with America's racial caste system and his faith that jazz critics could help in the process of integration: "Many of us who write about jazz have tried to upgrade the lot of the black musician, and we are happy to observe that in some respects that lot has improved." Furthermore, he once suggested with decided hyperbole that an appropriate solution for racism should be "the total merging of the races."[84] Despite his strong beliefs about race in America, however, Feather's tone throughout *Inside Jazz* is never polemical; the book proceeds with what might be considered an aesthetic of *musical* integration.

Feather cast a wide net: casual readers as well as musicians would find the book useful. Part 2 of the book presents Feather's "technical data" with accompanying musical examples; an exhortation to buy a projected book by Walter "Gil" Fuller, planned as a companion volume on bebop arranging and intended to encourage those who want to delve more deeply into bebop's musical language. If bebop symbolized the militancy and turbulence of the postwar moment, as Gillespie and others have suggested, Feather was either unaware of (or simply ignored) that notion. From Feather's perspective, bebop in 1949 represented simply a revolution of "musical style." Perhaps Feather believed that racial progress would be more easily achieved by attending to the serious, formal aspects of the "music itself" and to qualities that made the bebop world universal, rather than a clarion call for black nationalism, as writers after Feather have suggested.

MIXING HOT PEPPERS IN A DISH OF BLACK-EYE PEAS: "UN POCO LOCO"

I conclude this chapter's examination of the culture industry, society, and Afro-modernism with a brief discussion of a musical example from the period. The chapter began with a reference to Dizzy Gillespie's composition "A Night in Tunisia," which I interpreted as evidence of the expansion of Afro-modernism's musical parameters and of Gillespie's making the world his own within the intense modernization processes occurring during the 1940s. Most accounts credit Gillespie's experiments of the 1940s with successfully wedding the Afro-Cuban rhythmic approach to the emerging bebop language. He once characterized it as "mixing hot peppers in a dish of black-eye peas."[85] This combustible and appealing mixture, as Geoffrey

Jacques has recently argued, possessed both social and aesthetic functions. Although African American musicians had long been aware of Cuban music and had flirted with its elements throughout the early decades of the twentieth century, the complete consummation did not occur until the advent of Afro-Cuban jazz.[86]

Again, Arjun Appadurai's idea that migration and the mass media are important to modern subjectivity has significance here. During the years surrounding World War II, an increased pattern of immigration from the Caribbean reshaped the United States' demographic profile. This migration occurred at the same time as the intensified urbanization of African American communities outlined earlier in this chapter. The gradual acceptance of African American entertainers in the mass media extended to Latin American artists such as Desi Arnaz and to the lesser-known Cuban musicians who played with Gillespie and the other bebop musicians. Thus the seeds for an Afro-Cuban turn in modern jazz fell onto fertile ground and provided jazz musicians with more artistic options that signified profoundly for the musicians and audiences alike.

Afro-Cuban jazz linked two segments (Cuba and African America) of the African Diaspora primarily through the artistic agency of Gillespie and his migrant Cuban collaborators such as Chano Pozo and Frank Grillo, otherwise known as Machito. This coupling and the musical rhetoric that resulted can be, perhaps, best understood by the words of Machito, who believed that the bottom (or the rhythm) is what gave Cuban music its distinctiveness at the same time as jazz derived its depth of expression from its melodic and harmonic elements. He once stated: "Our music . . . occurs at the bottom, in the rhythm. [For example,] when there's a storm, then that's Cuban music. The rhythm moves you because it is where you're standing. You have to dance."[87] Thus, the move toward intensified rhythm and the dance impulse in modern jazz recentered the music within the legacy of African-derived principles and conceptualizations. As Lisa Brock has observed, "Cubans and African-Americans pulled from the same or compatible cultural memory bank."[88]

The storm-earthquake and hot peppers–black-eyed peas metaphors are convincingly realized in a recording by the great bebop pianist Bud Powell. If the first recordings of "A Night in Tunisia" represented the introduction of a novel stylistic element into modern jazz, then Powell's 1951 recording of his composition "Un Poco Loco" shows the Afro-Cuban turn settling into bebop's acceptable field of rhetorical conventions.[89] Interestingly, "Un Poco Loco" appears on the same session as his better-known rendition of Gillespie's "A Night in Tunisia." The piece was produced by Alfred Lion at

Blue Note, a label that, as I have discussed earlier, was known for its ad-
venturesome, high-quality work and its "musician-friendly" approach.
Throughout his career, Powell led a total of six recording sessions for Blue
Note. "Un Poco Loco" features bassist Curly Russell and the premier bebop
percussionist Max Roach.

As the paradigmatic pianist of the bebop movement, Powell's work as a
virtuoso soloist was pathbreaking. "The Amazing Bud Powell," as he was
known, helped to create a space for the bebop pianist to become the emotional focal point of a performance, a notion that went somewhat against the
grain of the wishes of the other musicians. According to Gillespie, "We
needed a piano player to stay outta the way. The one stayed outta the way
best was the one best for us. . . . Bud's importance was as a great soloist, not
necessarily an accompanist."[90] Indeed, Powell's dazzling technique allowed
him to create a solo rhetoric that set a high standard for all subsequent
instrumentalists—not just pianists—who would follow him.

In addition to showing prowess in bebop improvisation, Powell mastered
the necessities of composition in the bebop idiom. "Un Poco Loco" provides
a case in point. Like many bebop compositions, it is based on the same
rhetoric that characterizes bebop solos as modern: melodies that move
between fluid and rhythmically disjunctive passages within a sonic field
featuring an advanced harmonic language and dynamic, even obtrusive,
accompanying rhythms from the drummer. But even within the scope of
these challenging requirements, Powell's compositions always pushed the
envelope; his works always sounded distinctive and with a level of complexity, humor, and irreverence unmatched among that of his peers. Beyond
the improvisational and compositional elements, the most distinctive stylistic feature of "Un Poco Loco" is the hot peppers and earthquake—the Afro-
Cuban rhythm provided by the incomparable Max Roach. Thus, we have in
"Un Poco Loco" a performance that exhibits the traces of a historically specific, socially relevant modernism, one loaded with semantic content and
aesthetic interest. If ethnicity and other aspects of identity are processes
under constant construction, negotiation, and renegotiation in the social
world, then polysemous performances such as "Un Poco Loco" give us a
window into how they might work.

The "bricolage effect" is indeed in play here, since various aspects of the
tune seem to dialogue with other musical styles. While the Afro-Cuban
beat might signify an international element in Afro-modernism of the
1940s, the form of the piece suggests some other connections. Below we see
that the theme of the piece is made up of an AABA, thirty-two-bar structure
patterned on popular song form. Although this piece is original—that is to

say, not based on the harmonic structure of a previously existing song—the form of "Un Poco Loco" positions it in dialogue with bebop compositional practice. And again, the melodic content of the highly syncopated theme and the solo—their disjunctive phrases, rapid runs, bluesy licks and riffs, arpeggios on the upper partials of the chord changes—situate the piece within the classic bebop style. The interlude, which is heard twice in the tune, relates nicely to a similar interlude passage in Gillespie's "A Night in Tunisia," suggesting a direct line of influence between these two important musicians' compositional practices. Finally, the piece's macrostructure (theme-solos-theme), one that, in fact, frames or highlights the most important part of a jazz piece, the solo, is reflective of standard bebop performance practice.

Within the solo section, which is where the strongest "Diaspora dance" lies, we hear Powell arguably at the height of his inventive powers: a sense of urgency propels the solo, as he appears to push himself to the edge of his technical and creative capabilities. The piano solo takes place within a vamp centered in C minor. After an eight-bar setup that moves between C minor and G major chords, the section settles into a fifty-bar solo in which Powell plays fluid right-hand passages together with an ostinato pattern in his left hand. The harmony does not change during the fifty bars, and this repetition creates a tension that Powell exploits with the help of Max Roach's rock-steady and intensive support.

The solo section signifies in many different directions. Because of its length and the quality of Powell's melodic inventiveness, the rhetorical weight of the solo section threatens to overshadow the exquisitely crafted AABA theme. Furthermore, the static nature of the harmonic aspect of the section forecasts future directions in jazz, most prominently the modal movement of the late 1950s. The incessant repetition here also situates the music squarely within pan-African cultural practice. John Miller Chernoff reminds us that rhythmic repetition is an integral factor in sub-Saharan musical practice: "It is necessary to bring out the rhythmic tension that characterizes a particular beat. . . . The repetition of a well-chosen rhythm continually affirms the power of the music by locking that rhythm, and the people listening or dancing to it, into a dynamic and open structure."[91]

This same principle is at work in the harmonic domain, because repetition allows the soloist greater expressive freedom because of the lessened demand to keep up with the fast-moving harmonic changes of the typical bebop piece. The growth of emotional force also serves to better connect the audience to the sonic world and communal feeling created in the context of the repetition. Finally, since the cyclic solo creates a feeling of catharsis, bringing the piece to its emotional apex, it functions as many rituals do throughout the African Diaspora: within a binary frame that flows from the elements of the non-African culture to a more pronounced use of the African-derived cultural elements. Thus, although the Afro-Cuban quality of "Un Poco Loco" may not have retained the specific signifying function (Afro-internationalism) that Gillespie's big splash did in the mid-1940s, this rhetoric certainly signaled a "blackness" that became part of the language of subsequent expressions of modern jazz.

"Un Poco Loco" form

Intro	AABA	Interlude	VAMP	AABA	Interlude
4 mm	32 mm	4 mm	8-mm setup	32 mm	4 mm
			50-mm		
			piano solo		
			8-mm		
			drum solo		

Bebop musician Kenny Clarke's sentiment that he wanted to describe his own artistic expression as modern paralleled the sense of urgency and efficacy experienced in the social world of African Americans. The massive demographic shift of migration, the wartime economy, and the explosion (and the legacy) of new African American musical idioms marked the moment as exceptional in American music history. Just as Gillespie and his comrades navigated in their improvisations and compositions a maze of harmonic, melodic, and rhythmic procedures, African Americans negotiated a social world that held new challenges at midcentury. As we have seen, the culture industry responded to these historical developments and helped to create the context in which musicians' work was disseminated to and received by the public. The interplay of historical circumstances, of intra-group memories, of instrumental and lyrical gestures, and of personal agency and style created a powerful Afro-modernism at midcentury and a cultural scene of lasting consequence in the American consciousness.

6 "Goin' to Chicago"

Memories, Histories, and a Little Bit of Soul

> That's all we had. We had nothing but a piano.
>
> Auntie Ethel Ramsey

> Brother, we can't quit until we get our share.
>
> James Brown, "Say It Loud,
> I'm Black and I'm Proud"

> I have traced the course of this music from the colonial period to
> modern times, with conscious concern for its relationship to the
> general traditions of western music. I have been equally concerned
> with the social, political, and economic forces in American history
> that helped to shape the development of Negro music and to deter-
> mine the course it took.
>
> Eileen Southern, *The Music of Black Americans*

The male protagonist in the 1939 recording "Goin' to Chicago Blues"
expresses a sentiment found in many blues songs: a male fleeing an unful-
filling heterosexual relationship, escaping to another location, presumably
to reestablish himself in a new environment and, perhaps, love interest.
Cast in the familiar twelve-bar blues pattern, the song features the paradigmatic vocalist Jimmy Rushing supported by a small jazz combo led by
Count Basie. Black neighborhoods in urban centers such as Chicago,
Harlem, and Philadelphia began a steady decline during the Depression, a
pattern that would continue throughout the latter half of the century. But
these cities continued to attract thousands of black southerners, and the
years surrounding World War II saw an accelerated flow of black bodies,
hopes, and fears to northern cities. Much has been written in the historical
and social science literature about the economic and political reasons for
these citizens leaving the South. Clearly, job opportunities, racial oppression, and the promise of economic security influenced many to "go to
Chicago." And, as we shall see, other more deeply personal reasons

131

accounted for the demographic shift that is told in a small way in "Goin' to Chicago Blues."

Despite the varied and sundry motivations that caused migrants to swarm to Chicago and other urban destinations outside the South, new cultural and social formations flourished as a result of the mass movement. One of them is represented in the idea of a politically charged blackness in contemporary America—a notion grounded in the migration and related to developments in post-1950s American society. This radicalized black identity found expression in music, literature, and lived experience. We cannot overestimate the intense public and scholarly interest in black culture and the "Negro Problem" during the 1960s and 1970s—approximately one hundred years following the Emancipation Proclamation and some fifty years after the first migratory wave during World War I. Against the general tone of radicalism sweeping the country and shifts in governmental policies toward poverty-stricken African Americans, a growing black militancy and cultural nationalism dominated the social landscape. With a sense of urgency, policy makers, cultural critics, artists, scholars, and the public at large mulled over the question of blackness in American culture.

Some scholars questioned in print whether black culture was, in fact, myth or reality. Other researchers stormed inner-city ghettos in search of "authentic black culture," while still others wondered if recognition, let alone research, of such was "essentialist" and would ultimately work against the Civil Rights agenda that promoted integration through assimilation. Was the culture of United States blacks African, Afro-American, or simply American? Was the nature of that culture monolithic, diverse, or hybrid? Who were its most important culture bearers, males or females? Which cultural practices were best suited for the liberation agenda, the written/literary or the oral? Were expressions like jazz better thought of as "art for art's sake," as propaganda, or, as Amiri Baraka argued, as blacks' response "to the psychological landscape that is his [sic] Western environment"?[1]

In this chapter, I explore this watershed moment by juxtaposing three distinct community theaters. The first one continues the story of the Rosses as they migrated to Chicago in the late 1940s. The blending of historically specific northern and southern sensibilities that resulted from their move is suggestive of larger patterns of cultural synthesis in African American culture at this time. The Rosses were assimilated into an urban culture that had established itself during the World War I years. The negotiations taking place in various domains of life—the public and private spaces that made up the social world of these historical actors—are revealed in the stories below.

Through these stories and memories we witness identity and community building in progress during the postwar years. This process produced the fertile ground in which social meanings about music could germinate. It is important to note that the history of the "South in the city" constitutes the historical and material grounding of the ethnomemoir that opened this study and that shaped my critical and musical sensibilities during the 1960s and 1970s. Moreover, the story of intrablack acculturation surrounding the war years, the struggles for power in the face of oppression from outside (and within) African American culture, and the quest for pleasure and joy made possible the varied and new expressions of cultural blackness that would appear in later years.

The second community theater treated in this chapter takes place in the literary world. Scholars participated energetically in the struggle over or, perhaps better, the making of a new blackness during the 1960s and 1970s. Many voices contributed to this process. Black women writers were among the most important in the scholarly realm. While their efforts were not among the most popular, in retrospect, we see that they played a crucial part in redefining what blackness meant in the social world. Leading the way in this regard in the culture of musicology was the eminent scholar of black music Eileen Southern. Her work is positioned within the context of other black women writers at the time of the appearance of her book *The Music of Black Americans*. Indeed, the theater of the literary during this historical moment became and remains a very important site for understanding what blackness meant and means to many. The third community theater considered here is musical discourse itself. The music of a southern-bred entertainer of this period announced that a new world in black identity politics wasn't just "comin'" but had already arrived. James Brown's musical critique of culture is certainly suggestive of larger developments in the ongoing process of defining African American culture.

These three varied sites of cultural production—family narrative, historiography, and a recording—may seem disjunctive at first blush. What I hope to show, however, is that, taken together, they provide a realistic representation of a diverse African American culture always in the process of being made. I do not perform the cultural "smoothening" that Alain Locke did in *The New Negro* during the Harlem Renaissance. Instead I subscribe to a more accurate representation that highlights struggle both within a particular social setting and among the various discourses that surrounded it. My goal in this method is to move beyond "simplistic notions of black culture and creativity by insisting that African American cultural diversity become a conscious dimension of praxis."[2]

MAKING BRONZEVILLE BLUE(S)

As the subject of the interviews moved to life in the North, the storytellers began to talk about some of the changes they had confronted while adjusting to Chicago in the late 1940s and early 1950s. Some of the more prominent adjustments that surfaced among their memories had to do with food and music. Marjorie recalled, for example, that "the whole tone changed" for her after she moved. But what prompted her family's migration to the North? As the Ross children came of age and married, some of them experienced domestic problems around the same time as their parents did. Below, Celia and Marjorie tell their reasons for leaving the South; each story had to do with fleeing their troubled first marriages. Although some of these memories must have stirred negative feelings, you could never tell it, because these women kept the atmosphere buoyed with a lighthearted playfulness. They joked about each other's advancing ages, all the while boosting each other's egos. They spoke in matter-of-fact tones about their father's failed attempts at "making it" in Chicago and Bob's difficulty in remembering things the same way as they did. And they recalled gleefully a crucial mistake he had made almost fifty years prior to this interview. In the next passages, they respond directly to my questioning the order of their moves and the motivations behind them.

"Tell Your Father Good-Bye"

MARJORIE: Celia left first.

CELIA: Right. I was in a difficult marriage.

To whom? :GUTHRIE RAMSEY

Ah, what's his name? :CELIA

MARJORIE AND BOB: [sing-songy] Willie A. Jones.

CELIA: Willie, Jr. Willie, Jr. [She, Bob, and Marjorie laugh.] And my mother was already up here. My mother's brother was sick. At some point. Maybe we really need to go back. Actually my father came up here first, okay.

What year was that? :GR

CELIA: Oooh, I can't give you a off-hand . . . but I do know I was still in high school, so it had to be in the forties, okay. And, uh, he . . . 'cause I'll be out of high school fifty years, next year—

Good God. :BOB [makes a whistling sound and falls against Marjorie as if struck]

MARJORIE: [slapping Celia lightly on the knees] Guuurl!!? You tell[ing] people your age? [Strikes a pose, hands on hips.] We don't look it.

CELIA: [smiling] I know I don't look it.

Whoa. :BOB

CELIA: But anyway . . . [laughter]. But anyway, I was in high school, and I remember my father came up here, and he was working for Inland Steel in Chicago. Okay. And I remember because one year, I must was a junior or sophomore in high school, and he sent money home for Christmas. It was only twenty-five dollars and my coat at that time was twenty-four ninety-five.

MARJORIE: What about that time he bought one bicycle for the five of us?

CELIA: Well, he did do that, too. He bought one red. I mean one—

—yellow-and-green bicycle!!! :MARJORIE AND CELIA [in unison and with glee]

BOB: I don't remember [shaking his head and smiling; everyone laughs]. They always kept me out of it [makes a shoving motion with his hands]. I don't remember that. I don't remember the bike [talking stops as Marjorie and Celia crack up laughing].

CELIA: But anyway. My father didn't make it up here [in Chicago] . . . he came back for some reason. And then my uncle got sick and my mother come up here. And I guess there was a separation between her and my dad by that time.

Yeah . . . Yeah. :MARJORIE

CELIA: And she come up here and she was working and had got a job on Market Street being a seamstress and whatever. And because she loved her children so much and she never wanted us to go through any-thing, when the marriage was failing and every-thing, my mother knew that I was the puny one and that I was the one that would suffer the most, because I just wore everything on my heart and everything. So she came down and got me. Okay, and she brought me back up here on the *Greyhound bus* [emphasizing each syllable]. Okay, and that was nineteen . . . forty-nine. Forty-nine.

MARJORIE: I came here [to Chicago] after my first child was born because of marriage problems and whatever. When I left, I packed all my little stuff and put it under the house in boxes and bags and whatever. Oh, that's right. Bob was supposed to help me take it to the Trailways. You know, not the Greyhound. And he made a mistake and went to the bus station instead of coming to the house when Midge left home. That was my husband at that time. And I had to page him. And I had boxes and crates and sacks and everything. He finally came. We got on the Trailway. We went to—

—Waucissa. :CELIA

MARJORIE: Waucissa. We stayed there for a while and whatever. Then Mom called and said she wanted me here, because Midge was looking for us, and he thought that maybe we was on the street or whatever. So we . . . during the night, we caught a train and we came here.

She was running away from her husband. :CELIA

MARJORIE: I was running away from him. And when he got ready to play his cards and whatever, I said, tell your father good-bye [waving good-bye] and wave, and she [baby Lawedia] was like fourteen months. And I had my stuff packed up under the house and what-ever. I was making a getaway. That's why I say I migrated here [Bob laughs]. I came, you know . . . I mean . . . And then I left by night from Waucissa. So if they were looking for me on the street, well, they couldn't find me there either. And came but seven days, he was there. [Turns to Bob and puts a hand on his back. Celia repeats the gesture.] He got it out of Bob that I had gone to Chicago [Bob looks up and away]. I mean, he got it out of my brother. My brother. [Bob is rubbing his hand over his eyes.]

The one that we . . . . :CELIA

MARJORIE: The one that was not supposed to tell anything. He told him . . . he went with a sad story, saying that maybe your sister might be on the street with Lawedia and blah blah. Now I'm coming to Chicago where my mom, sister, and everybody is and my brother, whatever. And he let this man tell him all this. He had his stuff packed under the warehouse, so when he found out where I was, he caught the first thing smoking [Bob laughs]. They was having this house party that night, and somebody knocked on the door and Gloria went to the door—and that's my sister-in-law—and she said, "Marj, somebody's here looking for you." And I went there and I looked and I was so surprised. And that was him. I says, "What are you doing here? *What are you doing here?*" [emphasizing each word]. And he says, "I'll find ya. I'll find ya. If you got to hell and back, I'll find ya." And sure enough [looping her two index fingers near her head], he talked me on into going back down there. But then I made a getaway again, and I did not return that time.

"The Whole Tone Changed for Me"

MARJORIE: When I came here, then the whole tone changed for me. The music. Like the food. Now, chitterlings and all this kind of stuff, okay, we didn't eat that. And when I came here—

It was a delicacy. :CELIA

MARJORIE: All you could see is people saying about chitterlings and spaghettis and cole slaws and all this kind of stuff. And we didn't eat that. They threw that away because we could go to the—

Slaughterhouse. :BOB

MARJORIE: —slaughterhouse, and they would give it to you if you wanted it.

CELIA: We cleaned out the chitterling. We cleaned out the chitterling and we stuffed meat in them, and that became our sausage.

MARJORIE: But I couldn't understand, when I came here, then that's when I went into the Ella Fitzgerald and the—

Lady Day. :CELIA

MARJORIE: —Lady Day and all this. And it was a whole changeover for me, because I was there with blues and whatever.

B. B. King. :CELIA

MARJORIE: And Muddy Waters and all of them—

—Muddy Waters and all them. That's all we knew. :CELIA

MARJORIE: And I came here and they was coming to the houses and stuff. Meeting to the houses. And of course you had all of the night-clubs and things here. But then the families—

They called them house rent parties. :CELIA

MARJORIE: Yeah. House rent parties. You'd pay and come in—

A quarter. Quarter parties. :CELIA

MARJORIE: And then you'd see these chitterlings. People talking chitterling dinners and all of this. And I'm wondering, "Well, what's
so great about this?" You know. And then you'd go into
this jazz music that . . . And I'm looking, "Where's my type
music?" But you gotta mellow on down to the Lady Day and
the Ella Fitzgerald and all this. And the finger popping [snaps
her fingers] and the spoon popping and whatever.

CELIA: When we met the Ramseys, they introduced us to the jazz—

A whole different thing. :MARJORIE

CELIA: It was them. The Ramseys introduced us to jazz.

To the jazz [Celia joins her in the refrain]. I guess maybe
they had never . . . you know blues is everywhere, but
not so much as the way it was back there. :MARJORIE

Down South. :CELIA

MARJORIE: That was the thing there.

"I'd Rather Be in a Jail in Chicago Than in a Church in Alabama"

The black Chicago milieu in which the Rosses learned about "the jazz"—a
term that seems to serve as a metaphor for many aspects of northern life—
was the result of another black migration earlier in the twentieth century.
Certainly my most compelling interviewee for this part of the story was my
great-aunt, Mattie Ramsey Giles Harper (1895–1999). She was born in Geiger, Alabama, a racially segregated hamlet, which is where the family believes they started. Alabama's historical profile is embedded in its nicknames,
"the Heart of Dixie" and "the Cradle of the Confederacy." "Papa" William
Ramsey, Mattie's father, migrated to Chicago around 1916 from Geiger,
Alabama. Mattie, her daughter, Charlotte, and four of Papa's other grand-
children—Ethel, Doris, Russell, and Inez—were my primary storytellers.

The stories that the interviewees relate portray some of the experiences
that created the cultural space that so impressed the Rosses when they
migrated to Chicago. The family ethos that I sketched in the first chapter
was the result of the combination of these families and their respective
backgrounds and sensibilities. The episodes below provide various and
selected memories, fragments, and themes that the interviewees believed to
be important to their history, culture, and identity.

According to Mattie, Papa William was the offspring of an interracial couple—a white male landowner and a female servant. When the land-owner's parents "discovered" him, Papa was given land and livestock to raise his family in relative prosperity to other African American families in the community. But Papa would have to flee Geiger, because one night he shot a white intruder who was attempting to gain entry to his home, possibly to violate his daughter. One by one, the Ramseys would follow him to Chicago, sneaking northward in small groups so as not to draw unwanted and possibly fatal attention. They left behind their land for fear of the violence that would almost certainly be leveled against them because of southern custom. Once they were settled, Mattie and her brother, William, Jr. (my grandfather), would joke to each other: "I'd rather be in a jail in Chicago than in a church in Alabama."

A proud man, Papa, like many other African American men, secured employment in the Chicago stockyards and built a life in the North. He was described by one of his granddaughters as "a hard-working man." "He worked at Wilson stockyard for years and he got quite a number of his family there, 'cause my father worked there and another son. He was a church-going man; he'd frequent West Point Baptist Church, and he was a staunch member there. He liked good times like the Ramseys do like. You know, we played cards. We did innocent things. He was a good-hearted man." Times would get difficult, as they did for many families during the Depression. William, Jr., also worked in the meat-packing plants of the stockyards but got into "serious trouble" with the law, a situation that depleted his father's hard-earned savings.

After his wife, Cora, died, William, Jr., found himself a widower with seven children (Ethel, Earl, William [W. J.], Guthrie, Russell, Doris, and Inez). After moving his large, motherless family from home to home of relatives, he found himself in over his head and would ultimately have to surrender his children to social services. Living in the foster care system was often quite harsh for the youngest of the family. Like their ancestors who fled Alabama before them, the Ramsey children "escaped" their foster home one by one, eventually starting their own families, and they remained a close-knit clan. One of the results of this closeness is illustrated by the house party practices that the migrating Rosses recognized as part of Chicago's black culture. Below are some of the Ramseys' stories, gleaned from a set of interviews conducted in 1996.

"If You Don't Want the Truth, Tell Me Where to Stop At"

One of the most important issues raised for me throughout these interviews was the idea of "truth" among the interviewees. If social realities are indeed constructed and the result of myriad negotiations, then I saw a microcosm of this process during the course of these interviews. Because many of these conversations took place within a group context, many of the common or collective memories were processed, negotiated, adjusted, agreed and disagreed on before my eyes. In the following exchange between sisters, they negotiated the space between private truths and public expression. Interestingly, the women in each side of my family became the most vocal spokespersons and arbiters of the family truths that would be represented in the public forum.

DORIS: All this is being taped now.

ETHEL: Well, I'm telling the truth.

DORIS: I'm just letting you know.

ETHEL: Okay. I mean if you don't want the truth, tell me where to stop at . . .

DORIS: No, no. I'm just telling you it's being taped.

Territories, Cultures, and the Impractical Piano

The following passages confirm that historical actors are often very aware of the sociopolitical (and often hegemonic) factors that serve to restrict their mobility and life chances. In addition, they understand well the everyday manifestations of class stratification *within* urban black communities. One informant said that in the 1920s "everybody lived down 18th Street. 17th Street. 16th Street. That was like our South. That was the black people's area. That was as far as black people . . . They land. That's where they land. Just like they say black people come here now and land on the West Side, they all land down there . . . that was the territory."

Life inside the black territory, or black belt, as it is called in social science literature, could be harsh, requiring many survival skills. Despite the hardships of raising a large family during the Depression, William, Jr., purchased a piano for his children. This, in their view, was a very impractical investment, although some of them, including my father, learned to play some of the popular songs of the day by ear. A musically talented clan, they not only entertained themselves, but also some of them would play, sing, and dance in local talent shows. In addition, a recurring event of their childhood was "command performances" for their father and his drinking buddies.

ETHEL: That's all we had. We had nothing but a piano.

DORIS: That's all the music we had till you got to the Victrola.

ETHEL: Like I said. Daddy meant well, 'cause he knew I played piano. He knew I could play. And he went and got a thousand-dollar piano. A thousand-dollar piano! That was a *lot* [she stretches out the word] of money back in them days. And that's all we had was a piano. We had crates and five, six sleeping in one bed. But we had a piano [exasperated, she laughs]. And when he got evicted . . .

RUSSELL: [Daddy used to] wake them up whenever he got with whiskey, moonshine. He'd want to hear some music. They would be on the piano and play the music. They'd be in bed. He'd call Guff, Russell . . . Whenever he called, he called the whole family—

DORIS: He called everybody's name—

RUSSELL: Everybody's name.

ETHEL: Play!!!! Play the piano for some of his drunks. Play! Play!! Play!!! [Everyone laughs.]

ETHEL: [starts singing] "Music go round and round [Doris and Inez join her], oh-oh-oh-oh, and comes out here." That was Daddy's theme song.

INEZ: [sings] Piano!

DORIS: [echoes] Piano!

ETHEL: [chimes in, swinging her arms] Music goes round and round, oh-oh-oh-oh, and comes out here. Oh!! [In her seat, she starts twitching back and forth, moving forward and backward to the remembered music in her head, and Doris gets up to repeat the dance, standing. They laugh and act out long-ago movements and gestures.]

While the modest backgrounds of some of our greatest African American performers are well known, we rarely see how people beyond the press agents, managers, and biographers of these musicians remember them. Below, Ethel recalls her brush with one of the premier pianists and singers of the century, Nat King Cole.

GUTHRIE RAMSEY: Tell me about your piano lessons. When did you start?

ETHEL: I was still in grammar school. I was around six or seventh grade, 'cause I hadn't graduated. It was a piano room in Coleman School and they charged twenty-five cents a week. And I went—well, he [Nat King Cole] was gone already. But he could read music. See, I was playing by ear, but I wanted to learn music. I could bang out anything by ear. But my grandmother thought I was going to be a Nat King Cole. She was going send me to piano school to take piano lessons.

GR: Other Mama or your mother's mother?

ETHEL: My grandmother. Papa's wife. Daddy's mother. We call her Other Mama.

GR: So do you think she was behind you taking piano lessons?

ETHEL: I know she was. Well, she knew I was banging on that piano. And she always wanted me to be a genius, anyway. You know . . . I don't remember even how it came about. All I know is I wasn't in that room with Nat King Cole not too very long. Like I said, her quarters gave out. You know, I say that as a joke. I don't know whether she stopped it or the teacher thought I wasn't ready. I can't tell you. All I know is I didn't finish. I know that.

GR: It was through Coleman School?

ETHEL: No, it wasn't through Coleman School. It was a piano teacher in Coleman School. A room in Coleman School where you would take piano lessons.

GR: And it was the same teacher that Nat King Cole used?

ETHEL: Yeah. Same one.

GR: Okay. Tell me about Nat King Cole as a kid.

ETHEL: You know we all was rough and tough over on Dearborn and Federal. And he was one of the rough, tough . . . His father was a minister. Preacher. Preacher's son. And they said preachers' sons or children were always the worst kind. He stole as much coal as my brothers did.

GR: Tell me about playing the piano for school. Did you play the piano for Coleman School?

ETHEL: For Coleman School. Uh-hmmm. Nat Cole and I—

—for marches. :DORIS

ETHEL: Well, we did play for assembly. He did most of the assembly playing. They know I could bang out something. You had to march in by music. You didn't just come walking in. And you came in orderly. You came in either in twos or fours. You marched like soldiers marching in, and when you got to the door and then you heard the music, you walked in to the beat of the piano. And the piano sat right in the hall. In the

hallway. And each teacher would escort her class in.
Every teacher came outside and lined her class up.

GR: What tunes did you play when they came in?

ETHEL: [pretends to play the piano, humming a John Philip
Sousa march; everyone joins in, mimicking various
instruments] After I married and had Les, I thought
I was a grown woman. I wasn't but sixteen when Les
was born. So I must have been seventeen then. In the
meantime, I had left this man, and I was living in
Daddy's house. Like I said, we didn't have nothing but
that piano and some crates and three, four sleeping in
one bed—me, Inez, and Doris all slept together. And
the boys—all of them sleeping together. But we had
the piano. Les was born at 5:15 in the morning, December 20th. Listen. We didn't have not a stick of wood or
a lump a coal . . . Wasn't no heat. And Les was born at
5:15 in the morning. Well, me being a young woman, I
just pulled the cover over both of us and went to sleep.
When Les's father came, I said, "You call my grandmother." She lived right down the street, 4711 St.
Lawrence. We lived at 4527 St. Lawrence. I said call—
not call, we didn't have no phone. Send Earl and them
down there to get my grandmother, and call the doctor,
then call his daddy. That's the order I give it to him
[Earl]. When Other Mama got there, Les was two and a
half hours old. But his daddy beat him there first, and
the house was ice cold. He paid Earl and W. J. to get
some wood to make a fire to heat the house up. This is
the truth. This man came out the next morning to open
his garage [she starts laughing] and his car was sitting
right out—no garage. They tore that garage down.
Broke it down and brought it in the house, piece by
piece. By bushel basket. We had bushel baskets. That's
how you brought it in. By bushel basket. And we had
mucho heat.

DORIS: Didn't they vote us out the neighborhood?

ETHEL: The boys, they were tough. They were street . . . see,
we had jumped too far anyway. We had jumped from
Federal to St. Lawrence. That was too big a jump. Our
culture didn't go that far. And they were street. Earl,
W. J., and Guff. They were street boys. Federal and
Dearborn Street. The neighborhood got together and
petitioned the Ramseys out the block. They were causing so much trouble in the neighborhood, they got a

petition. And everybody on both sides of the street, 45th and St. Lawrence on to 47th Street, signed that petition to get the Ramseys off of St. Lawrence. And we had to go again.

Church Songs, Drunks, and Bribes

As I stated above, memories of various events and circumstances were often rooted in varying perspectives. The truth of each, if there is such a thing in these situations, probably lies somewhere in the spaces between these perspectives. When questioned about the extent of their father's musical talent, one of William, Jr.'s, daughters replied, "No more than singing when he was drunk."

DORIS: He'd sing them old church songs. He'd sit out there with the guys and they'd sing those . . . they used to be out front and they'd be singing quartet [music]. Long time ago, men used to sing in quartets.

ETHEL: I don't remember Daddy singing that.

DORIS: I remember he used to be out there with those men and they'd be singing . . . out there on the front.

ETHEL: They'd be out there drunk. Daddy didn't never go to church.

DORIS: They were singing those church songs, though.

As the interviewees recall, for all the importance of the black church in African American urban communities, attending church was not central to this family's lifestyle. At the same time, however, they recall with accuracy and glee the musical practices of the churches they did attend.

GUTHRIE RAMSEY: What church did you attend?

ETHEL: None. As a matter of fact, we were bribed—if you don't go to Sunday school, you don't go to the show. And that's how I went to Sunday school.

GR: Who would bribe you? Your father?

ETHEL: No. My father had nothing to do with it. His mother. His mother. That's how we went to Sunday school. We didn't go to church too much. When I started going into church . . . you know how teenagers group up now and go to church. And it's more of a social event. I remember we used to belong to a church called Sister August. Do you remember that [to Russell, who shakes his head no]? Sister August. And she used to give us free bread some day out of the week. And so we'd frequent that little church. It wasn't no bigger than right in here [she outlines the parameters of the seating area]. But we liked to go there. And we had church right in there.

GR: What kind of music was it?

ETHEL: Baptist service. Same music that they have now. But older, older songs.

DORIS: The songs we used to sing then, they pepped them up now. They don't sing the same songs that we sung. It's different. We sang songs like they originally were . . .

ETHEL: They sang songs like, uh [trying to remember], Dr. Watts. [Ethel and Doris break into a rendition of a Dr. Watts–style hymn.]

DORIS: We sang songs like they sing it now, they kind of jazz up now, like "Jesus Keep Me Near the Cross." [She and Ethel and Inez begin to sing their version of the song.] They just jazz it up some.

Mean Men and Good Providers

ETHEL: Daddy was a very poor provider. This has got nothing to do with love. It's the truth. He worked with Papa—Papa is my grandfather—and he had a good job. He and Uncle Delaware were beef-boners. They disjointed, uh, uh—

—stock animals. :RUSSELL

ETHEL: Yeah. And they had the highest-paying jobs that black men had in those days. They made hot money in those days. And Uncle Delaware, he was a provider. He was a provider. He kept a house. He kept his kids well-dressed and plenty of food. Daddy did not [shaking her head]. Daddy did not. It was my job to find another house to move in. It was always my job to cook food that wasn't there.

See, Daddy wasn't but twenty-one years old when I was born. Just made twenty-one May 26, and I was born June third. And then right after that, children started coming. And you know, some people just not equipped to take care of a whole bunch of children. Anyway. I told him . . . I said, "If you don't move me outta here, I'm gone. I am leaving here today. I'm not gonna stay here." And he knew I meant that. So he brought us all up and moved in Teddy's [and] them house. Uncle Tom's house [looking at Russell], 37 and Indiana. Well, now, Uncle Tom's wife, like Uncle Tom . . . Uncle Tom was sweet and he had a sweet wife—

Aunt Clara. :DORIS

ETHEL: Aunt Clara. Uh-huh. Right on the corner of 37 and Indiana. I never will forget. Everybody always kept a nice big house. And she welcomed . . . More came than was there. 'Cause it was just [she ticks off the names] Percy, Bernice, and Teddy. And Aunt Clara. Just five of them. He bringing five kids plus himself. So more of us came there than was already there. That was a beautiful thing.

Seven of us, wasn't there? :DORIS

ETHEL: Yeah. Yeah. Seven children and Daddy. Anyway. It was a beautiful thing that he did there, but . . . and Aunt Clara meant well. She cooked long meals for us. 'Cause Daddy worked in the stockyard and he'd bring any kind of meat and food home. It wasn't no problem bringing it home, if you'd bring it home. And she was swell. I remember good things about Aunt Clara. . . . But we stayed there and like I said, she would cook, cook, cook, cook. We didn't have no fancy dishes. We'd eat out of tin pans and bowls and just anything. . . . She didn't know all these people was gon' come to her house, and we was eating out of anything we could eat. Three days in a row—now Bernice and I was the same age. Same age. As soon as we'd get through eating, Bernice would get deathly ill. [Doris begins to laugh.]

INEZ: She didn't wash no dishes.

ETHEL: And, now, we ain't turning on no hot water. No dishwasher or lotion or all of this stuff. You going the hard way to wash these dishes. I did that three nights. And see, Clara was so naive [soft-voiced]: "Oh, baby. You'd better go lay down." [Everyone laughs.] "Go lay down and rest yourself, 'cause you, oooh." All these dishes.

DORIS: Yeah. And you see in those days, we didn't have no soap flakes either. You had the big bin—

—big bin of soap to wash them dishes. :INEZ

ETHEL: Half of 'em was making soap. Them folks was making soap. Making it out of grease and lye. So I told Daddy again . . . I said, well . . . I said, "I'm gonna come up out of here" [she chuckles]. I was young. I had to be smart for my age to realize this is a gimmick. Every time we get through eating, this woman gets sick. And her and I—out of the two of us, that means I got to go in the kitchen and do all the pots and pans and dishes and buckets and slopjars and all that. Uh-uh. This ain't gon' work. This ain't gon' work. But anyway, we moved from there.

During the course of these interviews, I never asked my informants directly about their views on race, identity, and culture. But clearly these are the issues that have emerged from the mix, jumble, and fragments of the memories. I have made no attempt in the representation of this data to present a seamless, realist ethnography. In fact, I want to draw attention to the collective process of memory and culture building among my interviewees. Moreover, I want to bring into high relief the role that the critic, ethnographer, or historian plays in constructing the social world of their "subjects" for reading audiences. Historical accounts that rely on interviews or an ethnographic stance are often filtered through numerous contingencies: gender, birth order, marital status, relationship to the interviewer or ethnographer, and other factors that relate, as Sherry Ortner notes above, to power struggles among subalterns.

What has emerged from these various stories are portraits of African American working-class sensibilities in the words of those who occupied that social station. As we study the cultural expressions of these communities, we must do so while recognizing how fluid and diverse they are. Many of them realized this diversity long before it became theoretically fashionable to recognize such. It was clear that some of these experiences were, in fact, painful to recall and reveal. I was surprised by many of them, since knowledge of some of these events was not passed along to subsequent generations. As one of my informants stated during an interview, "We just haven't talked about some of this stuff." I should point out, of course, the difficult stories were told with humor, self-effacement, and signifyin(g) of the highest and most profound order.

For that and other reasons, it is my belief that some of the resourcefulness, heroic resolve, and other sensibilities—especially those in the realm of expressive culture—were passed along, if transformed, to the next generation. Connections among artistic inventions such as music and the life experiences of audiences are not always pat and readily apparent, at least not to this writer. Yet when one digs below the surface and sees the similarities between the stated "artistic intent" of a musician and the truth claim of the stories recounted above, we perhaps move closer to understanding how meaning is generated. Specific audiences construct meanings about artistic culture in their everyday lives in much the same way as critics do: through the prism of their own life experiences and the webs of culture into which they have been socialized.

As the Ramsey siblings came of age, they married, started families, and passed many of their cultural practices and sensibilities along to the next generation. When they were joined to the migrating Rosses through marriage, one of the results was the down home–upsouth house party aesthetic that I described in the first chapter. In fact, one of the Rosses expressed a sense of elation upon witnessing the South in the city ways of the Ramseys, especially the house parties that they hosted in the 1950s. "We entertained,"

Figure 7. "Blues-ing" upsouth in Chicago. Siblings Earl and Ethel Ramsey enjoy a night out on the town in midcentury Chicago. Credit: Sina Rush.

one of the Ross sisters stated as she fondly remembered those times. They were proud that they always took the children to these affairs, sleeping us through the long night on the pile of coats that were laid on beds. Some of these parties even lasted until the next morning. Music for listening and music for dancing permeated the atmosphere. One Ross believed she even heard "a rhythm section" in the way that the Ramseys played cards, as each punctuated the game with dramatic card snapping on the table, with signifying, or, perhaps, even with a quote from a Signifying Monkey tale.

The syncretism and blending of down home and upsouth sensibilities formed the foundation of black Chicago family life depicted in the beginning of this study. It is important to remember, however, that while this story is a specific one, it has more general implications. As these families settled into the new Afro-modernism of the moment, the social status of African Americans moved steadily toward a crossroads that would dramatically appear in the 1960s. Gradually, the black archipelago created by

Figure 8.   Stomping the blues in the basement: learning
to stomp the blues begins early, as cousins Brenda Ramsey
Payne and Sheila Ramsey demonstrate in the late 1950s.
Credit: Brenda Ramsey Payne.

migration patterns in the early part of the century would be linked by mass-
media texts, which African Americans living all over the United States
would believe spoke to and about them as a group. The soul singer James
Brown became a very important voice in the 1960s, one that personified the
moment as a transitional one in black cultural politics. In my own recollections of that moment, it is important to note, James Brown ruled the private
and public cultural spaces of black Chicago. You heard him constantly on
the radio, at the block party, in roller rinks, homes, clubs, and stores.
Everywhere.

SAYING IT LOUD: THE NEW POLITICS OF BLACKNESS

"Uhh!! wit-cha ba-a-d self. Say it loud, I'm black and I'm proud." With
these lyrics, preeminent soul singer James Brown seemed to declare (in the
popular sphere, at least) that a new day had dawned in the world of African
American cultural politics.[3] Or better: The renewed thrust of black sociopolitical progress during the post–World War II period seems to erupt in this

Figures 9a–b. "We Entertained": Posing and "soul karaoke" continue the basement house-party culture of Chicago in the late 1990s. Credit: Brenda Ramsey Payne.

song's candid strut. J. Rosamond Johnson and James Weldon Johnson's hymn "Lift Every Voice and Sing," written in 1900 and originally sung by schoolchildren in Florida, had found a new and unlikely rival as the "Negro (or Black) National Anthem," as it was dubbed informally in black communities.[4] But "Say It Loud" was no hymn. Released in 1968, it became so emblematic of this era's new expression of black pride and Brown's presence became so ubiquitous in the American popular press that a mainstream publication, *Look* magazine, asked its audience the following year: "James Brown: Is He the Most Important Black Man in America?" While the query itself may have been rhetorical, no one denied the esteem in which Brown's fans held him; they christened him "Soul Brother No. 1," "the Godfather of Soul," and "the Hardest-Working Man in Show Business." Indeed, Brown personified these sobriquets, especially *soul, work, the show,* and *the business.*

In a string of hit recordings throughout the 1960s and 1970s, Brown's decidedly "southern-flavored" musical rhetoric galvanized African American communities, linking urban with rural, the North with the South, black revolutionaries with school children, militant, avant-garde artists with audiences possessing more "mainstream" tastes. Brown's star rose during turbulent times. Just as post-1970s rap music registers the shifting socioeconomic and cultural landscape of late capitalism, postmodernity, and the postindustrial, Brown's musical language, lyrical subject matter, public presentation, and cultural politics are saturated with the new consciousness of the late 1960s. Brown stood at the crossroads between the Civil Rights and Black Power movements; between the celebration of black sensuality and wholesome, Afro-styled family values; he stood between an urbanized Afro-modernism, which took definitive shape around World War II, and the blight associated with the postindustrial inner city after the 1970s. He was the 1960s version of a "race man," a determined black capitalist who fought for artistic and financial control over his career. He often spoke out publicly on behalf of those living in impoverished African American communities like the ones in which he had been born and raised. Brown lived a difficult, Depression-era childhood in the South, working numerous odd jobs to help his family meet ends. One of the ways he earned extra money was by performing for trains loaded with troops, who would throw spare change to young Brown as he danced, no doubt with the unabashed fervor that would one day define his energetic stage shows.

Brown always remembered the struggles of his early life, and this quality endeared him to working-class audiences. In December 1968, he even entreated Santa Claus in one recording to "go straight to the ghetto."[5] That

Figure 10. James Brown showed the world that soul did not come naturally but took lots of hard work. Credit: Chuck Stewart.

kind of down-home sentiment characterized many of Brown's recordings. The lyrical narrative of "Say It Loud" does not invoke, for example, the respectable, high-toned sentiments of "Lift Every Voice and Sing," which states in its second verse:

> Stony the road we trod, bitter the chastening rod
> Felt in the days when hope unborn had died
> Yet with a steady beat, have not our weary feet
> Come to the place for which our fathers sighed?

Like the Johnson brothers, Brown reflects on past struggles and stillborn hope, but he depends on an entirely different sense of poetic rhetoric. In one passage from the second verse, for example, Brown references a spiritual's text, mother wit, and colloquial expression:

> We've been 'buked, and we've been scorned
> We've been treated bad, talked about
> as sure as you're born

But just as sure as it takes two eyes to make a pair
Brother, we can't quit until we get our share

In another verse, Brown seems to speak of his personal experiences with manual labor. The lyrics can also refer to his earlier struggles for artistic control and an equitable financial relationship with his record company, the King label: "I've worked on jobs with my feet and my hands / and knew all the work I did was for the other man." Even the word *black* in "Say It Loud" represents a shift in African American sensibilities. During the 1960s it was radicalized and embraced as a politically charged designation for African American ethnicity. As a dark-skinned African American, Brown spoke to racial prejudice and to the "color-struck" element in African American communities.[6] So as Brown tropes the ideas of social justice and racial uplift that characterized "Lift Every Voice and Sing," he updates the message for his late-1960s audience. From Brown's opening trademark, "uhhh," to his half-spoken "call," "Say It Loud," and the response of a chorus of (white and Asian American!) children shouting "I'm Black and I'm Proud," we are drawn into a world that is, as one writer has described Brown's lyrical artistry, "far removed from the poetry of Western art song, the urbane witticisms and sentimentality of Tin Pan Alley, and the folksy, anecdotal narrative of country-western music."[7]

The musical rhetoric of this piece also breaks with and exploits tradition. Brown, as I mentioned, does not sing but speaks the lyrics of each verse, a gesture that both foreshadows the non- and semimelodic oral declamations of rappers in the next decade and recalls black "folk" preaching performance. The form of the piece comprises verses, a chorus, and a bridge section. The verses and choruses (the "say it loud" refrains) are each performed within the same choppy, repetitive "cut" groove that features an angular, prominent bass line, situating the piece firmly in B-flat.[8] The bridge, which is heard twice in the recording, moves to E-flat for a few measures, summons blues form, but is also reminiscent of similar harmonic gestures in gospel music.

Authorship of the piece is credited to Brown and woodwind player–arranger Alfred "Pee Wee" Ellis. As performers and composers, Brown and Ellis adorn the simple design of "Say It Loud" with shifts between what can be heard as two discrete tonal centers—relational but independent because of the repetitive quality of each. Brown and Ellis satisfy what Zora Neale Hurston calls the "will to adorn" in a number of inventive ways.[9] The small horn section almost competes with the bass line with melodic patterns that move between percussive, unison lines and chordal passages. The guitarist adds yet another "competing" pattern to the groove, which (like the horns) alternates between single lines and chordal punches but which fills in a different part of the rhythmic timeline. All parts of this instrumental tableau fit together like the pieces of a puzzle, and each supplies sonic variety within the mix. Audiences and musicians loved it. This division of sonic labor became the foundational elements of the funk genre, an approach to sound organization extending from the pronounced glorification of the strong backbeat in earlier R&B practices.

In my view, funk, or the "in the pocket" groove (explained earlier as the funk recipe), rivals in importance the conventions of bebop's complex and perhaps more open-ended rhythmic approaches. Each imperative—the *calculated-freedom* of modern-jazz rhythm sections and the *spontaneity-within-the-pocket* funk approach—represents one of the most influential musical designs to appear in twentieth-century American culture.[10] The "James Brown sound" inspired admiration, piqued the imaginations of black cultural nationalists interested in "African origins," and inspired contemporary dance crazes that swept across the country. One writer working at that time declared with deadpan sincerity that James Brown's horn section was "the most deadly and earthy music section in the history of American music." He writes further that "the James Brown band represents the quintessence of an African-directed movement in black music expression from the popular idiom, and it has influenced the latest dance styles."[11]

On this last point, Brown celebrates dance verbally in "Say It Loud," declaring at the end of the piece, "and we can do the Boogaloo," referring to an immensely popular African American dance of the late 1960s. His statement occurs in the context of the bridge, in which he had also earlier in the song broken from the lyrical narrative of the verses by performing various stock, but culturally rich, phrases like "ooo-wee, you're killing me, you're all right, and you're outta sight." This narrative respite, together with the harmonic move to E-flat and the rhythmic shift occurring in each bridge, was, in my own experiences, often accompanied by kinetic intensification by dancers or roller skaters, who often "helped themselves" to their own verbal declamations. Thus in terms of a typical in-the-moment musical experience, audiences freely participated in the recomposition of "Say It Loud." *"Go, girl!" "Look out!" "Don't hurt yourself,"* and *"Hey!"* one might hear on a crowded dance floor. *"Wall!"* one might hear at the roller rink if a skater wanted a slower skater to yield the fast lane near the wall so that he or she could get on with a more intense dance step. This collaborative act among dancers, skaters, listeners, and the mass-media musical text mirrors, in fact, how James Brown's band members created many of his late-1960s to

mid-1970s funky grooves. Part of Brown's reputation for being hard-working derived from his relentless touring, rehearsal, and recording schedules.
Within this context and under Brown's direction, his bands forged innovative approaches for complementing the singer's virtuoso improvisations. In
the process, they laid the musical groundwork for funk, jazz-fusion, numerous hip-hop idioms, and other styles of popular music.[12]

NOT JUST JAZZ, SPIRITUALS, OR MEN:
BLACK WOMEN CRITIQUE BLACK POWER

At the height of the Black Power movement, African American women novelists, scholars, and critics also seized the explosive moment. Writers such as
Alice Walker and Toni Morrison published novels that won Pulitzer Prizes
for fiction. In the 1970s black female critics Mary Helen Washington,
Barbara Smith, and Barbara Christian, among others, worked diligently to
define and institutionalize not only black feminist studies but also the
broader field of African American literary studies. Inspired in part by the
"discovery" of black female writers such as Zora Neale Hurston (who seized
the moment posthumously), African American women writers have
become, in the words of black female poet and literary scholar Ann du Cille,
"politically correct, intellectually popular, and commercially precious sites of
literary and historical inquiry." Du Cille, with more than a hint of asperity,
likens the fashionable interest in theorizing race, class, and gender in the
work of black women writers to standing in a dangerous, and suddenly busy,
three-way intersection with the likelihood of being run down by the
oncoming traffic.[13] (She calls the roots of this trend "Hurstonism.") The
contributions of black female writers through essays, anthologies, and
monographs over the last twenty-five years have institutionalized a
dynamic body of literature and, perhaps more important, championed
sophisticated frameworks that help us enjoy and understand it.

During the 1960s, populist black nationalism comprised various and
sometimes competing ideologies, which, taken together, articulated a desire
for varying degrees of cultural, political, and economic separation from the
dominant culture. Within this historical context, black feminists fought
against two kinds of invisibility. One kind involved distinguishing their
concerns from those of white feminism. The other involved exposing and
critiquing the masculinist emphasis of black nationalism, even as these
women drew energy from it. This second goal is instructive in understanding one aspect of Eileen Southern's work. The literature that grew out of the
freedom movement, while its authors struggled and waged war against

black stereotypes, erected other movements, the most notable of which centered the black male as the true subject of black culture, an attitude that marginalized African American women. Furthermore, the Black Aesthetic discourse privileged certain genres, preferring drama and poetry because of their direct, immediate, and oral impact. Black feminist (and "womanist") literary scholars have mounted creative and theoretical strategies in their fiction, poetry, and criticism that, according to one contemporary literary scholar, sought to "both restructure and supplement the ideological program of black cultural nationalism." In this artistic milieu, black feminists employed a "double gesture." They continued their "appreciation of the cultural history that has produced the black writer's strong investment in the model of a whole, cohesive self" and gave "a vigilant attention to the differences within the black experience that confound any totalized, unitary definition of black identity."[14]

It is within this historical "redefining blackness" context that Eileen Southern, one of the country's first African American and female musicologists, published *The Music of Black Americans: A History* in 1971. Southern should certainly be considered a "race woman." The appearance of her book in the wake of the Black Power movement, the turbulent social upheaval of the late 1960s, links it to an auspicious historical moment. As it does in "Say It Loud," the word *black* stands provocatively, even proudly, in Southern's main title. The book reflects some of the dramatic social changes of its day, such as the widespread student protests that led to sweeping curricular advances in colleges and universities across the nation and, most notably, the addition of courses in black history and culture. Designed to fill a void in the new curricula, Southern's work broke new ground in its focus, method, and scope, inspiring others (both directly and indirectly) to similar inquiry and helping to establish black music as a legitimate scholarly specialty. In a 1987 interview, Southern explained that attitudes expressed by her colleagues as she prepared to offer a course in black music fueled her resolve. Some of them contended that there was nothing to learn about the subject, because it constituted "just jazz and spirituals."[15]

Southern's study resonated with and challenged classic 1970s black cultural nationalism and its feminist response. In the preface to the 1971 edition of *The Music of Black Americans* she writes: "The black musician has created an entirely new music—in a style peculiarly Afro-American."[16] This statement clears a space for her exploration of a musical legacy that countered in scholarly terms sentiments like the "just jazz and spirituals" attitude or even the notion that a distinctive African American musical culture did not exist at all. Southern's scholarship reflected the notion of a unified, cohesive, and essentially male "blackness," using terms such as *"the"* *black community* and *the Black man* often. Other black female literary critics were intensely debating such representations in their work. Southern was, of course, not alone in this characterization. Many African American writers who contributed to academic discourse during the high years of the Black Aesthetic referred often to black male composers and performers to illustrate their rhetorical, musical, and polemical points. Aretha Franklin was a notable exception to this unspoken rule. Writers mentioned her music (along with that of James Brown and Mahalia Jackson), no doubt because of the symbolic currency of "soul music," an important idea in black nationalist discourse.[17]

There was, at the same time, a considerable critical gap between Southern's work and that of the Black Arts project, although she did not discuss this difference in print, as other female writers did. As a black female academic in an overwhelmingly white and male professional setting, Southern experienced racism, sexism, and even "the hostility of black male professors."[18] But she did not directly address these discriminatory practices in her work. In fact, as Samuel Floyd notes, her research "seems benign," because methodologically speaking, "she works squarely within the musicological tradition, cherishing its modes of inquiry and its scholarly products, with no desire to undermine or reject the accepted tenets and practices of the profession."[19] Southern championed a discrete Afro-American musical tradition, but she traced its historical trajectory in relationship to Western music traditions, a position untenable to the Black Arts project. If some black cultural nationalists valorized musical styles such as jazz for their rhetorical immediacy in the liberation struggle, Southern valued historical distance and exercised deliberate caution in her jazz discussions: "We are yet too close in time to this music to be able to view it in proper perspective."[20] If the Black Arts movement embraced a radicalized self-definition of black culture, Southern did not believe that her musicological project should venture into such a contentious, ideologically charged arena. She left that project to future scholars: "Since the immediate purpose of the present work is to record the facts of history, which must precede esthetic and stylistic evaluation, I have not tried to make explicit a definition of black American music. . . . I have tried to provide a solid and useful basis for discussion of the question of its definition."[21]

Southern's work contrasts sharply with an earlier book that fits squarely within the Black Arts movement ideology. Many recognize Amiri Baraka's *Blues People* (1963; written under Baraka's former name, LeRoi Jones) as a watershed publication in both black music historiography and American cultural studies.[22] Baraka understood well that an important relationship existed between black music's development and the historical trajectory of African American social progress. *Blues People* represents the first book-length study by a black author to theorize extensively about this connection.[23] As an African American writer, Baraka's "insider's" viewpoint was a novelty to jazz letters at that time. (However, it is also important to emphasize that Southern was equally rare in musicological circles.) If one could sum up Baraka's concerns as one research problem, it would be to trace the political economy of African American music, from slavery to freedom. That emphasis makes *Blues People* an important work in itself, a book that, because of the fundamental—not to mention controversial—issues it raises, one writer called "the founding document of contemporary cultural studies in America."[24]

Baraka's attention to the political economy of black music (and numerous related issues) was laudable. But his skepticism of the ever-evolving "modernist" profile of African American musical culture, of which he paints a rather static picture, is plainly and even painfully obvious. (By way of comparison, Eileen Southern celebrates this same modernist drive.) Baraka regretted key processes in black music culture, such as commercialism, urbanization, migration, and professionalization. He believed that they corrupted the "real" or authentic black aesthetic. That corruption thesis, as Ralph Ellison pointed out in an eloquent review of *Blues People* in 1964, thins out African American culture, fails to provide a full cost-accounting of its historical influence on "mainstream" American culture, and ignores the "intricate network of connections" that bind the two cultures together.[25] Moreover, I might add that a critique of commercialism, migration, urbanization, and professionalism should also show how these processes figured into what made these styles meaningful for African Americans and the larger American populace. Baraka sought to translate his idea of a collective and communal black experience into a cohesive aesthetic-political theory within an environment saturated with new interest in urban black culture.

The forcefulness of Baraka's critical writings resounds in his essay of 1963, "Jazz and the White Critic." Baraka discusses identity politics in jazz criticism and, in doing so, addresses many of the concerns that future writers would take up some thirty years later but with less political focus, in my view. Baraka distinguished "criticism" from the research of historians, whose work he praised. He argued that class and race in the American context should be central to jazz criticism and that writers on black music need to "set up standards of judgement and aesthetic excellence that depend on our [Negro] native knowledge and understanding of the underlying philosophies and local cultural referents that produced blues and jazz in order to produce valid critical writing or *commentary* about it."[26]

Despite Baraka's stringent critiques and belief that the personal identity and politics of the critic mattered, the notion did not, for the most part, appear to influence white writers, who continued to offer cultural translations of their own during the 1960s and 1970s. Consider, for example, four very important works, Charles Keil's *Urban Blues* (1966), Gunther Schuller's *Early Jazz* (1968), Dena J. Epstein's *Sinful Tunes and Spirituals* (1976), and Lawrence W. Levine's *Black Culture, Black Consciousness* (1977). In *Urban Blues,* anthropologist Charles Keil used social science methodology to explain "an expressive male role within urban lower-class Negro culture—that of the contemporary bluesman."[27] One cannot call *Urban Blues* unpolitical: it is, after all, dedicated to Malcolm X and is steeped in the imperatives of black cultural nationalism. But for unspoken reasons, Keil believed it best to suppress the personal, although his instincts pressed him otherwise. "I have restrained a strong impulse to write a soul barring [*sic*] autobiographical preface for the simple reason that much of who I am comes out in the book; how I got that way is probably irrelevant."[28] In the afterword to the latest edition of *Urban Blues* (1991), however, Keil wanted to set straight a misunderstanding among some of his readers concerning his racial background. He confesses "I AM WHITE" in one of the postscript's subtitles. He gets even more specific in this glib portrayal: he is "German and Yankee blue-eyed . . . an Aryan from Darien, Connecticut (no blacks or Jews allowed), who served time at Yale (a few of each allowed) and could afford to choose a deep identification with Afro-American values and aspirations."[29] These words are not exactly soul baring, but they do suggest a new attitude for a different time.

Keil also compares the work of white and black writers on the blues. "White writers . . . tend to be folklorizing, documenting, defining, and social scientific: let's pin it down."[30] In his study, *Early Jazz,* for example, Gunther Schuller transcribed recordings in order to bring *improvised* jazz into the realm of *written* scores, notated musical examples, and stylistic analysis. Schuller listened to "virtually every record made, from the advent of jazz recordings through the early 1930s."[31] The book can certainly be considered a key work in the contemporary era of jazz analysis—many scholars consider it a kind of standard for certain kinds of work in jazz research. Schuller couldn't have disagreed more with Eileen Southern's assessment that jazz was still too new to study in proper perspective. He did share her "objective" stance but threw in a dash of the personal—this *is* jazz, after all. *Early Jazz* combines "the objective research of the historian-musicologist with the subjectivism of an engaged listener and performer-composer."[32] However, the person who is listener, performer, and composer is not historically, culturally, or socially situated vis-à-vis the musical materials under discussion. Like Schuller, Dena J. Epstein also mentions her "occupational identity" (a librarian) but discusses no other aspect of her background in *Sinful Tunes and Spirituals*, a definitive, indeed monumental, study of black slave music in America.

Lawrence W. Levine's *Black Culture, Black Consciousness* treats music extensively, although it is not the primary focus of the study. Levine's book addresses a pressing question being taken up by the popular press, black cultural nationalists, humanists, and social scientists of the day: Did a black culture exist? Interestingly, Schuller, Levine, and Epstein each stressed the time and effort invested in his or her project, each confirming the "let's pin it down" sensibility. Schuller listened to "virtually every record made, from the advent of jazz recordings through the early 1930s"; Levine "worked [his] way carefully through thousands of Negro songs, folktales, proverbs, aphorisms, jokes, verbal games, and . . . 'toasts'"; Epstein's copious research took some twenty years.[33]

By way of contrast, "black writers are more inclined to celebrate blues as a core metaphor in process, the center of a worldview that incorporates jazz, literature, aesthetics, philosophy, criticism, and political strategy."[34] Albert Murray's *Stomping the Blues* (1976), is such as book, bringing a different set of concerns to the table than the white writers discussed above. At the same time, however, an underlying theme of *Stomping the Blues* emphasizes the "universal" implications of the specific blues culture ethos outlined in the book. It is instructive to compare Levine's thinking to that of Murray on this topic. Levine writes:

> I am aware that many of the materials I analyze have their origins or parallels in the folk thought of other peoples, and whenever it was relevant to my purposes I have explored these avenues, but for the most part I have assumed that once these materials made their way firmly into the network of Afro-American thought and culture they could be used to shed light upon black consciousness without constant reference to their existence in other cultures.[35]

Unlike Schuller's, Epstein's, and Levine's heavily documented studies, *Stomping the Blues* contains no scholarly apparatus to speak of; Murray's cultural experience stands for his "authority," although this sentiment is not addressed specifically. Murray's explicitly musical discussions in the chapters titled "Singing the Blues" and "Playing the Blues" sketch out important conventions of the blues and jazz aesthetic. In general, his musical discussion (based on recordings and live performances) coupled with his extensive use of illustrations, including "action" and publicity shots of musicians and the actual record labels of commercial recordings, gives the impression that he wanted to celebrate, not decry as Baraka does, the commercial status of blues-based art musics.

Black religious music attracted its share of scholarly attention in the 1970s. Portia K. Maultsby, an African American scholar, played an instrumental role in raising black music's visibility in the fields of ethnomusicology and black studies.[36] Maultsby's work is primarily historical in content and method rather than ethnographic or critical; it reflects the nascent status of black music study in academia and the practical needs of the field. Music theorist Horace Clarence Boyer, also an African American, provided his field with its first extensive look at the compositional, vocal, and instrumental traditions of the black church.[37] Of significance, he published some of his early work in *Black World*, one of the revolutionary periodicals of the Black Arts movement.[38] African American ethnomusicologist Jacqueline Cogdell DjeDje combined the historical and theoretical with fieldwork in her 1978 study, titled *American Black Spirituals and Gospel Songs from Southeast Georgia: A Comparative Study*.[39] Important to note, the work focused on her hometown of Jessup, Georgia, and included transcriptions. Maultsby and Boyer both have significant experience as performers in gospel music, and, like Murray, their cultural backgrounds informed their work.[40] Two other black scholar-performers working in the 1970s deserve mention here. Composer Olly Wilson and virtuoso pianist Pearl Williams-Jones each discussed the relationship of African music to that of African Americana, which had generated both scholarly and populist interest because of the Black Power movement.[41]

Although it is quite varied, all of the work discussed above—from the "academic" to the nonacademic, from Southern to Murray and beyond— laid out important groundwork, structure, and themes for future work. Because of these pioneering endeavors, black music became a truly open field of inquiry, attracting scholars from a variety of personal and disciplinary backgrounds. For the most part, it concerned the historical and the practical; writers outside the academy addressed the political import of black music. Ethnographic work represented a small portion of these studies. Whether writers chose to "say it loud" or revolutionize quietly, the work discussed above made possible today's growing criticism of African

American music in the same way that the blackness practiced in 1940s and 1950s family life helped to create the new blackness discourses of subsequent decades.

My discussion of memories, histories, and musical soul in the present chapter extends the notion of Afro-modernism framed earlier in this book. As we see, Afro-modernism had blossomed from the 1940s to the 1960s. Migration, economic and domestic relations, political, social, and class struggle, and musical practice itself contributed to the world of the Afro-modern in the United States. As southern and northern black cultural sensibilities (not to mention the international dimension of Afro-modernism at this historical moment) merged within private and public spaces, Afro-America changed. And the world changed with it. What is more, gender relationships were pressing issues in all domains, as the memories and histories discussed above show. Movement of all kinds infused a palpable energy into the historical moment. There was the migration and the class mobility that it symbolized for many. There was the movement of black females into the new blackness discourse at the same time as we saw black music move into the domain of formal study. And, of course, James Brown made everybody move on the dance floor. Through it all, musical practice and discourse in homes, schools, neighborhoods, churches, clubs, and the academy bore the traces of the cultural and social negotiations of the moment. As we shall see in the next two chapters, all of these issues will emerge in new figurations during the era of postindustrialism or, as I call it, the Age of Hip-Hop.

7   Scoring a Black Nation

Music, Film, and Identity
in the Age of Hip-Hop

We make our lives in identifications with the texts around
us everyday.
                Anahid Kassabian, *Hearing Film: Tracking Identifications*
                in Contemporary Hollywood Film Music

The 1990s will be remembered as a boom decade for black popular culture.
One might say that like New Negroes in the 1920s, African American performers were in vogue. By the century's end, black expressive culture had
become a pervasive factor in American society, fixed indelibly to the country's cultural profile. African American entertainers of all stripes are a commanding presence in the culture. In the post–*Cosby Show* era, cable television serves up a steady diet of situation comedies starring African American
casts, whose exaggerated performances sometimes come dangerously close
to worn-out, reliable stereotypes. Trumpeter and composer Wynton
Marsalis, whose tireless efforts to put jazz on an equal social standing with
Western art music, has been recognized with the most important distinctions and awards, including the prestigious Pulitzer Prize for composition in
1997.
    We celebrate and reward black sports figures such as basketball player
Shaquille O'Neal with huge salaries, unprecedented media visibility, prestige, iconic status, and power. The talk show diva Oprah Winfrey reigns
over daytime programming. She attracts a diverse international audience
and commands a paycheck that surpasses even NBA MVPs.[1] Whether executing a virtuoso instrumental passage, or dunking basketballs, or chatting
it up through tears and self-help philosophies, or slapsticking through formulaic situation comedies, the early-twenty-first-century black performer
is visible and getting paid.[2]
    Of all these entertainment activities, the musical arts is perhaps the one
in which African Americans exacted the greatest influence by century's end.
The importance of their music can be felt in many realms of American society as well as globally. For one, music scholars no longer have to apologize

or hide their passion for this music; they can earn academic credentials and advance professionally by writing about this topic. Furthermore, scholars in other disciplines have also found these musical genres rich in what they teach us about larger issues in culture and society. And African American musicians are a commanding presence in the marketplace: top-selling artists routinely sign multimillion-dollar contracts, and their fans fill stadiums and consume heavily promoted CDs by their favorite artists.

Black musical styles show up routinely as topics in the culture wars. Politicians of all persuasions have used the music to score rhetorical points with their various constituencies. Some comment on rap music's nihilism or debate whether it is music at all. Critics haggle over whether jazz is enjoying a renaissance or is a dead art. The demise of the American family, the angst of black middle-class citizens, juvenile delinquency, inner-city decline, the commodification of Jesus' gospel on *Billboard*'s rhythm and blues charts, and many other indictments have been saddled to the back of black popular music.

While many of the progeny of race music styles continued to flourish throughout the latter half of the century, certainly, the most prominent and controversial of these musical expressions in the 1990s proliferated under the cultural umbrella called hip-hop. If the 1920s were dubbed the Jazz Age and the 1960s marked the ascendancy of rock, then a strong case can be made for calling the last decades of the twentieth century the Age of Hip-Hop. Hip-hop culture is virtually everywhere: television, radio, film, magazines, art galleries, and in "underground" culture. It has even surfaced in congressional hearings. And even where hip-hop culture is not found, its absence may also be understood as a reaction against it. Wynton Marsalis and a host of other critics, for example, have positioned their musical work against hip-hop's musical and thematic conventions.

In the next two chapters, I explore two very important sites of cultural memory: the medium of film and the dynamic and contested cultural space we refer to as the black church. Rather than solely providing the typical biographical profiles and extensive discussions of hip-hop's canonical figures and musical works that one expects in a musicological study, I approach musical practice in the Age of Hip-Hop from a slightly different angle. I am interested in exploring not only what a musical performance means but also how it achieves a particular signifying inflection. Thus, in the same way that I used family narrative and the theater of the literary, I explore film and the church as two community theaters in which music or discourse about music inform the social reality of historical actors. Within these cultural contexts and social settings lies one of the keys to unlocking the door to meaning.

Although film and the black church may seem unrelated, they both provided twentieth-century African American culture with important contexts for the working out of cultural representation, social class debates, gender performance, spirituality, and various other issues associated with identity. Musical practice operates as an important medium for the circulation of social energy in film and in the church world. Below, I discuss how this is achieved in the content and context of hip-hop culture.

WHAT IS HIP-HOP CULTURE AND PRACTICE?

Hip-hop culture, according to Tricia Rose, one of the foremost scholars to address the topic, consists of three modes of expression: rap music, graffiti writing, and break dancing. It emerged, she writes, "as a source for youth of alternative identity formation and social status."[3] Disenfranchised youth created fashions, language, and musical and bodily performance styles and formed elaborate networks of posses (or crews) that expressed their local identities and affiliations through these modalities. While the origins of hip-hop expressions can be traced to specific locations, its mass-media coverage and broad-based consumption made it one of the most widely known popular musics of the late twentieth century.[4]

Rapping itself denotes a vocal performance in which a rapper uses spoken or semispoken declamations, usually in rhyming couplets. The "rap" is revolutionary: rather than a singing or instrumental performance, in this genre the rap is the emotional focal point of the presentation. The idea of rapping has deep roots in African American culture. Its stylistic and thematic predecessors are numerous: the dozens and toasting traditions from America and Jamaica; sing-song children's games; double-dutch chants; black vernacular preaching styles; the jazz vocalese of King Pleasure, Eddie Jefferson, and Oscar Brown, Jr.; the on-the-air verbal virtuosity of black DJs; scat singing; courtship rituals; the lovers' raps of Isaac Hayes, Barry White, and Millie Jackson; the politicized storytelling of Gil Scott-Heron and the Last Poets; and the preacherly vocables of Ray Charles, James Brown, and George Clinton, among many others. Historians of rap music trace its present-day form, however, to the mid-1970s hip-hop culture of African American and Afro-Caribbean youth living in the South Bronx and upper Manhattan neighborhoods of New York City. The commercial origins of rap began in earnest with the 1979 hit recording "Rapper's Delight," by the Sugarhill Gang.[5]

In the early days of contemporary rap, DJs working in clubs, parks, and local parties would establish reputations by mixing the beats and snippets of sound from various recordings to encourage their audiences to dance. Some of these DJs would perform simple "raps," a practice that soon became more and more complex. MCs (taken from the term *master of ceremonies*) or rappers specializing in the vocal performance of this convention emerged. Within this division of labor, the MCs became the focus of the performance, and they raised the artistic stakes in this realm by creating very elaborate lyrical feats. DJs also elevated the artistic demands in their performance realm: as technology became more sophisticated, DJs began to create stunning rhythm tracks by taking recorded "samples" from a variety of sources, mixing them in inventive ways over which rappers would perform dense, lyrical narratives. Over the last twenty years, rappers and producers (DJs) have developed many satellite idioms, each having specific stylistic traits that signify meaning in particular ways. Changes have occurred in all realms of rap music: in the lyrical focus, body languages, rhythm tracks, slang, and fashions. Regional styles emerged in much the same way as they did in other forms of black popular music of the twentieth century. Rap music and its attendant expressions became so prominent that by the mid-1980s they captured the imaginations of filmmakers.

FILM, MUSIC, AND HIP-HOP CULTURE

The medium of film has communicated, shaped, reproduced, and challenged various notions of black subjectivity in twentieth- and twenty-first-century America since D. W. Griffith's *Birth of a Nation* appeared in 1915. Writing in 1949, Ralph Ellison argued that *Birth of a Nation* "forged the twin screen image of the Negro as bestial rapist and grinning, eye-rolling clown—stereotypes that are still with us today."[6] Such depictions in cinema had already existed in print media; and they persisted in all mass-media contexts in varying degrees throughout the twentieth century.

Film, however, has provided a most salient medium for the visual representation of African American subjects. Cultural critic James A. Snead has written persuasively about the power of film and how it helps to shape both social reality and personal experience in this regard. "Even in the infancy of motion pictures, it was obvious that film, as a way of perceiving reality, opened up entirely new perceptual possibilities, giving the eye an augmented sense of visual mastery over its surroundings, preserving events in motion for a seemingly unlimited number of future replays, performing a wide variety of functions: education, propagandistic, recreational, aesthetic." If, as Manthia Diawara has argued, the camera is "the most important invention of modern time," then it becomes an even more powerful tool when its technology is combined with the powers of music. Indeed, when filmmakers combine cinematic images and musical gestures, they unite two of our most compelling modes of perception: the visual and the aural.

Below I consider three films produced during the Age of Hip-Hop: Spike Lee's *Do the Right Thing* (1989), John Singleton's *Boyz N the Hood* (1991), and Theodore Witcher's *Love Jones* (1997).[7] These films form a suggestive, if uneven, trio. *Do the Right Thing* takes place on the East Coast, in the multiethnic Bedford-Stuyvesant neighborhood of Brooklyn, New York. *Boyz N the Hood* paints a poignant picture of the emergence of "gangsta' land" South Central Los Angeles. *Love Jones* is situated in the heartland, in upwardly mobile Chicago. On an immediate level, I am interested in how music shapes the way we perceive these cinematic narratives individually; how music informs the way audiences experience their characters, locations, and plots. But I am also making a larger argument for how the musical scores of these films are sites for the negotiation of personal identity and self-fashioning, on the one hand, and the making and negotiation of group identity, on the other. Both of these activities inform "meaning" in important ways. Finally, I use this analysis to learn more about the process of "making" meaning in hip-hop musical practice generally.

Below, I address several questions with regard to this cinematic function of music in hip-hop film. What role does musical discourse play in cinematic representation? If one of the primary thrusts of black cultural production has been the resistance to and countering of negative black stereotypes forwarded since *Birth of a Nation*, how does the musical score of the film participate in this agenda? How does the music score or artistically (re)invent a black cinematic nation? The musical scores of *Do the Right Thing*, *Boyz N the Hood*, and *Love Jones* provide excellent examples of the fluidity and contestation embedded in the notion of black identity, a topic that became very compelling for theoretical, political, and artistic reflection in the late twentieth century. Before moving to the music in these films, I need to address an important topic raised in most discussions of them: the degree to which they accurately portray an "authentic" black cultural experience.

KEEPING IT REEL:
DIVERSITY, AUTHENTICITY, AND THE HIP-HOP MUZE

Hip-hop culture has taken on the profile of a cottage industry because of aggressive corporate commodification. The postindustrial decline of United States urban centers, a downward turn that ironically spawned hip-hop's developments, has been co-opted by corporate America and represented as a glossy, yet gritty, complex of music idioms, sports imagery, fashion statements, racial themes, danger, and pleasure. While history shows us the persistence of the exploitation of African American culture in the United States, hip-hop represents an exemplary case in this regard. As the historian Robin D. G. Kelley argues:

> Nike, Reebok, L.A. Gear, and other athletic shoe conglomerates have profited enormously from postindustrial decline. TV commercials and print ads romanticize the crumbling urban spaces in which African American youth must play, and in so doing they have created a vast market for overpriced sneakers. These televisual representations of "street ball" are quite remarkable; marked by chain-link fences, concrete playgrounds, bent and rusted netless hoops, graffiti-scrawled walls, and empty buildings, they have created a world where young black males do nothing *but* play.[8]

The omnipresence of such imagery in the media has made a strong impact on notions of "authenticity" in African American culture. And moreover, music and musical practices continue to play a crucial role in the creation, renegotiation, and critique of the authenticity trope.

The intersection of hip-hop musical practices and film serves as a cogent example. Hollywood in the early 1990s presented young fans with films like *New Jack City, Boyz N the Hood, Strictly Business,* and *Juice,* among others. Taken together, these films have helped to create a highly recognizable hip-hop mode of representing a one-dimensional black youth culture. As filmmaker Spike Lee notes, these "inner-city homeboy revues" created a world in which "all black people lived in ghettos, did crack and rapped."[9] As thematic heirs of the 1970s blaxploitation genre of film, the 1990s version has been dubbed "rapsploitation," or, as Henry Louis Gates, Jr., has labeled it, "guiltsploitation." Gates uses the latter term to characterize what he sees as a key message underlying many of these films: ambiguity about upward mobility. His observations about class status and black mobility are worth noting: "The politics of black identity, and the determined quest to reconcile upward mobility with cultural 'authenticity,' is a central preoccupation of these films. If genuine black culture is the culture of the streets, a point on which the blaxploitation films were clear, how can you climb the corporate ladder without being a traitor to your race? What happens when homeboy leaves home? A new genre—guiltsploitation—is born."[10] Gates sees this trend as directly linked to the attitudes and backgrounds of the filmmakers. Rapsploitation of the early 1990s occurred, in part, because of an emergence of young, black, college-educated, and middle-class directors. Gates argues that these auteurs did not choose to close "the gulf between the real black people behind the camera and the characters they've assembled in front of it."[11]

Critics have also raised questions beyond this underlying class-status tension, questions with respect to gender issues in these films. Feminist critics such as Valerie Smith, Michele Wallace, bell hooks, Wahneema Lubiano, and Jacquie Jones, among others, have noted that the perceived "realness" of the rapsploitation film genre is also real hostile to black women. But the class-based and feminist critiques of these films are sometimes difficult to articulate because of the compelling nature of the film experience itself and what Smith has identified as a documentary impulse. Wallace, for example, admitted: "The first time I saw John Singleton's *Boyz N the Hood*, I was completely swept away by the drama and the tragedy. It was like watching the last act of *Hamlet* or *Titus Andronicus* for the first time. When I left the theater, I was crying for all the dead black men in my family."[12] Upon subsequent viewings, however, Wallace noticed the strain of misogyny running throughout much of the film. She perceived that *Boyz* and other films like it seemed to be saying that the dismal social conditions depicted in these films were due to character flaws in the women.

Feminist critic Valerie Smith has argued that a documentary impulse authenticates these films with claims that they represent the "real." They achieve this documentary aura through an uncritical use of various aural and visual markers of "real" black living conditions, reproducing stereotypical ideas about African Americans. The boundaries separating fact and fiction, truth and artistic invention, become blurred. Smith notes that critics, reviewers, and press kits assure audiences that these black male directors were "endangered species" themselves and are thus "in positions of authority relative to their material."[13]

While the importance of film cannot be dismissed, we should be careful to recognize the difference between cinematic entertainment and the "truth" of lived experience. There does not exist a one-to-one homology between lived experience and representations of such in film. At the same time, we should keep in mind that the same social energy that sustains ideologies like misogyny and other forms of discrimination also circulates in the narratives of these films. In other words, these directors didn't invent the misogyny, but they help to reproduce it. In this sense, they—perhaps unconsciously—kept it real, as the saying goes.

Writer Lisa Kennedy has argued that the complex of money, narrative, and pleasure bound up in film experiences makes them "extraordinarily powerful." Film, she writes, "is how America looks at itself." Nonetheless, she warns us against confusing the "individual vision" of an artist like a filmmaker with "the" collective reality of a group of people. Despite this warning, the dialogic interplay between "real" lived experience and film narratives (and for that matter, television shows, news programs, independent documentaries, print media, and music) remains an important fact of early twenty-first century life. In the case of film, "the real lives of people are substantiated by their reel lives."[14]

And as I will argue over the next few pages, the nexus of "reel life" and music and musical practices has import on the topic of black music and meaning. What interests me here is not so much the critique of monolithic representations of black class status and life expectations represented in these films. Nor do I want to question Hollywood's capital-driven fixation to exploit these topics. Rather, I want to explore film as one way to enter into an analysis of the intersection of black identity and musical practice. When writers, directors, producers, and composers work together to create convincing characters and story worlds for audiences, they do so with the help of musical codes that circulate and in some ways create cultural knowledge, in the present case about how "blackness" is experienced in the social world at the historical moment in question.

WHAT'S THE SCORE?: DEFINING THE PARAMETERS AND FUNCTIONS OF MUSIC IN FILM

Before turning to the specific films in question, it is necessary to provide a brief overview of how music in cinema works generally. Broadly speaking, music works to enhance the story world of the film; it deepens the audience's experience of the narrative and adds continuity to the film's scene-by-scene progression, providing what Claudia Gorbman calls the "bath of affect."[15] Anahid Kassabian argues that the study of music in film should not be an afterthought to what might be considered the more important areas of plot and characterization: "Music draws filmgoers into a film's world, measure by measure. It is . . . at least as significant as the visual and narrative components that have dominated film studies. It conditions identification processes, the encounters between film texts and filmgoers' psyches."[16]

The music in contemporary Hollywood films divides into two broad categories. The first is the composed score, which consists of music written specifically for the film. The second category is the compiled score: songs collected from sources that often preexisted the film. According to Kassabian, these two modes of musical address are designed to generate different responses from the perceiver. The composed score, she argues, is usually associated with the classical Hollywood score and encourages "assimilating identifications"; that is, it helps to "draw perceivers into socially and historically unfamiliar positions, as do larger scale processes of assimilation."[17]

The scoring techniques of the classical Hollywood cinema can achieve this end because of their unconscious familiarity to filmgoers: They have become naturalized through constant repetition. With few exceptions, the musical language of nineteenth-century Romanticism forms the "core musical lexicon" of American films. Music's cultural and cinematic work depends on its ability to signify an emotion, a location, a personality type, a frightening situation, and so on. The specific musical language of nineteenth-century Romanticism works well in this function, because it has been used in this way repeatedly since the 1930s. This repetition has produced a desired result in film scores, since, as Gorbman notes, "a music cue's signification must be instantly recognized as such in order to work."[18]

We can experience the hallmarks of these scoring techniques in the classic Hollywood film *In This Our Life*.[19] As the opening credits roll in this black-and-white film, we hear Max Steiner's familiar orchestral strains, typical of films during this era. The string section bathes the soundscape with sweeping melodies and a Wagnerian orchestral lushness that signals to the audience intense emotion and melodrama. Throughout the film, orchestral codes sharpen our perception of characters' interior motivations, propel the narrative forward, and help to provide smooth transitions between edits. During the plot exposition of the film, for example, we met the vixen Stanley, played by the inimitable queen of melodrama Bette Davis. Although the other characters' dialogues have revealed some of her less than desirable personal qualities, the orchestral strains of the score reveal to the audience much more than mere plot exposition could ever suggest. In her first appearance, Stanley drives up to the house with a male passenger. Viewers hear an ominous-sounding minor chord that is scored in the lower registers of the sounding instruments. As it turns out, the male passenger is her sister's husband, a man with whom Stanley is having a torrid affair. After a brief dialogue between the two reveals Stanley's manipulative personality—emphasized, of course, with melodramatic orchestral passages— the score transitions into animated rhythmic gestures that dissolve into an ascending pizzicato string passage as Stanley leaves the car and bounds up the steps into the family's spacious Victorian home. The music has helped to situate us in the plot and to identify with its characters despite our own subject positions, which may be quite different from those depicted in the film.

The compiled score, a staple feature of many Hollywood films since the 1980s, brings with it "the immediate threat of history."[20] It encourages perceivers to make external associations with the song in question, and these associations become part of the cultural transaction occurring between the film and its audience. Compiled scores produce what Kassabian calls "affiliating identifications." The connections that perceivers make depend on the relationship they have developed with the songs outside the context of the film experience. "If offers of assimilating identifications try to narrow the psychic field," Kassabian argues, "then offers of affiliating identifications open it wide."[21] The discussion that follows will explore how such distinctions bear on the interpretation of music in hip-hop film, a body of cinema having obvious and strong associations with a genre of music that has a discrete history.

Both the classic score's and the compiled score's relationship to the story world of the film can be divided into two primary modes of presentation: diegetic and nondiegetic music. Diegetic (or source) music is produced from within the perceived narrative world of the film. By constrast, nondiegetic music, that is, music produced from outside the story world of the film, serves the narration by signaling emotional states, propelling dramatic action, depicting a geographical location or time period, among other factors. Most of the music in a film fits into this category. Another kind of musical address in film blends the diegetic and nondiegetic. Earle Hagen calls this type of film music source scoring. In source scoring the musical cue can start out as diegetic but then change over to nondiegetic. This often occurs with a shift in the cue's relationship to onscreen events, usually when the narrative world and the musical score demonstrate a much closer fit.[22] With these ideas about music in film in mind, I turn to Spike Lee's now classic film *Do the Right Thing*.

DO THE RIGHT THING

As I stated above, Griffith's *Birth of a Nation* stands as the symbolic beginning of American cinema, providing a grammar book for Hollywood's historical (and unquestionably negative) depiction of black subjects. Likewise, Spike Lee's *Do the Right Thing* (hereafter *DTRT*) may be viewed as a kind of Ur-text for black representation in the so-called ghettocentric, New Jack flicks of the Hip-Hop Era. This film is important for a number of reasons. Lee succeeded in showing powerful Hollywood studios that this new genre of comparatively low-budget films could be profitable to the major studios. *DTRT*'s popular and critical reception (it earned millions and an Academy Award nomination) caused Lee's star to rise to such a degree that he became the most visible black filmmaker of the past decade. Hollywood studios tried to duplicate *DTRT*'s success, thus allowing other black directors access to the Hollywood production system, albeit within predictably prescribed limits.[23] Lee's use of rap music (and some of the musical practices associated with it) demonstrated how it could be used to depict a range of associations. Some of these include black male and female subjectivity, ethnic identity, a sense of location, emotional and mental states, a specific historical moment, and the perspectives of age groups. In these realms, DTRT cast a long shadow over the repertory of acceptable character types, plots, and themes in subsequent ghettocentric films during the Age of Hip-Hop.

Scoring the Right Thing

DTRT conforms to some of the conventions of classical Hollywood cinema discussed above but with marked differences. Victoria E. Johnson has recognized the importance of music in DTRT, calling it Lee's most musical film.[24] Johnson identifies two primary modes of musical rhetoric in the score. What she calls the "historic-nostalgic" strain encompasses, for the most part, orchestral music written by Lee's father, Bill Lee. The sound is reminiscent of some of the chamber music by African American composer William Grant Still—quaint, genteel, and staid. Interestingly, Branford Marsalis's jazz-inflected saxophone and Terrance Blanchard's trumpet perform the melodies.[25] This music is always nondiegetic and, in Johnson's view, serves to convey a romanticized vision of community in the ethnically mixed neighborhood in which the story takes place. This use of music corresponds to the classical approach.

Rap music rests at the other end of the aesthetic continuum in this film. The group Public Enemy's rap anthem "Fight the Power" (1989) is heard diegetically at various points in the film as it pours out of the boom box of the character Radio Raheem. Johnson argues that the other musical styles heard in the film, which include jazz, soul, and R&B, mediate the two extremes represented by rap and Bill Lee's original score. (There is one exception to this observation, however. Jazz is also used nondiegetically to help depict flaring tempers between characters.)

While I generally agree with Johnson's reading, I depart from it on several points. Johnson stresses that Lee is conversant with classical scoring conventions and that he "manipulates convention in a traditional manner to orient spectators within the film story."[26] I experience DTRT somewhat differently here. The somewhat unconventional approach of the score disorients the audience in my view. This musical strategy is joined to unusual cinematic techniques such as unrealistic visual angles that call attention to the camera and a use of music that moves back and forth between "bath of affect" and "listen to me" narrative positions.

The three modes of musical language in the film—the orchestral music of the Natural Spiritual Orchestra (nondiegetic), the popular music played by WLOV radio station (diegetic), and the rap music from Radio Raheem's boom box (diegetic)—create a rather hectic and conflicted semiotic field. Consider, for example, the first five scenes in which we hear the orchestral music that Johnson believes signals a romanticized community. During a monologue in front of the Yes, Jesus Light Baptist Church, the speech-impaired character Smiley talks about the futility of hate in society while holding up a small placard of Malcolm X and Martin Luther King, Jr. Smiley's stammering seems somewhat at odds with the placid musical gestures heard in conjunction with it.

The next time we hear this mode of music, the Italian pizzeria owner, Sal, and his sons, Vito and Pino, drive up to their shop, which sits on a garbage-strewn corner of a primarily black neighborhood. (Ironically, other scenes in the film portray the neighborhood as whistle clean.) In this scene we learn of the deep hatred Vito harbors for this neighborhood and for the people who live there. Although Sal admits with glib resolution that the air-conditioner repairman has refused to come around without an escort, he can barely contain his anger over Vito's attitude about working in the neighborhood. This scene does not, in my view, conjure a romanticized community. Again, the placid strains of the score seem strangely at odds with the narrative world on the screen.

When the character Mookie (played by Spike Lee) exits his brownstone into the morning sun, the neighborhood is stirring with Saturday-morning activity. The orchestral strains do portray a cozy, communal feeling in this third instance of hearing this mode of music. But in the very next scene in which music of this type is heard, the characters Mother-Sister and Da Major, the neighborhood's matriarch and patriarch, respectively, trade insults with one another. The fifth time the orchestra is heard, Jade, a young woman who is Mookie's sister, is lovingly combing Mother-Sister's hair on the sun-baked front stoop of a brownstone. The communal feeling created by the music and the scene quickly dissipates, however, as Mother-Sister deflects a compliment from Da Major, responding to his polite advance by hurling more insults. Thus, I see the score not so much signaling community as functioning to highlight conflict and tension in the narrative world of the film. This strategy sets the viewer on edge and frustrates any settled feeling that might be forwarded in the scene.

But the music that Mister Señor Love Daddy plays on radio station WLOV *does* seem to signal community. It marks the geographic space of the neighborhood and underscores his references to love and the importance of community togetherness. In the early scenes of the film, the radio music, which consists of various styles of R&B—replete with gospel singing and funk beats—is heard in sundry settings. We hear it in Da Major's bedroom as he rises, in Mookie and Jade's apartment, in a Puerto Rican home, and in a Korean-owned grocery store—in every cultural space except Sal's Famous Pizzeria. This compiled score inspires the idea of a community, one created by the spatial boundaries of the radio station's broadcast span.

Nonetheless, WLOV's programming inspires one instance of community conflict. When Mookie, an African American, dedicates a song (Rubén Blades's "Tu y Yo") to his Puerto Rican girlfriend, Tina, a group of Puerto Rican young men enjoy the tune on a front stoop. As Radio Raheem passes by playing "Fight the Power," a battle of decibels ensues. "Fight the Power" wins the bout when Radio Raheem's boom box overpowers the scene with one turn of the volume knob. This confrontation contrasts with the first meeting of Radio Raheem's music and that of WLOV. (I discuss this brief meeting below.) Community alliances, like Lee's cinematic uses of various musical styles, are fluid and situational. Why, one might ask, didn't the Puerto Ricans identify with the "Fight the Power" message?

Gorbman writes that "music is codified in the filmic context itself, and assumes meaning by virtue of its placement in the film."[27] Because of the audience's familiarity with rap music and the dynamic formal qualities of the music, Lee is able to highlight its "difference" from other musical styles in *DTRT*'s score. As the film progresses, however, the audience experiences a level of familiarity with "Fight the Power" because of its persistent use. Lee is able to reencode rap music's signifying effect during the film's narrative.

Lee can achieve this because he capitalizes on the history of Public Enemy's reputation outside the use of "Fight the Power" in this film. Clearly, this use fits into the affiliating identifications category. At the same time, repetitively hearing the piece also allows us to spill over into the assimilating identifications arena. I argue this because the repetitive use of "Fight the Power" allows Lee to manipulate audience members of different subject positions to relate to the musical conventions and political message of the piece through their understanding of what it means cinematically. Thus, they have been assimilated into a particular reaction or identification with the music and, perhaps, the story world and its characters as well.

If the typical classic Hollywood film score renders the audience "less awake," as Gorbman contends, then Lee's use of rap music breaks that pattern. He positions it as an intrusive, embodied presence in the film. We see Lee setting the tone for this cinematic treatment during the opening scene of the film, which features a dance sequence by the actress Rosie Perez.

Doin' the Outside Dance!: "Fight the Power" and the Body Politic

DTRT's unusual opening has received attention from other scholars, but I want to respond to a critique by the feminist critic bell hooks. Hooks has leveled scathing criticism at this scene, and I quote her at length:

> The long beginning sequence of the film (rarely mentioned by critics) highlighting an unidentified black woman [Perez] dancing in a manner that is usually a male performance is a comment on gender and role playing. Positively, she has "mastered" an art form associated primarily with male performance. Yet to do so, she must stretch and distort her body in ways that make her appear grotesque, ugly, and at times monstrous. That she is attempting to appropriate a male style (we can see the "female" version of this dance in the Neneeh [*sic*] Cherry video "Kisses on the Wind") is emphasized by her donning the uniform for boxing, a sport most commonly associated solely with males, even though there are a few black female boxers. By evoking the boxing metaphor, this scene echoes Ishmael Reed's new book of essays, *Writin' Is Fightin'*, with its exclusive focus on black males, associating the pain of racism primarily with its impact on that group. Alone, isolated, and doing a male thing, this solitary dancer symbolically suggests that the black female becomes "ugly" or "distorted" when she assumes a role designated for males. Yet simultaneously the onlooker, placed in a voyeuristic position, can only be impressed by how well she assumes this role, by her assertive physicality.[28]

Hooks's discussion does not mention several issues with regard to the expressive practice at the heart of the scene and thereby misses some of its signifying potential. While it is true that boxing is an important metaphor in the performance, I see the role of *dance* as even more significant. If we begin, as hooks does, with the correct observation that the brand of black nationalism echoed in *DTRT* downplays the role of women in that struggle, then one is tempted to read everything in the film through that particular lens. But this performance is first and foremost a dance—the kind of social dancing that has been labeled "the vernacular." Perez moves with agility and authority through many of the hip-hop-inspired dance moves that appeared during the 1980s. We see her moving between the Womp, the Charleston, the Running Man, the Cabbage Patch, the Kid 'n Play, the Fight, the Roger Rabbit, the Elvis Presley, and various other highly stylized pelvic thrusts, shuffles, jumps, and "up-rocking" movements that are closely associated with break dancing and other hip-hop-inspired movements.[29]

Perez is quite simply working it. At no time during this sequence, in my view, did Perez assume the ugly or monstrous bearing noted by hooks. She looks totally engaged, especially near the end of the performance, when she appears to be smiling—as if to say, "I *know* I'm working it!" Although this sequence is not, as hooks points out, in the film narrative proper, it does serve the film's narrative.

When we identify this dancer as a black Puerto Rican in the film, I cannot help but collapse this knowledge into the history of break dancing itself. This important art form has had its Puerto Rican origins erased or at best eroded in the popular imagination, although research is beginning to correct this cultural amnesia.[30] That Perez went on to be the choreographer of the black-variety television show *In Living Color* in the early 1990s is also significant to the multiethnic, hybrid landscape of what has been called the hip-hop nation. We must take seriously the historical role of black vernacular dancing. To say that in Western discourse issues pertaining to the body have been valued less than those of the mind is an understatement. One example of this is hooks's failure to see the political dimensions of Perez's performance. Although there is no doubt that Spike Lee possessed a good deal of control over the representation of that performance, we cannot discount the historical, signifying, and liberating tradition of black dance, a tradition in which Perez is expertly participating and upon which she is nonverbally commenting.

Black social dancing circulates social energy. Females have played and continue to perform key historical roles in the creation and dissemination of these dances. For this reason, I see Perez as doing a very female thing rather than an exclusively male one. While it is true that at points in the dance sequence, which consists of a series of jump cuts, Perez wears boxing gloves and shorts, her costumes in other frames are more typical of the late-1980s fashions. Since the boxing movements (mostly jabs, uppercuts, and shuffles) are so similar to hip-hop dance movements, especially the upper-body gestures, I experience a strong political connection among the lyrical and instrumental import of "Fight the Power," the sport of boxing, and Perez's expression of hip-hop dance.

The lyrics of "Fight the Power" are given life by Perez's kinetic narrative. In fact, at one point during the dance she mimes the lyrics of a particularly salient political statement. Perez's lip-synching, together with her gestural emphasis on the words, unlike any other sequence in the dance, connects her unquestionably to the song's overtly political sentiments. Moreover, this recognition of "self-consciousness" invites the viewer to make an explicit connection between the flowing words and the moving body. Thus, rather than seeing Perez's performance as extratextual or as merely objectified by the camera's lens, I believe she "subjectifies" a distinctly female presence into Public Enemy's somewhat phallocentric nationalism.

I want to point out that cultural memory also plays a strong role in my reading of this scene. Because she is alone, as hooks points out (alone with an audience, I might add), Perez's performance recalls for me a line from James Brown's "Lickin' Stick."[31] In the song's lyrics, Brown comments that "sister's out in the backyard doing the outside dance." Presumably, sister's "outside dance" takes place beyond the gaze of parental judgment and censure.

During Perez's "outside dance," her body's center and extremities provide a catalog of 1980s hip-hop body attitudes. Viewing this scene in the late 1990s makes this point even more salient, since hip-hop's body grammar has changed significantly over the years. The dance is performed against the backdrop of classic brownstones, and we conclude from this forecasting that the film's story world will somehow be linked to urban America generally and to New York City specifically. The lyrics of "Fight the Power" scream 1989! at the beginning of the piece. The immediacy of Perez's dance "says" the same thing. We are in the present, a present that has urgency, particularity, politics, *and* pleasure.

This interpretation of Perez's performance supports an important observation by feminist salsa scholar Frances R. Aparicio. She argues: "Latinas who are active listeners and consumers of salsa music continuously rewrite patriarchal and misogynist salsa texts. They engage in 'productive pleasure,' which allows them as culturally bound receptors the opportunity to produce meanings and significations that are relevant to their everyday lives."[32]

The fact that Lee does not sustain within the film's narrative all of the political force that my interpretation lends to this opening does not weaken the dance's import, nor does it strip Perez of all her agency and its implications. Much of the power that I perceive in the dance is unquestionably derived from Perez's creativity and the histories it invokes. One might associate this move with affiliating identifications in the same sense that Kassabian uses the term to describe the effective result of a compiled score.

As myriad black cheerleading squads, drill teams, and popular dance troupes do, Perez probably choreographed and improvised (some of) the sequences herself. Lee's choice to introduce in the context of a dance an entire song that will be central to the film's story line works well. Because music with lyrics (not to mention a rap performance with numerous lyrics) would lose some of its communicative effect if it were heard within filmic dialogue or action, the "wordless" (yet very semantic) dance allows viewers to experience the full impact of the sentiments of "Fight the Power." When we do hear this song (nine other times) during the film, we can then focus almost exclusively on the *cinematic* meanings it generates.

Radio Raheem: Bigger with a Boom Box

With respect to filmic association, Perez's body is replaced during the film by Radio Raheem, a key character who speaks sparingly but signifies much. In the climatic scene of *DTRT* Raheem is killed by police officers trying to quell a riot outside Sal's Famous Pizzeria. Radio Raheem, a Bigger Thomas with a boom box, is represented almost in shorthand by Lee. He rarely speaks and doesn't have to. The song "Fight the Power" "speaks" for him. And what is more, his body is objectified as an imposing presence that is to be taken seriously, if not feared. The sonic force of producer Hank Shocklee's innovative and explosive rhythm track combines with the lyrics to create a palpable and, if you love this groove, pleasurable tension. More so than any other musical form heard in the film, rap music stands alone because of its singular cinematic treatment. In fact, because Radio is associated with rap music, no other character measures up to the intensity that his presence achieves.

A good deal of the dramatic thrust of Radio Raheem's character is due to how he is framed musically. When we first meet him, no music has underscored the two previous scenes. This strategy works well in establishing Radio Raheem as an important presence in the film. Radio never responds to the tune by dancing or even moving to its rhythm. Yet because of Perez's opening dance performance, I believe that its bodily connection is never lost on the audience. After we meet Radio Raheem, he has a brief but very important interaction with one of the characters that symbolizes an important message in the narrative.

Earlier in the film we have met Mister Señor Love Daddy, the DJ at the neighborhood's radio station, which programs various popular musical styles throughout the day (one assumes no rap music is programmed). It is important that the music of the station, as I have already mentioned, is for the most part heard diegetically, situating this neighborhood in a specific cultural space, not a universal one. The radio station and the music it plays show the degree to which mass media can unify and demarcate a sense of the local for listeners. The music and the ethos it creates in the film's narrative point to a community with a common past and present. Love Daddy's on-the-air patter, for example, belongs to a long tradition of black radio jocks.

When Love Daddy and Radio Raheem share a scene, one would expect the stationary and mobile DJs to have an unpleasant confrontation. But as he passes the control booth's exterior window, Radio Raheem salutes Mister Señor Love Daddy. Love Daddy responds in kind with a verbal on-the-air greeting. This exchange, together with the opening scene, connects rap music to the cultural orbit of other black vernacular traditions.

At the same time, its cinematic use singles rap out in this story as hyper-political, especially when compared with the treatment of other musical styles in the soundtrack. I argue that this discourse spilled out of the reel world and into the real world, proving that expressive culture has the power to make worlds and worldviews, even as it is shaped by the social world. The singularity of this artistic and political construction by Lee insists on the silencing of rap music, a move that, in turn, depends on the death of Radio Raheem's body for the sake of narrative closure.

The political insurgency of Public Enemy's lyrics encouraging listeners to stand up to hegemonic forces in society and the dense musical play in the rhythm track that makes use of sampled excerpts from black music history (most prominently James Brown) signify profoundly. If you silence this music, you have effectively silenced the past, present, and future of the community. Despite numerous critiques that Radio Raheem's character is too simplistic, I see the cultural work he symbolizes as complex and signif-icant.[33] The cinematic and, most important to my discussion, the *musical* construction of this character provides an important commentary on race, class, and gender in American society.

BOYZ N THE HOOD: THE WEST COAST RESPONDS

The film *Boyz N the Hood* (1991), written and directed by John Singleton, appeared in 1991 and earned over fifty million dollars at the box office, making it one of the top-grossing films of its kind. Critically acclaimed, the film was received as a convincing portrait of urban black America. *Boyz* (hereafter *BNTH*) tells the story of three young black men coming of age in South Central Los Angeles. Just as Lee did in *DTRT*, Singleton uses the opening of the film to create a specific ethos.

As the film begins we hear, against a black screen, the audio of an activ-ity for which South Central had become known in recent years: the drive-by shooting. A cacophonous mixture of angry male voices, gunshots, police helicopters, sirens, chaos, and violence assaults the viewers and thrusts them into a 1990s version of a high-noon Wild West showdown. And just in case we don't connect inner-city "blackness" to this violent scenario, these words appear across the screen: "One out of every twenty-one Black American males will be murdered in their lifetime. Most will die at the hands of another Black male." Thus, with these sentiments and the opening drive-by voiceover, "black on black" crime, "black men as endangered species," senseless violence, and youthful nihilism foreground important themes of the plot, setting, and characters we will experience in the film.

The film's narrative proper begins in 1984 South Central with a group of young black children walking to school along garbage-lined streets. The historical and physical settings of this film allow us to speculate that we are also experiencing the "coming of age" of one of the most controversial idioms of hip-hop: gangsta rap. This leap is not a large one, for, as Valerie Smith notes, the directors of rapsploitation "position themselves in a common enterprise with black musicians in the frequent use of rap and hip hop in soundtracks, and with the visible presence of rappers on screen as actors."[34] During the opening scene we meet Tre, one of three preadolescent boys around which most of this story revolves. We also hear for the first time Stanley Clarke's original score, which plays an important role in *BNTH*'s dramatic thrust.

One of the schoolchildren announces that he wants to show the others something. The something turns out to be a blood-soaked walkway riddled with bullet holes. Somebody got "smoked." Clarke underscores nondiegetic suspenseful-sounding music in the spirit of the classic Hollywood film tradition: minor mode, synthesized strings, percussion, and soprano saxophone. We also hear gunshots during these passages. Serving as metacommentary on the world outside the film, the gunshots and the holes they make are experienced as the camera scans their target: Ronald Reagan reelection campaign posters. The musical score connects us emotionally to the children and their plight.

Singleton's and Stanley Clarke's scoring is somewhat more traditional than Lee's in *DTRT*. Nondiegetic music functions as a bath of affect, drawing us into the spell of the film's narrative, and heightens its dramatic import in a time-proven, "unheard" way. Such moments occur during scenes in which Tre's parents are interacting with him. We are to relate to them as working- to middle-class subjects who are doing the best they can to make it in the world.

The music—often scored with strings or harp as background and simplistic melodies usually played by a single saxophone, trumpet, or flute— sounds like soft pop ballads. It conjures the innocence of childhood, parental love, feelings of neighborhood and friendship. One notable exception in the film, however, occurs in a scene in which an intruder has broken into the house and is shot at by Tre's father, the provocatively named Furious Styles. The music underscoring the scene features a jazz tenor saxophone soloist playing agitated, wailing passages in the upper register. As Furious protects his home and family, the music causes the viewer to identify with the former's state of fear and adrenaline-induced excitement. That this particular style of music could serve in this way demonstrates the degree to which some African American styles have become naturalized—they can assimilate the viewer in much the same way as classic Hollywood scoring can.

If the nondiegetic music is used to represent work ethics, family values, and civic pride in *BNTH*, then the diegetic music articulates more specific ethnic and class affiliations. The scene in which Tre's mother drives him to his father's home near the beginning of the film demonstrates this usage. As they arrive in the sun-drenched neat neighborhood, we hear Clark's nondiegetic scoring of sentimentality and nostalgia. At other moments, we hear diegetic soul music in the distance, marking this as a working-class African American neighborhood. When Tre and his father bond during a "birds and the bees" discussion while fishing, the sentimental scoring returns. The composed and compiled scores together with the narrative work to create an African American community, albeit a male-dominated one, with the typical challenges facing working- and middle-class families: how to maintain or better their status and pass these values along to their offspring.

When Tre and Furious drive home from the fishing trip we experience what is perhaps the most complex use of music in the film. Kassabian writes that film music has three primary purposes: identification, mood, and commentary. All three are achieved in these next scenes. During the ride, a 1970s hit by the R&B group the Five Stair Steps is heard diegetically from the car's radio. "Listen to this song," Furious entreats his son. "I love this song." The song, "Ooo, Ooo Child," a medium-tempo ballad features a soul singer and oooing and ahhhing background vocals in the same stylistic vein as the music first heard from the radio station WLOV in *DTRT*. We witness father and son interacting through this mass-media music. Furious is enjoying his son's company; he hums and sways to "his" music, celebrating soul music's conventions and, no doubt, finding pleasure in the personal and cultural memories they evoke. Tre seems comfortable and amused.

The song performs two other cinematic functions. As Furious and Tre drive past Doughboy's house they see him and another boy being escorted by police into a waiting squad car. At this point, the lyrics of "Ooo, Ooo Child" become a compelling commentary on the unfolding drama:

Ooo, ooo child, things are gonna get easier
Ooo, ooo child, things'll get brighter
*
Someday, yeah, we'll walk in the rays of a beautiful sun
Someday, when the world is much brighter

By the end of the scene, as the squad car disappears into the dis...... with Tre watching intently from the curb, the song is no longer diegetic; it is heard only by the audience as its strains fade into the sound of a police siren. This poignant scene ends the depiction of Tre's young life. The remainder of the film, which takes place seven years later, deals with the lives of Tre, Doughboy, and Ricky (Doughboy's brother) as young men coming of age.

BNTH provides a cinematic mediation on how various rap idioms signify in the real world. Two styles are heard in the soundtrack: New Jack Swing and gangsta rap.[35] Each is heard diegetically and shapes the viewer's perceptions of setting and characterization. Immediately following Doughboy's childhood arrest scene, the film cuts to the story world's present.

The adult Doughboy has been given a homecoming cookout to celebrate his release from his latest prison stint. The party takes place in his mother's backyard. An upbeat New Jack Swing recording (featuring female rapper Monie Love) frames the scene; it is heard diegetically from a very large speaker system. (The recording is "Work It Out," written by Jazzy Jeff and Monie Love.) Animated African American teenaged bodies crowd the space with youthful exuberance and bravado. Some are playing dominoes and card games; others drink malt liquor out of forty-ounce bottles. Many of the teenagers dance to the infectious rhythms of the song, executing individualized versions of some of the dances performed by Perez in *DTRT*. The young men and the women verbally tease one another with the dozens; at the same time, they scope the backyard for potential romantic interests.

Through the cultural practices taking place at the party—and music plays a central role here—Singleton creates a sense of community in the scene. Despite Doughboy's troubles with the law, we empathize with him and situate him into this web of culture and the communal feeling evoked. Like Radio Raheem, Doughboy never *moves* to the music, but he obviously relates to it strongly. He is the only character, for example, that comments verbally about the diegetic hip-hop music in the film, taking note of the music emanating from a passing car: "Damn, that shit [is] bumpin'." This gesture may be interpreted as a kind of metanarrative comment on Ice Cube's primary career in gangsta rap, a connection that the primary audience of the film would easily make and identify with strongly.

Hip-hop music, as I mentioned, is always heard diegetically in the film. When the less dance-oriented forms of gangsta rap are heard, they denote the menacing aspects of male nihilist culture, including threats of drive-by

shootings or other "hard-core" youth cultural spaces. In one scene, for example, Tre is almost hit by a passing car as he crosses a residential street.
When he gathers himself to fashion a response, without ceremony one of
the male passengers points a shotgun barrel at his face at point-blank range.
In another scene, gangsta rap plays diegetically in Compton, depicted here as
a "rough" neighborhood. The sparse, funky, and at once ominous-sounding
strains of gangsta rap signify in this film the destruction of a community.

Singleton uses jazz in *BNTH* to signify class status in Tre's mother, Reva
Styles, who becomes solidly middle-class by the end of the film. During one
scene, Tre is on the telephone with his girlfriend when his mother calls. As
the dialogue switches back and forth between the bachelor's quarters he
shares with his father and his mother's very chic dwelling, the music moves
between R&B for the men's space and urban contemporary jazz for Reva's.
This particular use of jazz-related practices will be extended into the next
film under discussion: *Love Jones*.

MUSICAL CONSTRUCTIONS OF BLACK BOHEMIA
IN *LOVE JONES*

The film *Love Jones* expands the hip-hop lexicon of acceptable black subjects
and their corresponding musical associations. The film is an urban, Afro-
romantic comedy, written and directed by Theodore Witcher, and set in contemporary Chicago. Darryl Jones, a bassist and native Chicagoan, scored the
original music. *Love Jones*'s eclectic soundtrack and the "musicking" practices associated with the music distinguish the film from run-of-the-mill
romantic comedies.

Consider the first few minutes of the film, in which Witcher (like Lee and
Singleton before him) sets the tone for the story that follows. During the
opening, Witcher strings together a jumble of short urban scenes, including
the Chicago skyline, the El train, a run-down neighborhood, a modest storefront shop, trash-lined railroad tracks, a Baptist church, the hands of a
shoeshine man, and the faces of black people—old, young, some profiling,
others showing no awareness of the camera at all. But all of them striking.
Filmed in black and white, Witcher's stylish montage forecasts an approach
to the presentation of inner-city blackness that departs from and is, in my
view, more expansive than the two previous films I have discussed.

The music underscoring the opening features the genteel song "Hopeless," performed by singer Dionne Farris. The tune borders on soft rock and
has virtually none of the hip-hop conventions heard in *Do the Right Thing*
and *Boyz N the Hood*. The lyrics of "Hopeless" play a slight trick on the

viewer, because we hear the lyric "hopeless" against the first few scenes in the montage, which at first appear to paint a somewhat bleak depiction of inner-city life. But as the visual sequences progress, smiles begin to spread across the subjects' faces. And as the musical narrative spins out, we learn that Farris is singing about romantic love and not social commentary: she's as "hopeless as a penny with a hole in it."

Love Jones features an attractive posse of educated, well-spoken, widely read, comfortably middle-class twenty-something Generation X–styled characters. Their hairdos (always a political statement with regard to African American culture) cover the spectrum: close-cropped, dreadlocks, braids, chemically straightened. They live in tastefully appointed homes, lofts, and apartments that are lined with books and stylishly decorated with modern and African art. They are dressed for success and "wearing the right thing," if I might borrow Lee's title for the moment. Intrablack diversity is the feeling. The characters listen to jazz, the Isley Brothers, and urban contemporary music. Their calculated and robust funkiness translates into frank talk about sensuality. They read Amiri Baraka, smoke, drink, swear, play cards, and talk a boatload of shit in grand style. Like carefree adolescents, they delight in playing the dozens with each other. And with fluency they pepper their musings on poetry, sexuality, Charlie Parker, gender relations, religion, and art with spicy, up-to-the-minute "black-speak" rhetoric. Witcher apparently wants us to recognize these verbal exchanges and their accompanying body attitudes with a contemporary performance-oriented African American culture.

Love Jones's characters portray a hip "big shoulders" black ethnicity that insiders recognize as realistic in cultural spaces like contemporary black Chicago. In this setting, the film's narrative winds through various venues and situations wherein acts of ethnic performance can take place. One such space is a nightclub called the Sanctuary. Modeled after a jazz club, the Sanctuary features spoken-word poetry and live music. The Sanctuary appears to cater to black Generation X-ers. Its audience respects the performers, paying rapt attention to the time, timbre, lyric, and substance of each poet's offering. Quiet diegetic music from the bandstand and jukebox envelopes the Sanctuary with the soundtrack of hip, polite society.

The film tells a love story between Darius Lovehall, an aspiring novelist and spoken-word poet, and Nina Mosley, an ambitious freelance photographer. Darius is a regular performer at the Monday-night open-mike session; Nina, who is on the rebound from a bad relationship, is there relaxing with a female friend. Nina and Darius meet. Nina initiates a conversation, following their exchange of curious glances. Shortly thereafter, an emcee invites Darius to the stage, and he performs a sexually explicit poem, which he titles at the last moment (in true "Mack Daddy" fashion) "A Blues for Nina."

The performance itself is, in fact, not blues or jazz performance but what might be described as easy-listening funk: an ostinato bass pattern in D-minor splashed with subdued colors from a saxophone's soulful riffing. References from black music history inform the poetry; in one line Darius says that he's "the blues in your left thigh, trying to become the funk in your right." The audience, which is depicted in a series of very flattering close-ups that are reminiscent of the opening montage, responds with sporadic declamatory affirmations. These vocables provide an obligatory bow to the southern past, even if they may no longer signify that history solely.

Music in *Love Jones* works overtime. Its characters are more fully constructed, engaging in more musical practices and cultural spaces than in the previous two films discussed. Music in the pool hall, the nightclub, the house party, the WVON "stepper's set," the reggae club, and the residences expands the representations of Hip-Hop Era blackness on screen. While this depiction of black bohemia may be a caricature itself, when compared with contemporaneous visions of black life in America (like *DTRT* and *BNTH*, for example), *Love Jones* can be viewed only as a counterweight to those characterizations.

Although contemporary R&B forms the core musical lexicon of *Love Jones*, jazz references surface in the Sanctuary's performance space and as a way to show how "enlightened" the characters are. In one case, the jazz/blues piece "Jelly, Jelly, Jelly" becomes the soundtrack of sexual frustration as Darius and Nina try to suppress their lust for each other. Important to note, rap music is heard only one time in the film: during a car scene in which one of Darius's friends is courting Nina behind his back. In this very brief scene, rap music becomes quickly associated with a questionable character trait.

Interestingly, in all three films, music is linked to other black cultural practices such as the dozens, dance, card playing, and so on. Music is central to constructing black characters within these films' narratives. Rap music, for example, helps to create specific kinds of character traits in (male) subjects: politicized, nihilistic, or underhanded. Various styles of jazz are used for their identifications with middle-class culture or to enhance the audience's experience of emotional states. R&B styles, for the most part, are used to depict communal associations. The quasi-orchestral music linked most closely to the sound of classic Hollywood scoring, when it does appear in these films, is used in traditional ways: to assimilate audiences into a particular mode of identification with characters and plot situations.

During the Age of Hip-Hop, filmmakers such as Spike Lee and John Singleton worked to create what they thought were realistic portraits of urban life. While their portrayals were popular, many critics believed that they helped to erect harmful stereotypes. Witcher, director of *Love Jones*, for example, had trouble convincing Hollywood executives that his kind of story could find a niche in the market or was even plausible because of the ghettocentric focus of so many black films of the early 1990s.[36] Thus, despite the way in which directors might have positioned their work as countering hegemony in Hollywood, their approaches and the repetition of them became conventions against which those interested in other kinds of representations would have to struggle.

The juxtaposition of different black musical styles in these films demands that audiences grapple with the ways in which numerous musical developments have appeared under the cultural umbrella of hip-hop. How these styles relate to one another cinematically represents only one arena of interest. These expressions have enlarged the boundaries of hip-hop, and this expansion has inspired celebration, dissent, and, of course, debate on exactly where these boundaries lie. Because of the persistence of older styles of black music and their continual evolution of meanings during the Age of Hip-Hop, filmmakers are able to use these external associations as part of the way in which audiences experience these scores, and thus their cinematic representations.

The music, modernism, and modernization processes discussed earlier in the book provided the historical, social, and cultural foundations for what has developed during the Age of Hip-Hop. If we consider, for example, the way in which jazz in the 1940s represented the quintessential Afro-modernist expression of black urbanity, we can better understand how the musical styles most closely associated with hip-hop represent "the urban contemporary" for the present generation. If the blues muse of the World War II years existed as a basic ingredient in various styles, then we need to try to identify, codify, and theorize the elements that make up the decidedly hybrid hip-hop sensibility and "worldview." One might learn, for example, that the idea of Afro-modernism might be extended into the late twentieth century. Indeed, the question might be posed: Does Afro-modernism exist as an unfinished project?

The three urban landscapes portrayed in *Do the Right Thing, Boyz N the Hood,* and *Love Jones* are meditations on how modern blackness is experienced in cities that in the 1940s represented the promised land—the cultural spaces to which black humanity flocked in order to participate fully in modern America. The urban conditions recently called postindustrial and the artistic responses to these conditions reflect the changing social configuration of the late-twentieth-century American city. Just as Dizzy Gillespie's Afro-Cuban experiments participated in a new demographic shift in the 1940s, today's musicians mix hip-hop conventions with other expressions to reflect the configuration of their own social worlds and the statements they want to make in them.

If it is indeed true that contemporary people fashion their lives with the texts around them, as this chapter's epigraph proposes, then the study of hip-hop film provides a fruitful site of inquiry in this regard. In the three films discussed in this chapter, directors and composers worked together to create narratives in which audience members can engage and with which they can form identifications. These texts become ways through which some understand themselves and others in the social world. Music forms an important component in these narratives, serving to order the social world in both the cinematic and real-life domains.

Notwithstanding the scene in *Do the Right Thing* in which Smiley performs his opening dialogue in front of a Baptist church, the black church is invisible in the three films I have discussed. No one appears to go to church, and this is unfortunate, because in reality the black church has been a central institution in the development of African American culture. The ring shout rituals that produced the spirituals of the "invisible institution," the independent mainline denominations that published their own hymnal traditions, and the storefront Pentecostal denominations that infused their services with fervor and dramatic worship patterns point to a vibrant and varied legacy of culture building. Have these practices become outdated in today's social environment?

Musical practice has been central to the formation and relevance of the black church. Innumerable African American performers, for example, have noted their debt to singing in or playing for choirs and the foundational role that these experiences played in their musical development. Just as hip-hop culture's voracious muse has reshaped the contemporary music scene, black gospel music has proven to be just as permeable, flexible, and defiant, despite conservative ideologues who have defended its borders. In the next chapter, I examine, among other things, how the collision of these sensibilities encourages new ways of thinking about the late-twentieth-century black church as a vibrant community theater of African American culture. This cultural space is not, as many believe, any more a "folk" world closed off to commercial and artistic interests than any other music in the marketplace is. On the contrary, contemporary gospel musicians may well be at the forefront of innovation and artistic risk, even as they ground themselves firmly in history and tradition.

8 "Santa Claus Ain't Got Nothing on This!"

*Hip-Hop Hybridity
and the Black Church Muse*

From the outset, rap music embraced a variety of styles and cultural forms, from reggae and salsa to heavy metal and jazz. Hip Hop's hybridity reflected, in part, the increasingly international character of America's inner cities resulting from immigration, demographic change, and new forms of information, as well as the inventive employment of technology in creating rap music.

Robin D. G. Kelley, *Yo' Mama's Disfunktional!
Fighting the Culture Wars in Urban America*

Before the church really accepted gospel music, [people] were saying it wasn't nothing but the blues—playing the blues and stuff in the church—especially the older heads. But of course it didn't phase me one way or the other. I enjoyed playing. Whatever they said play, I'd play it and get enjoyment out of it. I never thought to compare whether this is right for church, because the music carries words or praises. It's still gospel music, whether it's an anthem or spirituals. It's still the gospel being sung.

Thomas A. Dorsey, *The Rise of Gospel Blues*

Policing the boundaries of black religious expression in the West is an activity that reaches back centuries. The historical record documents negative reactions to black religious practices from a range of detractors that includes both black and white critics. A self-conscious hybridity has marked the development of African American religious practices since their appearance in the New World. Scholars trace many of these tendencies back to the ring shout of slave culture. Accounts describing the ring shout abound in the literature of missionaries, travelers, and abolitionists, among others. A typical report describes religious services that combine elements of dance, storytelling, singing, and shouting from the African heritage within the context of a Christian worship service spoken in English. From the beginning, the syncretism that characterized the ring shout was condemned as heathenish, barbaric, and profane in much the same spirit as miscegenation was.

Most scholarly explanations of the ring shout highlight the collision of European and African practices embedded in the ritual. But another mixture is just as important. Practices like the ring shout together with other expressive practices of early African American culture resulted from the blending of many ethnic groups among the enslaved Africans. Moreover, the continual flow of blacks from the Caribbean to North America during the years of the slave trade brought another dimension of cultural negotiation to the process of African American culture. Hybridity, in other words, has always been a part of the background and pedigree of African American culture.

Hybridity has clearly shaped the religious realm. Thomas Dorsey's mix of blues and gospel in the 1920s and 1930s; Rosetta Tharpe's blend of jazz and gospel during the 1940s; Edwin Hawkins's and Andre Crouch's pop-gospel of the late 1960s; and the Winanses' smooth-soul gospel of the 1980s were all seen as hybrid—and quite controversial—expressions in their day. Few social or musical boundaries have been considered too contentious to cross in black religious music's quest for expressive resources. This tendency for hybridity links gospel to the larger world of black diasporic religious practices to which it belongs. This system, as Mintz and Price have described, existed as permeable and additive with respect to its relationship to other cultures.[1]

The most recent musical juxtaposition in the history of gospel music is represented by the intersection of hip-hop culture and black gospel. It is important to note here that while elements of black vernacular music can be traced, in part, to a central pool of cultural resources from the African continent, the various genres of African American music have also managed to maintain distinct conventions and profiles. Each genre represents specific constellations of a basic set of conceptual approaches to music making. As we shall see below, much of the rhetorical power of these stylistic juxtapositions in black gospel music has relied on the audience's ability to recognize that some kind of mixture or boundary crossing is taking place when they hear a performance.

The tension existing between tradition and innovation (or, as Susan McClary has recently characterized these dialogical terms, convention and expression) is one of the reasons the church has remained a hotbed of musical creativity through the years.[2] While church leadership has generally guarded and cherished the notions of tradition and convention, forces from within the church (more often than not the younger generation) have defied the older heads, as Thomas Dorsey called them in the second of this chapter's epigraphs, and claimed stylistic change as an artistic priority. The interaction of these two impulses (tradition and innovation) has provided a creative framework through which musicians have continually pursued new musical directions, despite the inevitable controversies that these innovations are sure to inspire. What is more, the proven commercial viability of these musical mixtures has also provided grist for the mill in historical critiques of gospel. Can gospel exist as entertainment and fulfill its worship status simultaneously? Can it do cultural work beyond its implicit goals of evangelism, supplication, and exhortation? Or to put another aspect of this controversy in terms more specific to Afro-modernism, can gospel be art and "folk" at the same time?

Despite its overwhelming popularity, rap music has also faced challenges about its pedigree, but the battle lines have been drawn along other issues. A key issue surrounding rap music has been whether it can be considered music per se. Robert Walser has demonstrated, however, that rap's qualities are grounded in black cultural imperatives and the creative agency of rappers and the producers who pull together the rhythm tracks over which the raps are performed. In other words, hip-hop practitioners, in true Afro-modernist fashion, have resisted some of the parameters set by the "standard" musical system and have created a new approach that is pushed so close to the edge of established convention that even its status as music has been questioned.[3]

As early as 1933, decades before rap's appearance, writer Zora Neale Hurston proposed in the brief article "Characteristics of Negro Expression" some of the thematic and musical qualities of hip-hop music. Anti-essentialists will be wary of my present strategy—linking in a seemingly ahistorical way rap music and a Depression-era exegesis of black culture. Yet Hurston's prescience cannot be denied. Her list of characteristics moves across musical, linguistic, bodily, visual arts and other modalities of expression, capturing some of the historical hallmarks of black expressive practice, ones that have been passed from generation to generation. These qualities and tendencies include a dramatic mode of presentation; the mimicry and revision of previous expressions; the will to ornament convention through improvisation; an additive approach to "languaging" that inspires dense narratives with dense layers of meanings; male braggadocio; angularity and asymmetry; frank approaches to sexuality; and the importance of the local cultural space, among others.

While the congruency between Hurston's ideas and hip-hop is clear, the meanings generated by these qualities are dependent on the contingencies specific to historically situated, geographically placed musicians and listeners. Like the muse of gospel music, the hip-hop muse has shown similar affinities for permeability and the additive imperative, but with differences. Like jazz's multiethnic, omnimulatto origins, hip-hop's emergence in the 1970s was nurtured by a multiethnic collection of African American, Afro-Caribbean, and Latin American youth.

As I've noted, hip-hop has undergone numerous stylistic transformations since it burst onto the national scene commercially in 1979. Its thematic content reflects this hybrid profile, encompassing myriad topics in its lyrics: social responsibility, calculated nihilism, cultural criticism, black self-help, misogyny, both male and female braggadocio, artistic rivalry, violence, gender relationships, religion, homophobia, leisure and party life, and parental control, among many others. In both hip-hop and black church music, the twin modalities of history and memory animate themes and musical gestures as their various stylistic idioms invoke and sometimes critique previous (and contemporary) genres of the last fifty years, especially soul and funk.

I turn now to some recent examples of contemporary gospel music appearing during the Age of Hip-Hop. Hip-hop music has been put to multifarious uses in gospel's stylistic domain. It has transformed the community theater that is the black church. While the examples that I discuss below do not make equal use of hip-hop's most prominent stylistic features, they do, however, demonstrate the additive, permeable quality and preoccupation with history and cultural memory found in the many expressive practices that have appeared during the Age of Hip-Hop.

CELEBRATING SOUL, SIGNIFYIN(G) HANDEL: A DISCURSIVE COLLISION

The project *Handel's Messiah: A Soulful Celebration*, which appeared in 1992, is ambitiously drawn from a complex of musical, social, and ideological sources. *A Soulful Celebration* essentially sets Handel's composition *Messiah* in the modes of jazz, rhythm and blues, and gospel. Although set in these varied styles, the project was marketed under the label "gospel." Dorsey's axiom is apparently true: it's still the gospel being sung. Thus, the project is grounded in flaunting the juxtaposition of gospel music and Handel's *Messiah*, written at a time when chattel slavery was settling into high gear in the American colonies. On the one hand, gospel music reigns as a powerful sign of ethnicity among African Americans. Faithful Christian believers and nonbelievers alike have long recognized the genre as an important cultural symbol, loaded with both social and eschatological meaning. On the other hand, Handel's *Messiah* has virtually no musical parallel in the history of American concert life. The composition formed an important part in this country's establishment of a "classical" repertory and became an important tool in American "musical evangelism."

From its pastiche "Overture" representing "a partial history of black music" to its finale—a brassy, percussive, techno-funked, piano-slamming rendition of the "Hallelujah! Chorus," *A Soulful Celebration* is a postmodern wonder. The duets, airs, small group pieces, choruses, and accompaniments of *A Soulful Celebration* provide a window into the specific traditions of black gospel composition, arranging, and performance practice. Moreover, the theory of "repetition and difference," an idea taken from black literary studies and recent musical studies, helps to highlight the cultural dialogism standing not only at the heart of this work but in African American music making in general.

I find two aspects of *A Soulful Celebration* compelling. First, this project stands as a stellar example of Signifyin(g), a term that originated in black vernacular speech but has been engrafted into the world of literary criticism by the critic Henry Louis Gates, Jr., in his important book *The Signifying Monkey* (1988).[4] Music scholars have responded to Gates's work enthusiastically. Scholars who work on jazz and popular forms, such as David Brackett, Samuel A. Floyd, Jr., Ingrid Monson, and Robert Walser, have contributed persuasive arguments for the value of Gates's Signifyin(g) theory.[5] Indeed, the notion of Signifyin(g) explains the cultural relevance of *A Soulful Celebration* even before the first downbeat sounds. The other aspect I'll discuss is how some of the pieces work well as examples of gospel composition and performance practice. I argue that, despite the commercial profile of the project, in form and practice many of these pieces conform to the ideals of gospel music and to the cultural imperatives of what is considered "the core culture" black church.

Matthew Baumer has provided a descriptive history of the *Soulful Celebration* project, heavily based on interviews with Mervyn Warren, one of the coproducers of the work.[6] Conceived with popular and widespread success in mind, the project was ensured of public interest through its corporate backing and performer name recognition. *A Soulful Celebration* was a collaborative recording; that is, many artists from both the secular and sacred worlds contributed as performers, arrangers, and producers. The stellar lineup includes Mervyn Warren and Cedric Dent of the a cappella group Take Six, Stevie Wonder, Quincy Jones, Vanessa Bell Armstrong, Al Jarreau, Tramaine Hawkins, George Duke, Richard Smallwood, Tevin Campbell, Patti Austin, and a host of others.

The project consists of sixteen discrete pieces. According to the liner notes, each is considered an "arrangement" rather than a composition. As Baumer has shown, the new arrangements vary in the degree to which they follow the formal plan of the original work on which each is based. Some, like the "Hallelujah! Chorus," arranged by Mervyn Warren, Michael O. Jackson, and Mark Kibble, adhere to Handel's basic outline, despite their creative reharmonization. Other pieces, such as George Duke's arrangement of "Behold, a Virgin Shall Conceive" and Robert Sadin's "Glory to God," take considerable liberties with the materials.[7] Both of these practices are typical in the practice of gospel composition, especially among contemporary musicians.

A Soulful Celebration represents one of the latest musical installments of a cultural dialogue begun in nineteenth-century America. The *Messiah*'s historical role as an important symbol of musical, political, moral, and civil health has been documented in histories of American music. The composition was a favorite of the Boston Handel and Haydn Society, founded in 1815. In its mission statement, the society pronounced its members' desire that the "science" of music would excite the feelings and exercise the powers "to which it was accustomed in the Old World."[8] While many of the meanings once generated in this context by the *Messiah* have vanished, others remain intact. Numerous annual Christmas performances of the work are offered by community groups, churches, and other organizations that seem to inspire the same sense of musical well-being and accomplishment.

And it is important to note here that many African American congregations in particular present the *Messiah* with zeal, enthusiasm, and the same sense of ownership. As cultural historian Bernice Johnson Reagon has noted of a black Methodist congregation in the Eastern Shore region of Maryland:

> Music of all kinds was performed at Tindley Temple, and behaviors toward music and worship service were not stratified. The church that sang Handel's *Messiah* at Christmas and Rossini's "Inflammatus" on Sunday morning also held Eastern Shore–style, all-night tarrying services and testimonials and expressed a strong belief in Holiness. Each member could receive it all in his or her own way, shouting or getting happy or being more quietly stirred.[9]

A Soulful Celebration, I would argue, presents an interesting twist on all these sentiments.

The writers and musicians represented on this project "Signified" on the symbolic American origins of the *Messiah*, and they did so with a cogent "black" difference. The result provides listeners with the feelings and power of the Old World, indeed, but not solely the world that the Handel and

Haydn Society longed to emulate. These worlds are of both African and European provenance. Of course, as part of African American traditions, black gospel music represents a synthesis and consolidation of sensibilities that can be traced to both Europe and Africa. Thus *A Soulful Celebration* is a work of western European origin, appropriated by a nineteenth-century American audience for its own purposes, and then transformed, in this case, by musical techniques and practices that themselves represent an aesthetic complex from both Europe and Africa but that symbolize something quite specific for the audiences that it has reached. Samuel Floyd's work suggests generally, and I concur about the specific case presented here, that this project represents an extension of the syncretism and synthesis that created African American music itself. Floyd writes:

> From my examination of the syncretic process as it occurred in nineteenth-century America, I conclude that the emerging African-American genres were not formed by the insertion of African performance practices into the formal structures of European music, as the conventional wisdom would have it, but were molded in a process that superimposed European forms on the rich and simmering foundation of African religious beliefs and practices. The foundation of the new syncretized music was African, not European.[10]

Allow me to outline a working definition of the concept of Signifyin(g). The term is based on the standard English word *signification*, which "denotes the meaning that a term conveys, or is intended to convey."[11] *Signifyin(g)*, on the other hand, is a black revision of the standard English term. It is a homonym that, according to Gates, "seems to be intentionally inscribed within . . . [but is] remarkably different from that concept represented by the standard English signifier, 'signification.'" He goes on to explain, "Whereas signification depends for order and coherence on the exclusion of unconscious associations which any given word yields at any given time, Signification luxuriates in the inclusion of the free play of these associative rhetorical and semantic relations."[12]

As I've noted earlier, Floyd has extended the tropes of Gates's Signifyin(g) theory into an allegorical musical theory he labels Call-Response, which is the trope of tropes or the master trope. Subsumed under this rubric are all "the elements we have come to know as the characterizing and foundational elements of African-American music."[13] The use of these tropes in Handel's framework gives the entire *Soulful Celebration* project its power and unity.

I consider below a few musical specifics of the project in light of its Signifyin(g) potency. As I stated above, the project itself Signifies on

Handel's original work. Furthermore, and perhaps most important, it depends on both the audiences' familiarity with the original Messiah and the recognition of its musical syntax for its Signifyin(g), telling effect (although it is possible to enjoy it without knowing the original). Consider, for example, the irony and postmodern cachet of Mervyn Warren's musical rhetoric in the opening measures of "Every Valley Shall Be Exalted." The piece opens with a sample of the English Chamber Orchestra and Choir performance of the original score. After that opening gesture, Warren's rhythm track, a cyclic, nonteleological groove in E with ostinato bass, causes a rupture, a symbolic clash of syntax and rhetoric in which the perpendicular worlds of signification and Signification collide gloriously. It is, indeed, a gesture that exists at the nexus of Culture and culture.

Baumer describes this gesture as "crushing" the sample, and he interprets the cadential chord before the singers enter as "the musical equivalent of the Road Runner sticking his tongue out at Wile E. Coyote before leaving him in a cloud of dust."[14] I concur with Baumer, especially since the F7-sharp 11 chord situated a half step above the tonic, which Warren uses as a subtle dominant substitute, seems to momentarily suspend the entire sound world of the piece a few inches above ground level.

I'd like to offer another interpretation of this rhetorical gesture, however, one that is perhaps more consistent with and grounded in the black vernacular. In *The Signifying Monkey,* Gates recalls a brief story from 1983 in which a group of black high school students from North Carolina, dismayed by their poor performance on standardized examinations, responded by devising "a test to measure vocabulary mastery in street language."[15] One of the test questions asks: "Who is buried in Grant's tomb?" The students' answer was "Your Mama," a verbal response used in black vernacular speech either as a conclusion of a healthy round of Signifyin(g) duels or as a challenge to heighten its intensity.

Seen through this lens, and with the help of Samuel Floyd's Call-Response model, the opening gesture of "Every Valley" opens up to numerous readings. First, in the broadest sense, it might be seen as positioning the new version "against" the backdrop of the old: in other words, the new version self-consciously invites attention to itself as a foil to the former. This is a common practice of Signifyin(g) in the black literary and musical traditions. On the other hand, if one accepts my hypothesis, the gesture may be seen as setting the tone for the musical duel that occurs between the lead singers in this piece, Lizz Lee and Chris Willis. With dramatic melismatic runs, astounding rhythmic agility, intense use of their respective vocal ranges and improvisational abilities, and their interlocking calls and responses, these performers exemplify the game rivalry and individuality within collectivity tropes as identified by Floyd. They seem pitted both against the unyielding "funky as raw chitlins" groove and against one another. The intensity of this duel-duet serves the performance well (one might even say it's the central attraction of the piece), and it makes the work aesthetically pleasing in the same way that instrumental duels and multiperformer solos have accounted for some of the most exhilarating performances in jazz.

I should point out that each level of Signifyin(g) here, Warren's rendition and the performers' game rivalry, should be considered unmotivated Signification, "or refiguration as an act of homage."[16] In the liner notes, for example, Warren thanks Handel "for writing such wonderful music"; and then he acknowledges the artists "whose gifts brought these arrangements to life."[17]

Floyd links the emergence of Signifyin(g) as we know it today to a modernist shift in black mass consciousness during the postslavery era and to psychological responses to white supremacy and racial segregation. These dual factors caused African Americans to develop self-defensive and self-empowering strategies, one of which is Signifyin(g), "the tool of the human, urban trickster, whose general behavior is symbolized in the toast of the Signifying Monkey." Floyd argues that "the toast itself is a metaphor, a symbol for the state of things—for the American condition as seen and experienced by sophisticated urban African Americans, the new city slickers—and the Monkey's strategy is symbolic of a way of coping with that condition through trickery."[18] The Monkey's strategy—using clever language and wit to gain advantage—is directly related to those of earlier trickster figures of African origin, one of which was Esu, according to Floyd. Thus he sees the rhetoric embedded in the Signifying Monkey tales and the repetition thereof as serving a specific function at a particular historical moment.

W. E. B. Du Bois identified another contemporaneous African American response to America's institutionalized systems of hegemony at the turn of the twentieth century. He forwarded his well-known idea of double consciousness to describe African American twoness: "an American, a Negro; two souls, two thoughts, two unreconciled strivings; two warring ideals in one dark body, whose dogged strength alone keeps it from being torn asunder."[19] What Du Bois described as a historically specific, class determined, masculinist, sociocultural and psychological condition, scholars have extended into practically every domain of African American life since. Along with Signifyin(g), double consciousness has become a master trope for the formation of

African American culture, as a way to explain the actions of numerous historical actors and as an guiding principle for cultural production.

But what are the musical implications of these observations? And what can they tell us about the cultural work of the Signifying Monkey and the usefulness of the idea of double consciousness during the Age of Hip-Hop, a world in which "the state of things" is much different from their state in the era in which these ideals emerged?

The rhetorical use of the musical tropes, indeed, the musical Signifyin(g) taking place in the *Soulful Celebration* project, while drawing on historically specific ideas of the past, is embedded with contemporary social energies. As we have learned, hip-hop, one of the dominant musical cultures of the moment, has been marked by hybridity since its inception. (Modern jazz's embrace of Cuban music in the 1940s demonstrates this same capacity for hybridity.) Gospel music, too, has proven to be just as malleable over the years. In fact, both of these musical worlds are essentially the result of such mixing, matching, and juxtapositions.

Because of the accelerated rate at which mass-media images and sounds circulate and the power of the global market assuring their influence during the Age of Hip-Hop, the borrowing has intensified greatly since the high years of Afro-modernism outlined in earlier chapters. Thus the North-South dialogue of the 1940s grew exponentially over the years into an international, intragenre, interracial, intracoastal, intrahistoric conversation fueled, in part, by technological advances that have made access to musical gestures of the past (and contemporaneous "distant" ones) more available and elastic. The musical tropes of Signifyin(g) have been wedded to innumerous styles and practices, demonstrating the bricolage, mosaic, pastiche, and additive impulses of contemporary hip-hop culture. The *Soulful Celebration* project exemplifies this mosaic approach. For all the above reasons, I believe that the concept of double consciousness no longer captured the complexity, elasticity, or "additive-ness" to describe black cultural production or identity in the late twentieth century. The combination of performers whose professional affiliations represent both the secular and sacred camps serves as one example of this mindset. Indeed, the mass-media texts of recent years circulate complex mixtures of styles and genres, and thus more heterogeneous possibilities for group and self-fashioning.

The arrangement of "Comfort Ye My People" provides an excellent example of some important elements of contemporary gospel composition and performance practice. The piece concludes with a repetitive section comprising a four-bar loop, a nonteleological, cyclic groove that provides compressed displays of the call-and-response tropes, especially among the singers. These troping cycles are musical and ideological remnants of the ring shout from the slave past. As other scholars have observed, troping cycles are derived from other aspects of African culture, such as cyclic conceptions of time reckoning. As I've noted earlier, the twelve-bar blues, black sermons, and the two-bar "shoutin' music" forms in the black church exemplify this sensibility.

Troping cycles work as microrepresentations of the syntax of rituals present throughout the African Diaspora. Walter Pitts has identified a "binary structure" in these ceremonies, in which two metaphoric frames combine to provide a ritual syntax. He writes that "African-American rituals have a universal predisposition to flow from a formal, tightly structured, constraining, European frame toward an emergent, less constricted expression of the African-self . . . the outward shell gives way to the inner being as emotional intensity increases."[20] Morton Marks calls this technique "switching," a communicating device prevalent among societies where two cultures have come in contact, especially in situations involving trance induction.[21]

A representation of this activity can be heard in "Comfort Ye My People," sung by two of the most capable and expressive singers in gospel music, Vanessa Bell Armstrong and Daryl Coley. The piece begins in the style typical of a soulful "power ballad," or what is referred to in vernacular argot as a slow jam. The accompaniment is rather sparse, allowing the musical soundscape to breathe, and a soprano sax adds to the pastel blankets of colors evoked by the rhythm track. Although the singers display moments of intensity marked by melismatic vocal work and loud, chesty singing near the top of their respective ranges, they are clearly saving their call-and-response reserves for the troping cycle at the end of the piece.

The composition moves to the second frame of the metaphorical syntax during its final passages. This section of the piece is typically referred to as the vamp. In Chicago's gospel community the term *special chorus* was most frequently used for this kind of section. As noted in chapter 3, I use the academically arid term *troping cycle* to describe it (1) because *vamp* seems to denote only the harmonic successions and melodic patterns typical of the section; and (2) because the term *troping cycle* points not only to its function but also to the aesthetic demands and requirements placed on the singers or instrumentalists. In order for the section to really work, the performers must use all of the Call-Response tropes they can successfully execute.

I want to stress that my interpretation of the piece as conceptually comprising two frames is not meant to dismiss or undervalue traditional methods of musical analysis—that is, accounts that may specify the particulars of Warren's melodic, rhythmic, and harmonic plan. In his groundbreaking work, Horace Clarence Boyer has offered paradigms for the analysis of gospel music, and it is especially helpful in understanding how *A Soulful Celebration* operates as contemporary gospel music, as opposed to traditional. Matthew Baumer, for example, has transcribed a big chunk of "Comfort Ye" and has shown that Warren's adherence to Handel's original plan frustrates the typical verse-chorus structure found in traditional and contemporary gospel as outlined by Boyer.[22] Warren himself describes many of the pieces as situated somewhere between through-composed and verse-chorus types.[23]

In the troping cycle of "Comfort Ye," Armstrong and Coley bring all of their expertise in the call-and-response framework to the forefront through four elements that Boyer argues distinguish gospel singing: timbre, range, text interpolation, and improvisation. Although the piece begins in E major, like Handel's, the harmonic cycle at the end comprises a four-bar repeated succession centered on A. The accompaniment, indeed, has intensified in contrast to the opening of the piece; yet the musician's sense of "pocket," the vernacular term used to describe a rhythm section's absolute control of a groove's volume, rhythmic nuance, harmonic and melodic accuracy, and mechanics of delivery, is strictly maintained.

Armstrong and Coley have center stage. Their work exploits Boyer's four elements with maximum effect: their vocal timbres are varied and self-consciously strained and full-throated, and they move between singing comfortably within their respective ranges and reaching for their upper limits; their improvised note choices, especially within scalular melismatic passages, shift between bluesy declamation and sprightly beboplike runs that would rival experienced jazz musicians. Mastery of textual interpolation, especially as a form of call and response, constitutes an important activity for successful troping cycles. Another level of textual interest is added by Armstrong and Coley's shift between various modes of direct and indirect discourse, a strategy that allows immediate communication to their listening audience.

"I WON'T COMPLAIN":
A GOSPEL DIVA SANCTIFIES THE BLUES

Historian and singer Bernice Johnson Reagon argues that the African American "singing tradition announces the presence of our community. It is a way in which we nurture and heal ourselves. It is an offering to the celebration of life and the lifting of the spirit."[24] In his book *Stomping the Blues,* Albert Murray explores this singing tradition and connects it explicitly to the instrumental expressions of blues performances. He explores important modes of musical signification, including the lyrics, the music, body language, formal conventions, technical devices, and other aspects of blues performance practice. Murray's observations amount to something he calls a "specific technology of stylization."[25] In this technology of stylization, vocalists and musicians must collapse "artifice" and "direct emotional expression." They must also call attention to the semantic gap existing between the "concrete information" referenced by the lyrics and the musical rhetoric accompanying them.

I am particularly interested in Murray's comparison of the cultural spaces he calls "the Saturday Night Function" with "the traditional down home Sunday Morning Service." Murray writes that the church can "generate paroxysms of ecstasy that exceed anything that happens in the most gutbucket-oriented of honky-tonks." Like so many other writers, he positions the church as the probable originator of such techniques as "the solo-call/ensemble-riff-response pattern" that is so prevalent in many forms of African American music.[26]

But origins of influences are difficult to trace. I am convinced, moreover, that origins have little to do with the meanings generated in many musical performances of black vernacular music. What is more important is the signifying effect a musical gesture produces in a specific context. In other words, historical origins matter less to audiences than what they perceive as a performer's self-conscious mixing, matching, juxtaposing specific musical gestures from disparate stylistic, historical, and idiosyncratic sources. One such example of this kind of cultural work can be heard in the work of the Clark Sisters. Their sanctifying blues provides an excellent example of Murray's technology of stylization. Their style not only purifies but also shows how artifice, emotion, function, and taste cohere into a specific kind of elegance.

The Clark Sisters are recognized as arguably the leading all-female gospel singing group of the last two decades. They are the talented daughters of Rev. Elbert Clark and the formidable and late Mattie Moss Clark, who for years served as director of the Church of God in Christ's National Convention and as leader of the Southwest Michigan Choir. The Clark Sisters are celebrated for their musicianship as well as for the religious fervor created within their performances. Although often overlooked and underexplained, their unrivaled musicianship sits at the center of the fervor. Their mastery can be attributed to many factors: the legacy of gospel singing in the family, early training in their parents' church, and not least, the immense gifts of one sister, Elbertina "Twinkie" Clark. Along with her sisters, Twinkie began singing in her mother's choir and later accompanied her on the organ during the "Midnight Musicals." These after-hours talent showcases demanded that musicians and singers be on their mettle during planned and impromptu performances. Twinkie Clark's compositional work positions her as one of the most important writers in late-twentieth-century black gospel music.[27] Some of the sisters have recently begun to produce solo work, confirming their enduring appeal. Any performance by the Clark Sisters will demonstrate many of the definitive elements and conventions of black vernacular music and how innovation can intensify these techniques.

Karen Clark-Sheard is the youngest of the Clark Sisters, and a particular recording proves that she has artistically come into her own. She performed a version of Don Johnson's song "I Won't Complain" on a project titled "Twinkie Clark-Terrell Presents the Florida A&M University Choir." Recorded live on October 28, 1995, on Florida A&M's campus, the song was released on video and CD in 1997.

Clark-Sheard's rendition stands in the nexus of several traditions. She sings only half of one stanza of the piece. The rubato tempo of "I Won't Complain" represents a long tradition of singing that serves as a showcase of the vocalist's spiritual conviction as expressed through musical technique and mastery. Singers sometimes sing snippets of these songs, as in the present case, or sometimes they sing the entire composition. The audience's continuous reaction to the textual narrative and the musical and kinetic rhetoric of Clark-Sheard's performance represents one of the more powerful aspects of this particular recording. The audience provides a collective and continuous critique of the various parameters of her singing. A reading of the performance against their reactions provides us with insight into the horizons of expectations within gospel singing. Explanation of this performance also lends Albert Murray's technology of stylization a needed musicological dimension.

In a foundational article on black religious music, the late pianist, singer, and scholar Pearl Williams-Jones provides a useful lexicon of gospel vocal techniques.[28] Published in 1975 around the same time as *Stomping the Blues,* Williams-Jones's work expresses many of the historical idiosyncrasies of that time. "Blackness" is defined as having the qualities of an African-derived "folk" ethos, and the political import of such is of central importance to any aesthetic theory. Moreover, the ancestral lineage of this ethos is found in "folk tales, speech patterns, religious beliefs and musical practice."[29] Proclivities for these sensibilities are passed along from generation to generation through oral transmission. The black church operates as an enclave of this cultural reproduction. William-Jones's black community is not engendered but spoken of in very broad and generic terms. At the same time, she is concerned with historical specificity. She writes, for example, about the role of black religious music during Reconstruction and the Civil Rights movement.

Williams-Jones's catalog of the specific techniques, requirements, and typologies of black gospel singing is invaluable. In the gospel music tradition we experience a "colorful kaleidoscope of black oratory, poetry, drama and dance." Audiences prize personalized renditions in this tradition. They expect singers to demonstrate multiple timbres, an exceptional range, and vocal agility, among many other dramatic vocal devices. The improvisational parameters of the performance should also include stock rhetorical expressions, prescribed bodily movements, and charismatic zeal. Yet this zeal should be controlled and work within a requirement that Ben Sidran has called "stage presence," which he explains as "the ability to perform music at the peak of emotional involvement, to be able to maintain the pitch of this involvement, and continue the process of spontaneous composition."[30]

Williams-Jones positions the gospel singer as a symbolic combination of the black preacher and the congregation. The melismatic, improvisational aspects of gospel vocalizations can sometimes achieve "dizzying heights of virtuosity," incorporating "a barrage of pyrotechnics into a gospel song which lifts the simplest one to aria status in mere moments."[31] The charismatic appeal generated by the total performance not only dramatizes a song's lyrics but also serves as a way for audiences to gauge the singer's degree of emotional immersion.

We experience the full range of these conventions in the approximately two minutes of Clark-Sheard's performance. The audience is obviously thrilled about her rendition, in part, perhaps, because of her culturally specific virtuoso status. The A&M choir is, without doubt, well known in the area and having a bona fide star in their midst generates excitement and anticipation. They express this appreciation vocally. After the pianist's brief introduction, containing hints of the melody and establishing the key center of C major, Clark-Sheard enters, singing the beginning of the refrain softly: "God has been good to me." This is an immensely popular song within black Pentecostal circles. A simple, reflective statement of Christian faith in the face of adversity, the tune belongs to the compositional legacy of Charles Tindley, Lucie Campbell, and, most notably, Thomas A. Dorsey.

Line 1. God has been good to me

Line 2. He's been so good to me

Line 3. More than the world could ever be

Line 4. He's been so good to me

Line 5. He dried all my tears away

Line 6. Turned my darkness into day

Line 7. I'm gonna say "thank you, Lord"

Line 8. And I won't complain

Although her performance here serves as introductory material to a more upbeat composition written for the choir, it still presents, as Williams-Jones points out above, a set of musical requirements and challenges for Clark-Sheard. She is what I would call a soul coloratura. She must set the stage for the subsequent choral material and, at the same time, inscribe her virtuosity within the framework provided by the eight brief lines of the chorus. Her work is a model of emotional compression in this regard. Clark-Sheard's mastery of several aspects of gospel singing deserves attention: timbral variation, melismatic runs, asymmetrical phrasing, bodily gestures, and textual invention. All of these parameters stack up to dramatize the lyrics, to demonstrate her spiritual commitment, and to self-consciously establish her command over the tradition in which she is participating.

The first line of the song draws a concerted response from the audience when they recognize the tune and appreciate Clark-Sheard's tone and timing. This is her setup. Her timbre is sweet, somewhat breathy, and understated; she takes a breath in the phrasing between "God has" and "been good to me." She will "take her time," as the old adage of exhortation states. In line 2, Clark-Sheard again breaks the brief statement in half with a breath but not before melodic invention on the long "o" vowel sound of the word "so." The crowd talks back immediately with sporadic applause and various exhortations: "sing, Karen" "all right," and "yes." Line 3 contains an arpeggio spanning a tenth. Again, Clark-Sheard separates the idea with a breath between "more than the world" and "could ever be." The word *could* is a high G, a half step below the highest note in the song. She sings it with a breathy tone, tossing off another melismatic phrase on the words *ever be.* Clark-Sheard pauses after line 4's "He's been," taking a breath before a downward melodic flourish on the word *so* that contains four basic asymmetrical units. The remainder of the phrase, "good to me," is almost thrown away, because after a quick breath, Clark-Sheard launches into an ascending line on the word *He,* which textually belongs to line 5. The quick melodic phrase complements the secondary dominant (C7), underpinning it perfectly: her inclusion of the ninth scale degree (D) suggests a sophisticated harmonic sense. Moreover, the inclusion of the phrase in line 4 red-flags it as rhetorically significant.

Line 5 is loaded with semantic content and marks a transitional moment in the emotional trajectory of Clark-Sheard's performance. Standing in contrast with the truncated "He" in line 4, she stretches out this "He dried." Her held note on the word *dried* contains two sounds: the long *i* in *dried* and a long *e* that she achieves by closing the throat and producing a very nasal quality. During the melodic invention on this same word, Clark-Sheard shifts back and forth between the two vowel sounds, exploiting their timbral contrast. Juxtaposed to this vowel contortion, she sings a descending line on the word *all* that can be explained only as a hollow, stylized growl with a slight flutter. The crowd, which has been drawn gradually into this spectacle, roars its approval to line 5's rhetoric. Line 6 contains another harmonically rich statement on the word *darkness*, which Clark-Sheard sings over the pianist's F13-sharp 11 chord, riffing on the chord's extensions with all the skill of a bebop instrumentalist.

One of the key phrases of the solo occurs within a kind of suspension of time created by a brief cadenzalike move. As the pianist shifts harmonically between A7-flat 9 and an E-flat 11-sharp 13 chords, Clark-Sheard executes a much longer than practical melodic passage on the word *I*. Several aspects of this particular passage make it important to the overall effect of the performance. Again, she exploits the diphthongs in order to maximize the emotive content of line. The Clark Sisters patented this type of execution, but it also indicates a regional trait among native Detroit singers. Aretha Franklin, Vanessa Bell Armstrong, and CeCe Winans, all hailing from Detroit, are among those who have also perfected this style. As gospel journalist Anthony Heilbut once noted: "Detroit singers enjoy vocal contortions that make Stevie Wonder sound restrained."[32] The passage shows off her range and her intricate, melodious, instrumental-like conception of the entire performance.

Clark-Sheard's body language adds another level of semantic content to the performance. It speaks volumes. During the "I" passage her left hand gestures along with the run, moving it in sync with the melodic direction. The audience voices its approval of both the bodily and the musical gestures. Along with her wide-eyed, concentrated expression, the hand motions make the melodic run a visible and material entity. Jacqui Malone's recent study of black vernacular dance characterizes these forms as making rhythms visible.[33] I see Clark-Sheard's vocals and bodily gestures operating similarly: the full scope of her body language indexes the numerous cultural stances that are available to female singers. She grips the microphone like a pop performer; she sings with her eyes closed, squinting, or looking into the distance, signifying spiritual preoccupation. On high notes, her eyebrows raise and shoulders shrug; during dramatic, emotionally charged passages, her head tilts at an awkward angle. At some points during this section Clark-Sheard's free hand rests open-palmed on her diaphragm, a typical stance of many female gospel singers. Clark-Sheard's body language cuts many ways: religious reverence, coy show-business sass, ethnic solidarity, and artistic concentration. Taken together, these gestures add dimensions of emotional import and cultural relevance to "I Won't Complain."

In his chapter titled "The Blue Devils and the Holy Ghost," Murray writes that "the definitive devices of blues musicianship were already conventions of long standing among downhome church musicians long before Buddy Bolden, Jelly Roll Morton, King Oliver, W. C. Handy, and Ma Rainey came to apply them to the dance hall."[34] One such device is what he calls the "call/ensemble-riff-response pattern." He illustrates the convention with the following passage:

Solo-call: On the mountain.

Congregation: I couldn't hear nobody pray.

Solo: In the valley.

Riff: Couldn't hear nobody pray.

Solo: On my kneehees.

Riff: Couldn't hear nobody pray.

Solo: With my Jesus.

Riff: Couldn't hear nobody.

Solo: Oh, Lord.

Riff: I couldn't hear nobody.

Solo: Oh, Lordahawd!!!

Riff: Couldn't hear nobody pray.

Everybody: Way down yonder by myself I couldn't hear nobody pray.[35]

Murray offers some discussion of the kinetic impetus behind such call-and-response patterns, their comparative roles in secular and sacred cultural spaces, and what he calls the shameless transgression of such artists as Ray Charles, Aretha Franklin, and James Brown, who built careers crossing these socially recognized boundaries. I want to explore some of the underlying cultural imperatives in Murray's example to analyze the remainder of Clark-Sheard's performance. The variation seen in the solo-call lines ("on the mountain," "in the valley," "on my kneehees," "with my Jesus," etc.) suggests the endless improvisational expectations of the gospel soloist. This improvisational imperative feeds off the congregation's vocalized and kinetic energy. As we have seen in the first half of Clark-Sheard's rendition, a soloist's invention may involve the contortion of standardized pronunciations, a convention that Murray represents with unconventional spellings of the words *knees* and *Lord*. The "couldn't hear nobody pray" lines provide a sonic anchor and framework for the soloist to riff within and against. As others have noted, this practice can be heard in many forms: we hear it in blues, in jazz, and in most styles of gospel music. In the last line of Murray's example, the soloist and congregation become "sonically one." I would extend this metaphor and suggest that they become socially, emotionally, and spiritually one as well.

We hear these imperatives boldly realized in the remainder of "I Won't Complain." After Clark-Sheard's "I" passage between lines 6 and 7, she immediately riffs, "I'm gonna say 'thank you, Lord.'" The word *I* becomes *I'm* and represents a profound example of the wordplay suggested by Murray above. Clearly, in this instance the musical opportunity presented by the vowel sound *had to be* exploited; there was no apparent rush to "return" to the actual lyrics of the piece. Moreover, the riff on the word *I* invites speculation that the individualized, musical Self that Clark-Sheard forwards in the performance skirts close to the secular transgression that Murray mentioned earlier. Yet the immediate shift to the line "I'm gonna say 'thank you, Lord'" moves us out of the realm of virtuoso spectacle and into one of worship and adoration.

At this point in the performance, "I Won't Complain" becomes a truncated model of the call/ensemble-riff-response convention. Yet the cultural requirements are fulfilled by Clark-Sheard's capable musicianship. Between lines 7 and 8, she creates a call-and-response pattern but supplies both solo riff and response.

(Line 7)	I'm gonna say "thank you, Lord"
Response	Thank you, Lord
Call	When I look back over my life
Response	Thank you, Lord
	(Modulation to E-flat major)
Call	When I see how far He's brought me *from*
Response	Thank you, Lord
Call	*Oh, oh, oh*
Response	Thank you, Lord
(Line 8) Call	And I won't complain

In several of the call lines, Clark-Sheard intensifies her melismatic invention (indicated by italics). The modulation from C to E-flat also adds an additional boast to the performance's emotional course of action. Moreover, the succession of musical phrases has sped up considerably from the previous sections of the piece. The audience's collective critique follows suit: they verbally evaluate every parameter of the performance. Organist Twinkie Clark-Terrell, Karen's older sister, inconspicuously drifts into the piece at an earlier point and by the modulation becomes the predominant voice in the accompaniment. During these final passages, she supplies another item of response to the singer's calls, riffs, and runs. In the best of improvisational comping traditions in African American music, Clark-Terrell spurs on Clark-Sheard's vocalizations and stirs the crowd with her strong rhythmic punctuation. Clark-Terrell sets the Hammond B-3 organ at its most biting timbre, one which would overpower a lesser singer. It almost competes for the emotional center of the performance. The harmonies she chooses are complex: 9ths, 11ths, and 13ths abound. The vocal, instrumental, emotional, and spectacular energy explodes in the final line. Again, on the word *I* Clark-Sheard allows us to measure just how far we've come in two short minutes. She sings the highest note of the performance, a high A-flat. The melismatic, multidirectional pattern, the subtle slip between major and "blues scale" modalities, the timbral shifts between a pinched head voice to a chesty gruffness, and the almost fierce facial expression purify the cultural space. The audience erupts before the final vocal strain has dissipated. Crowd and performer have affirmed their community. God is in the house. The blues have been sanctified and sufficiently stomped.

I have pointed out some of the usefulness of Albert Murray's work in *Stomping the Blues* for the analysis and interpretation of a musical performance. I want to conclude this section by acknowledging some of its limits. In *The Hero and the Blues*,[36] which appeared in 1973, three years before *Stomping the Blues*, Murray continued to clean some literary house, so to speak, a task that he had begun in his book the *The Omni-Americans: Some Alternatives to the Folklore of White Supremacy*.[37] Clearly, both *The Hero* and *The Omni-Americans* may be read as counterstatements to the prominent African American literary discourse of the day, the Black Arts movement. "All statements," as Murray writes in the introduction to *The Omni-Americans*, "are also counter-statements." Murray's intention was to counter what he called "race-oriented propagandists, whether black or white."[38] If Amiri Baraka argued against a criticism of black music informed by "Western" philosophy, Murray sought the opposite, constantly referring to a range of Western playwrights, authors, and musicians to support his arguments. Murray and Ralph Ellison shared contempt for what the latter called the "burden of sociology" in black music inquiry. Murray's counter, however, sometimes carries, in my view, a "burden of universalism."

"SANTA CLAUS AIN'T GOT NOTHING ON THIS!": KIRK FRANKLIN'S HIP-HOP GOSPEL MESSAGE

Contemporary gospel performer Kirk Franklin's song "Jesus Is the Reason for the Season" provides an excellent opportunity to discuss some pertinent issues surrounding the idea of spirituality and secularism in African American culture, among other issues, during the Age of Hip-Hop. Through the song's formal conventions, its appearance at a specific historical moment, and through Franklin's self-conscious manipulation of the visual aspects of his performances, which include distinctive body attitudes, we have before us a profound example of musical self-fashioning in contemporary gospel. Moreover, "Jesus Is the Reason" provides a musical critique of the perceived boundaries separating sacred and secular life, entertainment and ministry, and the supposed gulf between the so-called folk, mass, and high cultures.

Kirk Franklin was arguably one of the most visible contemporary gospel performers in the 1990s. When he burst onto the national scene in 1993, few had heard of him outside his native Dallas, Texas, church circuit. His debut album, titled *Kirk Franklin and the Family*, was a top-ranked recording on the gospel charts for more than one hundred weeks, eventually going platinum. Formed in 1991, Kirk Franklin and the Family is a seventeen-piece ensemble that electrifies audiences with its dramatic vocal precision supported by sleek funk accompaniment. The stylish elegance of their look in publicity photos and live performances represents a convergence of traditional black church "Sunday go to meeting" and big-business entertainment sensibilities. Big hair, bright colors, designer fashions, and bold jewelry make a statement: contemporary gospel music is a glamorous and lucrative endeavor. If the meek are going to inherit the earth, they will be dressed to the nines and cleaner than the board of health when they do.

As Franklin's star rose, he ventured into various musical and entrepreneurial activities, including the formation of production units called Nu Nation and Fo Yo Soul. One of the groups associated with his companies is God's Property. Formed in 1992 by Linda Searight, God's Property is made up of black young adults who range in age from sixteen to twenty-six. Primarily serving Franklin as a tool for evangelism, their sound has received widespread attention and recognition. God's Property has appeared on *The Late Show* with David Letterman, they have performed with pop sensations

Celine Dion and Stevie Wonder, and their music was featured in the sound-track of Spike Lee's film *Get on the Bus.*

The song "Jesus Is the Reason for the Season" appeared on the *Kirk Franklin and the Family Christmas* project in 1995.[39] The CD was hugely successful for the group and solidified Franklin's reputation as a premier composer, arranger, and performer of contemporary gospel. Of the eleven songs on the recording, "Jesus Is the Reason" is the only one featuring both the family and God's Property, the latter listed as supplying additional back-ground vocals. My analysis of this recording examines the lyrical, the musi-cal, and the visual. These components combine to make "Jesus Is the Reason" a strikingly hybrid text.

Opening gestures of the piece set up the listener for the eclectic mix that follows. An E-flat major chord sounds on the harpsichord, arguably one of the most fragile instruments associated with Western art music. The singers are heard for the first time quoting or, perhaps more appropriately, sampling the French Christmas carol "Angels We Have Heard on High." The full-bod-ied three-part singing is reminiscent of the barbershop quartet singing that stressed sentimentality or nostalgia. This approach is a staple in the gospel singing tradition. At the end of the phrase, the singers unexpectedly tumble into a downward portamento. The spill doesn't land us into the next phrase of the Christmas carol but "drops us off into some funk," in the words of George Duke's funk classic "Reach for It." Instrumentally, the piece sounds identical to any of the contemporary jazz-funk and jazz-rock ensembles, fea-turing electric bass, drums, and various synthesizers and guitars.

The remaining vocals in this introduction add another important layer of sonic interest and cultural meaning to the recording. In stark contrast with the phrase sampled from "Angels We Have Heard on High," the vocals in the funk portion of the introduction feature Franklin's emphatic declama-tions and exhortations together with what I'm calling sanctioned and unsanctioned choir noise. The sanctioned utterances are the typical "go ahead!" and "all right!" one hears within spirited, youth-oriented black core culture churches. But the unsanctioned oral declamations push this piece right out of the "respectability" zone. God's Property's mix of rhythmically coordinated and spontaneous chants—whoops, hollers, and other vocables—creates a wash of youthful exuberance that sounds like a victory party after a football game. This sonic backdrop is also reminiscent of the party noise that begins Marvin Gaye's "What's Going On?" or "Got to Give It Up," or D'Angelo's "Brown Sugar." Franklin's vocal work isn't sung but spoken—he eggs on the imagined audience with stylized declamations that evoke James Brown: "put your hands together," "uggh, good God!" "You better ask somebody," and "come on." He concludes the introduction with the curious exclamation "Santa Claus ain't got nothing on this!"

The Santa Claus exclamation is loaded with cultural significance. As a Christmas project this recording celebrates the miraculous birth of Jesus Christ, one of the most important observances on the church's calendar. Yet in much of the Western world, the beloved mythical character Santa Claus attracts equal attention as the secular spirit of the holiday. But there are dissenting opinions throughout Christendom concerning this partnership. Some believe that the emphasis on the materialistic impulse of Christmas, for which Santa Claus stands, has eclipsed the religious meaning. Moreover, many Christians believe that this situation symbolizes a broader pattern of secular humanism becoming a dominant factor in the church. Such sentiments have spawned maxims like "Jesus Is the Reason for the Season." These kinds of phrases also show up as sermon titles or as "hooks" within the sermon proper. So when Franklin exclaims, "Santa Claus ain't got nothing on this!" he instantly accesses a community of Christians who are united in a common theological stance.

I hear Franklin's exclamation making musical claims as well. An important sentiment behind contemporary gospel is that Christian artists should "take back what the Devil stole" from the church. Within African American music history there exists a long-standing tension between Western ideas about the secular and the sacred and between other cultural sensibilities in which the split is not as profound. The appropriateness of certain musical gestures for worship, the secular nature of a song's subject matter, dress, body language, and the proper venue of presentation have become lightning rods for controversy.

At the beginning of his famous recording "Stomp," Franklin addresses these historical tensions directly by declaring: "For those of you who think that gospel has gone too far—you think that we've gotten too radical with our message—well, I've got news for you. You ain't heard nothing yet. And if you don't know, now you know. Glory, glory! Whooo. Ha, ha, ha. You better put them hands together and act like you know up in here. GP [God's Property]!" I should mention that the remix of "Stomp" is based on a sample of "One Nation under a Groove," a hit recording from the secular funk group Funkadelic. The video of this version features a prominent female rapper. Although the "Santa Claus" exclamation does not register as explicit a challenge as the introduction of "Stomp" does, I believe it is loaded with similar content. And what follows throughout the song rivals for brassy funkiness any project in the secular marketing category.

How is this achieved? The form of "Jesus Is the Reason" can be described as comprising three large sections. Section I contains the introduction, three choruses, and two verses. Section II embodies two interludes and two "special chorus" subsections. Section III is a spontaneous-feeling funk groove that contains layers of vocal and instrumental call-and-response devices. This sectional form can be found in many gospel compositions. The structure is "improvisation friendly." In live performances a director is free to shuffle and repeat various sections to create contrast and excitement.

Section I
Intro   chorus   verse   chorus   verse   chorus
Section II
Interlude   special chorus   interlude   special chorus
Section III
The shout: spontaneous-sounding call-and-response declarations

Section I is united musically by a technique that is found in many hip-hop and R&B recordings of the mid-1990s, in which the verses and choruses are essentially the same harmonic progression. The verses and choruses are distinguished only by variance in their melodic lines and instrumentation. This kind of repetition provides the singers with a harmonic setting for improvisation and sets up the listener for the intensification of musical resources that will surely follow. The chorus, or hook, of the song is made up of two alternating lines that shift between a unison melody sung by the females and a passage that is divided between soprano, alto, and tenor parts. Each is punctuated with Franklin's vocal exclamations.

a. (Unison, soprano, and alto)   Jesus is the reason-nah for the season, yeah

b. (Alto, soprano, tenor)   Yes He is, oh yes He is, oh yes He is, yeah

(Franklin's metasong text)   Come on, come on, come on—ah!

a. (Unison, soprano, and alto)   Jesus is the reason-nah for the season, yeah

b. (Alto, soprano, tenor)   Yes He is, oh yes He is, oh yes He is, yeah

(Franklin's metasong text)   Yo Chris, kick it.

These passages achieve their emotional immediacy from a number of resources. Because part of the melodic line is sung in unison, the vocalists can deliver it with a force that rivets listeners' attention to the lyrics. The extra syllable added to the word *reason* provides an off-beat rhythmic lift to the first phrase, ignoring the rules of "proper" pronunciation. The female singers perform in what vocal teachers refer to as chest voice, a technique common in gospel and one that produces a hard timbre. Gospel audiences love this sound, and it constitutes one of Franklin's signature compositional gestures. The soul singing of Chris Simpson on the lead vocals creates a stunning affect, and for all of the sonic tug-of-wars occurring in the piece, it remains the emotional focal point.

In Section II, the interlude and special chorus provide a contrast of musical materials from Section I that intensifies the emotional thrust of the song. In the interlude, the singers perform a reharmonized snippet of the familiar refrain of the carol "Angels We Have Heard on High." The soundscape becomes awash with crowd noise as the singers whoop, holler, and bray various spontaneous chants. The special chorus comprises a new repetitive groove over which the singers move back and forth between unison and three-part vocals. It is important that during the second interlude of this section, the bassist plays the bass line of a 1970s funk piece, "School Boy Crush," by the Average White Band. This kind of rhetoric is also heard during the verses in which the guitarist plays a gesture from jazz guitarist George Benson's song "Give Me the Night."

Section III is meant to sound completely spontaneous. It features various call-and-response vocalizations from the choir layered over the funky groove being played by the rhythm section. This section has the feeling of the "reprises" of many live gospel recordings that capture the improvised music making and preaching that usually precede the shouting dance in Holiness churches. In a striking moment, Franklin exclaims: "I love it when you call him your Savior!" This gesture is an obvious reworking of a line ("I love it when you call me big Papa") made famous by the late and infamous rapper Notorious B.I.G., perhaps one of the most controversial performers to appear in the hip-hop canon. This kind of performance strategy has drawn negative criticism to Franklin's work from the traditional gospel music advocates.

Finally, God's Property is an important ingredient in this recording's sonic recipe. As I stated above, the soprano and alto parts are written so that the singers execute these melodies in their chest voices. Younger singers can sing in this fashion with greater ease than older ones. By combining this youthful exuberance, popular fashions, secularized body languages, "sampled" musical gestures from a wide musical spectrum, and a grounding in the traditional performance practices of gospel music, Franklin has crafted what might be called a hip-hop-inspired "New Jack gospel" sound.

The heightened visibility and commercial viability of African American music in the late twentieth century produced an atmosphere of prolific creativity. Some observers charge that the particularly intense involvement of a global music industry has exacted a toll on creativity in African American culture. This may be true to a point. But the appearance and fluidity of hip-hop music culture confirm that music will continue to be as important an activity for practitioners and fans as it has been in the past. But, as I have shown throughout this book, the increased visibility of African American expressive culture from the Harlem Renaissance to the present has also given rise to controversies surrounding what and how it "represents."

Indeed, its representational capabilities appear infinite. In films created in the Age of Hip-Hop, we saw how musical practice could inform our perceptions of a diverse set of social factors, in this case, cultural nationalism, nihilism, and bohemianism. We saw how, through rhetoric and performance practice, musicians continued a tradition of referencing and revising European and Euro-American culture for present needs. Moreover, by mixing and matching musical genres with distinct histories, musicians such as Karen Clark-Sheard and Kirk Franklin could powerfully critique current ideas about secularism, sacredness, and the intense commercialism that is part and parcel of hip-hop culture.

In all these examples larger issues emerged with respect to race, gender, and class, often without direct verbal comment from the performers; the critiques were leveled through performance itself, as in Rosie Perez's dance in *Do the Right Thing*. History and memory have played powerful roles in the generation of meaning in the race music constellation of styles. This has continued in Hip-Hop Era musical practice; in fact, this predilection to use the past to comment on the present appears to be one of the defining features of late-twentieth-century African American music.

"Do You Want It on Your Black-Eyed Peas?"

A Tag

Vocalist and poet Jill Scott, a Philadelphia native and the anointed princess of hip-hop's recent neosoul movement, asked the question in this epilogue's title in one of the songs on her celebrated debut recording, *"Who Is Jill Scott?"*[1] Her work is a stunning synthesis of the dense narrative themes of rap music, hip-hop recording techniques, and musical conventions from the soul and funk genres of black popular music. At the same time that it is forward-looking, her music seems like a throwback to days gone by. As I discussed in the first chapter, Stevie Wonder announced in the 1970s that African Americans were no longer interested in "baby, baby songs." His pronouncement sought to capture the political urgency of that moment. Poet Gwendolyn Brooks, as well, stated (quite ironically) about those years that it wasn't a "rhyme time." Jill Scott's work seems to circle back to certain aspects of that past. For example, she writes in "He Loves Me (Lyzel in E-flat)":

> You love me especially different every time
> You keep me on my feet
> Happily excited by your cologne, your hands, your smile, your
> intelligence

And in "Brotha" she declares:

> So many times you tried to cut we
> You wanna tear we down but you can't touch we
> We ain't invincible but Lord knows we're beautiful and blessed
> Check the affirmative

Scott's thematic mix of politics, gender struggles and triumphs, nonrhyming lyrical couplets, and Fender Rhodes–inflected social critiques highlights how structures of feeling from the past can serve present needs and pleasures.

Poet Sonia Sanchez, a leading figure of the Black Consciousness era and an icon of the spoken-word movement in which Scott cut her teeth, recently interviewed the singer for *Essence* magazine. Sanchez mused: "I know Jill Scott. She is pot liquor and corn bread. She is caviar and champagne. She is a blues song and a spiritual. She is Nina, Leontyne, Sarah, Aretha."[2] This description seems to capture the hybridity of Afro-modernism, indeed, the genre crossings and southern memories that I have explored in this book.

Proud of her roots in black Philadelphia, a place that has captured the imaginations of cultural theorists from W. E. B. Du Bois and beyond, Scott proves that the creative energies in the network of urban spaces formed by the Great Migration have not been completely gentrified by broad mass-media coverage. Undoubtedly, other Jill Scotts will continue to appear in New York, Chicago, Philadelphia, Detroit, Baltimore, and so on. Each blending her own mix of pot liquor, corn bread, caviar, champagne, blues, spirituals, Nina, Leontyne, Sarah, and Aretha. These unnamed artists will continue to trope their ancestors, pin themselves down in history, mark their space in the present, and map a passage to their future.

My twenty-two-year-old second cousin Robert Payne II, great-great-grandson of William "Papa" Ramsey and hip-hop producer–beat maker, appreciates both the "hip-hop flavor" and soul–R&B feeling in Scott's work. He further asserts, "You have to be aware of other genres of music . . . you have to look at other ways that people express themselves." At the same time he believes that hip-hop musicians should stay in touch with "the roots" and learn from "the old-time stuff" that is always making a comeback.[3]

In other words, you can go anywhere, but don't never leave home.

Notes

CHAPTER 1. DADDY'S SECOND LINE

1. Reebee Garofalo, *Rocking Out: Popular Music in the United States* (Boston: Allyn and Bacon, 1997), 261–62; Brian Ward, *Just My Soul Responding: Rhythm and Blues, Black Consciousness, and Race Relations* (Berkeley: University of California Press, 1998), 366; Mark Anthony Neal, *What the Music Said: Black Popular Music and Black Popular Culture* (New York: Routledge, 1999), 110–12; Craig Werner, *A Change Is Gonna Come: Music, Race, and the Soul of America* (New York: Plume, 1999), 187–91; Nelson George, *The Death of Rhythm and Blues* (New York: E. P. Dutton, 1989), 126; Rickey Vincent, *Funk: The Music, the People, and the Rhythm of One* (New York: St. Martin's Griffin, 1995), 131–33.

2. Quoted in Ward, *Just My Soul Responding*, 366.

3. Paul Oliver, *Songsters and Saints: Vocal Traditions on Race Records* (Cambridge: Cambridge University Press, 1984). In Jerry Wexler and David Ritz, *Rhythm and the Blues: A Life in American Music* (New York: Alfred A. Knopf, 1993), 62–63, Wexler recounts how he encouraged *Billboard* to drop the "race records" label for one "more appropriate to more enlightened times." For a brief historical overview of various designations for African Americans, see, for example, Joseph Holloway, ed., *Africanisms in American Culture* (Bloomington: Indiana University Press, 1990), xviii–xxi.

4. The term *dusty* is used among many African Americans in Chicago to denote historical recordings that continue to appeal to contemporary audiences but are no longer popular in the sense of still being commercially viable.

5. Michael P. Smith, "Behind the Lines: The Black Mardi Gras Indians and the New Orleans Second Line," *Black Music Research Journal* 14, no. 1 (spring 1994): 49. While I am not drawing a direct link between the New Orleans second line and what happened on that particular evening, there appears to be a strong connection between the two.

CHAPTER 2. DISCIPLINING BLACK MUSIC

1. Alan P. Merriam, *The Anthropology of Music* (Evanston, Ill.: Northwestern University Press, 1964), 3.

2. Joseph Kerman, *Contemplating Music: Challenges to Musicology* (Cambridge, Mass.: Harvard University Press, 1985), 159.

3. Albert Murray, *Stomping the Blues* (1976; New York: Da Capo Press, 1987); and Samuel A. Floyd, Jr., *The Power of Black Music: Interpreting Its History from Africa to the United States* (New York: Oxford University Press, 1995).

4. See Doris Evans McGinty, "Black Scholars on Black Music: The Past, the Present and the Future," *Black Music Research Journal* 13, no. 1 (spring 1993): 1–13, on the idea of black researchers as "trusted insiders."

5. Richard Crawford, "On Two Traditions of Black Music Research," *Black Music Research Journal* (1986): 5.

6. Floyd, *The Power of Black Music,* 6.

7. Henry Louis Gates, Jr., *The Signifying Monkey: A Theory of Afro-American Literary Criticism* (New York: Oxford University Press, 1988), 53.

8. Floyd, *The Power of Black Music,* 226–66.

9. Evelyn Brooks Higginbotham, "African-American Women's History and the Metalanguage of Race," *Signs* 17, no. 2 (winter 1992): 5–6.

10. Hazel Carby, "Policing the Black Woman's Body in an Urban Context," *Critical Inquiry* 18 (summer 1992): 754.

11. Evelyn Brooks Higginbotham, "Rethinking Vernacular Culture: Black Religion and Race Records in the 1920s and 1930s," in *The House That Race Built: Black Americans, U.S. Terrain,* ed. Wahneema Lubiano (New York: Pantheon, 1997), 159.

12. Sherry B. Ortner, "Resistance and the Problem of Ethnographic Refusal," *Comparative Studies in Society and History* 37, no. 1 (January 1995): 173. Ortner's definition of the ethnographic stance is instructive: "Ethnography of course means many things. Minimally, however, it has always meant the attempt to understand another life world using the self—as much of it as possible—as the instrument of knowing." For more on ethnography and popular music, see Sara Cohen, "Ethnography and Popular Music Studies," *Popular Music* 12 (May 1993): 123–38. See also Marcus M. J. Fischer, "Ethnicity and the Postmodern Arts of Memory," in *Writing Culture: The Poetics and Politics of Ethnography,* ed. James Clifford and George E. Marcus (Berkeley: University of California Press, 1986), 198. For recent discussions on ethnography in the field of ethnomusicology, see Gregory F. Barz and Timothy J. Cooley, eds., *Shadows in the Field: New Perspectives for Fieldwork in Ethnomusicology* (New York: Oxford University Press, 1997).

13. Ortner, "Resistance and the Problem of Ethnographic Refusal," 176–77.

14. Robert Walser, *Running with the Devil: Power, Gender, and Madness in Heavy Metal Music* (Hanover, N.H.: University Press of New England, 1993), xiv; Samuel A. Floyd, Jr., "Ring Shout! Literary Studies, Historical Studies, and

Black Music Inquiry," *Black Music Research Journal* 11, no. 2 (fall 1991): 278. For an example of recent discussions of this cultural transaction, see David Brackett's brilliant essay on James Brown's recording "Superbad," in Brackett, *Interpreting Popular Music* (Cambridge: Cambridge University Press, 1995), 108–56. Brackett explores the relationship among the linguistic, cultural, and musical processes involved in the meaning of this piece through analysis of Brown's use of repetition and recombination of musical figures and his explosive approach to pitch, rhythm, and timbre. For more on music and meaning, see Simon Frith, *Performing Rites: On the Value of Popular Music* (Cambridge, Mass.: Harvard University Press, 1996), 249–78; Brackett, *Interpreting Popular Music*, 1–33; Richard Middleton, *Studying Popular Music* (Philadelphia: Open University Press, 1990), 249–58.

15. Farah Jasmine Griffin, *"Who Set You Flowin'?" The African-American Migration Narrative* (New York: Oxford University Press, 1995), 3–12.

16. Ibid., 4.

17. Geneviève Fabre and Robert O'Meally, *History and Memory in African American Culture* (New York: Oxford University Press, 1994).

18. For discussions of black music and its relationship to various notions surrounding modernity, see Samuel A. Floyd, Jr., ed., *Black Music in the Harlem Renaissance* (Westport, Conn.: Greenwood Press, 1990); Paul Gilroy, *The Black Atlantic: Modernity and Double-Consciousness* (Cambridge, Mass.: Harvard University Press, 1993), 72–110; Ronald M. Radano, "Soul Texts and the Blackness of Folk," *Modernism/Modernity* 2, no. 1 (1995): 71–95; Ronald M. Radano, "Denoting Difference: The Writing of the Slave Spirituals," *Critical Inquiry* 22, no. 3 (spring 1996): 506–44; Krin Gabbard, "Introduction: The Jazz Canon and Its Consequences," in *Jazz among the Discourses*, ed. Krin Gabbard (Durham, N.C.: Duke University Press, 1995), 1–28; Mark S. Harvey, "Jazz and Modernism: Changing Conceptions of Innovation and Tradition," in *Jazz in Mind: Essays on the History and Meanings of Jazz*, ed. Reginald T. Buckner and Steven Weiland (Detroit: Wayne State University Press, 1991), 128–47.

19. Hans A. Baer and Merrill Singer, *African-American Religion in the Twentieth Century: Varieties of Protest and Accommodation* (Knoxville: University of Tennessee Press, 1992), 3.

20. See Griffin, *"Who Set You Flowin'?"*

21. James Baldwin, *Nobody Knows My Name: More Notes of a Native Son* (New York: Dial Press, 1961), 5.

22. Maya Angelou, *Singing' and Swingin' and Gettin' Merry Like Christmas* (New York: Bantam, 1976), 28.

23. Toni Morrison, *Jazz* (New York: Plume Books, 1993), 79.

24. Toni Morrison, "The Site of Memory," in *Inventing the Truth: The Art and Craft of Memoir*, ed. William Zinsser (Boston: Houghton Mifflin, 1987), 85–102.

25. Ibid., 95, 97.

26. Henry Louis Gates, Jr., *Colored People: A Memoir* (New York: Vintage

Books, 1994). Gates discusses writing his memoir in "Lifting the Veil," in *Inventing the Truth*, ed. Zinsser, 141–58.

27. Gates, *Colored People*, 64–65.

28. Deborah E. McDowell, *Leaving Pipe Shop: Memories of Kin* (New York: Scribner, 1996); and Spike Lee, *Crooklyn* (film, University City Studios, 1994).

29. Lawrence Kramer, *Music as Cultural Practice, 1800–1990* (Berkeley: University of California Press, 1990), 9. Kramer, one of a growing number of music scholars who combine the tools of musicology and cultural studies, has proposed a helpful way to discuss meaning in European art music written between 1800 and 1900. Based on J. L. Austin's influential book *How to Do Things with Words*, Kramer's theory stresses the performative aspect of music. Austin distinguishes between two kinds of speech acts: constative utterances that make truth claims that are evaluated as true or false, and performative utterances that inspire some kind of action in the world. Likewise, Kramer wants us to look beyond the surface "truth claims" that a musical text or gesture forwards and to consider other kinds of cultural work it may perform. Kramer suggests three kinds of windows: (1) textual inclusions, or the text, titles, epigrams, program notes, and expressive markings; (2) citational inclusions, or titles that link a work with literature, visual image, place, or historical moment; musical allusions to other styles of music and the inclusion of other styles of music; and (3) structural tropes, or the structural procedures in a work that may be viewed as typical within a specific cultural-historical framework. Structural procedures are defined and made powerful by their performative success.

30. See Christopher Small, *Musicking: The Meanings of Performance and Listening* (Hanover, N.H.: University Press of New England, 1998).

31. Floyd, *The Power of Black Music*, 10.

32. Susan McClary, "Paradigm Dissonances: Music Theory, Cultural Studies, Feminist Criticism," *Perspectives of New Music* 32, no. 1 (winter 1994): 78.

33. See Robin D. G. Kelley, "Writing Black Working-Class History from Way, Way Below," in Kelley, *Race Rebels: Culture, Politics, and the Black Working Class* (New York: Free Press, 1994), 1–13.

34. The glossary in John Langston Gwaltney's ethnographic study *Drylongso: A Self Portrait of Black America* (1980; New York: New Press, 1993), xv, defines the term *drylongso* as meaning "ordinary." As one of Gwaltney's informants puts it: "Since I don't see myself [in] most things I see or read about black people, I can't be bothered with that. I wish you could read something or see a movie that would show the people just, well, as my grandmother would say, drylongso. You know, like most of us really are most of the time—together enough to do what we have to do to be decent people" (xix). I thank Robin D. G. Kelley for bringing this reference to my attention.

35. Sherry B. Ortner, "Making Gender: Toward a Feminist, Minority, Postcolonial, Subaltern, etc., Theory of Practice," in Ortner, *Making Gender: The Politics and Erotics of Culture* (Boston: Beacon Press, 1996), 1–2.

36. Gates, *The Signifying Monkey*, 1988, ix.

37. Floyd, *The Power of Black Music,* provides the most detailed explanation of the processes of repetition and revision in black music history.

38. LeRoi Jones, "The Changing Same (R&B and New Black Music)," in Jones, *Black Music* (New York: William Morrow, 1967), 180–211; quotations from 181, 186–87.

39. Blackness, or, more precisely, African Americanness, has been a singular entity among other ethnicities in American society. No one believes that white ethnics, for example, have remained essentially the same over the course of their historical American experience. But a static blackness looms over the American consciousness like a black cloud ready to empty rain on the national parade or enrich the soil, depending on one's viewpoint. One can proudly exclaim in the public sphere, for example, "Love me, I'm Italian!" without being perceived as mounting a challenge to any particular political ideology. But such sentiments about blackness are routinely scrutinized for any hint of subversive critique of the democratic, pluralistic ideals of our nation.

40. Benjamin B. Ringer and Elinor R. Lawless, *Race-Ethnicity and Society* (New York: Routledge, 1989), 1; Werner Sollors captures this dualism when he describes ethnicity as "belonging, and being perceived by others as belonging to an ethnic group." Shibutani and Kwan also recognize the we-ness and they-ness of ethnicity as being mutually dependent ideas: "An ethnic group consists of those who conceive of themselves as being alike by virtue of their common ancestry, real or fictitious, and who are so regarded by others." Stuart Hall pushes the importance of this relationship to the limit when he argues that "there is no identity that is without the dialogic relationship to the Other. The Other is not outside, but also inside the Self, the identity." Werner Sollors, ed., *The Invention of Ethnicity* (New York: Oxford University Press, 1989), xiii; T. Shibutani and K. M. Kwan, *Ethnic Stratification: A Comparative Approach* (New York: Macmillan, 1965), 47, quoted in Ringer and Lawless, *Race-Ethnicity and Society,* 1; and Stuart Hall, "Ethnicity: Identity and Difference," *Radical America* 23, no. 4 (1987): 9–20. I thank Timothy D. Taylor for these references.

41. Robin D. G. Kelley, "Notes on Deconstructing the Folk," *American Historical Review* 97, no. 5 (December 1992): 1400–1408. Kelley's observations confirm Stuart Hall's notion that the Other and the Self are inextricably connected. Sollors (in Sollors, ed., *The Invention of Ethnicity,* xiv–xv) writes that "ethnicity is not so much an ancient and deep-seated force surviving from the historical past, but rather the modern and modernizing feature of a contrasting strategy that may be shared far beyond the boundaries within which it is claimed. It marks an acquired modern sense of belonging that replaces visible, concrete communities whose kinship symbolism ethnicity may yet mobilize in order to appear more natural. The trick that it passes itself off as blood, as 'thicker than water,' should not mislead interpreters to take it at face value. It is not a thing but a process—and it requires constant detective work from readers, not a settling on a fixed encyclopedia of supposed cultural essentials."

42. George Lipsitz, *Time Passages: Collective Memory and American Popular Culture* (Minneapolis: University of Minnesota Press, 1990), 99–132. Audi-

ences understand this dialogue, because as musical gestures are repeated over time, they ultimately generate agreed-upon signifying values or materiality. As Eric Hobsbawm put it, a tradition is "a set of practices, normally governed by overtly or tacitly accepted rules and of a ritual or symbolic nature, which seeks to inculcate certain values and norms of behaviour by repetition, which automatically implies continuity with the past." Eric Hobsbawm and Terence Ranger, eds., *The Invention of Tradition* (Cambridge: Cambridge University Press, 1983), 1. The formal qualities and conceptual frameworks that make up black vernacular musical traditions congeal into Ortner's concept of "key symbols . . . which, by their redundancy, pervasiveness, and importance can be seen as capturing and expressing a society's focal cultural concerns." This definition is offered by José E. Limón, "Representation, Ethnicity, and the Precursory Ethnography: Notes of a Native Anthropologist," in *Recapturing Anthropology: Working in the Present,* ed. Richard G. Fox (Santa Fe, N. Mex.: School of American Research Press, 1991), 118. See also Sherry B. Ortner, "On Key Symbols," *American Anthropologist* 75 (1973): 1338–46.

43. As Charles Hamm notes, for example, the musical interaction between early European settlers and Native Americans was negligible because of irreconcilable "cultural differences." Music was profoundly symbolic of these differences. See Charles Hamm, *Music in the New World* (New York: W. W. Norton, 1983), 23. And even among the first settlers themselves, controversies about music arose. The well-documented conflict between proponents of the "regular singing" and "common way" sacred singing style, for example, clearly illustrates how music became a cultural site in which the notions of "tradition," aesthetic standards, theology, and class-consciousness seemed to forecast future debates about the importance of music in American cultural politics. See Gilbert Chase, *America's Music: From the Pilgrims to the Present,* rev. 3d ed. (Urbana: University of Illinois Press, 1987), 19–37.

44. Earl Lewis, "Connecting Memory, Self, and the Power of Place in African-American Urban History," *Journal of Urban History* 21 (March 1995): 348. Historian Earl Lewis stresses the importance of memory in this intergenerational reproduction because it "functions as a contested area of deeply held but at times highly idiosyncratic beliefs. At the same time, a society's cohesiveness hinges on its ability to create national or group memories, which enlist the support of large segments of the population. Few have studied the nexus between individual memories and group behavior."

45. Dizzy Gillespie and Al Frazer, *To Be or Not to Bop: Memoirs* (Garden City, N.Y.: Doubleday, 1979), 279, 280–81.

46. Kelley, "Notes on Deconstructing the Folk."

47. The polemics surrounding these labels have also cut other ways. Scholars have uncovered the historical origins and trajectories of these categories, revealing how they serve as buffers around power and privilege. Another mode of intervention comprises arguments for the value of vernacular expressions in written discourse. Since the vernacular-folk-popular-mass constellation of styles emerged as culturally valuable, scholars have sought to illuminate the compet-

ing and interrelated sensibilities *within* them. In black vernacular studies, for example, scholars have argued for the place and contributions of intrablack "Others" in the history of African American vernacularism. Questions of class status, sexuality, geographic location, and logocentrism, among other issues, have opened up penetrating analyses of both the policing forces of terms such as *vernacular* and the ways in which labels can gloss over differences within a cultural group.

48. St. Clair Drake and Horace R. Cayton, *Black Metropolis: A Study of Negro Life in a Northern City* (1945; Chicago: University of Chicago Press, 1993); Gunnar Myrdal, *An American Dilemma: The Negro Problem and Modern Democracy* (1944; New Brunswick, N.J.: Transaction Publishers, 1996).

49. See Griffin, *"Who Set You Flowin'?"*

50. Susan McClary, "Constructions of Subjectivity in Schubert's Music," in *Queering the Pitch: The New Gay and Lesbian Musicology,* ed. Philip Brett, Gary Thomas, and Elizabeth Wood (New York: Routledge, 1994), 213.

51. Lila Abu-Lughod, "Writing against Culture," in *Recapturing Anthropology: Working in the Present,* ed. Richard G. Fox (Santa Fe, N. Mex.: School of American Research Press, 1991), 141.

CHAPTER 3. "IT'S JUST THE BLUES"

1. Dinah Washington, *Dinah Washington on Mercury,* vol. 1 (Mercury, compact disk, 832–444–2).

2. See Hazel Carby, "Policing the Black Woman's Body in an Urban Context," *Critical Inquiry* 18, no. 4 (summer 1992): 738–75.

3. Henry Louis Gates, Jr., "The Trope of a New Negro and the Reconstruction of the Image of the Black," *Representations* 24 (fall 1988): 129–55.

4. Samuel A. Floyd, Jr., *The Power of Black Music: Interpreting Its History from Africa to the United States* (New York: Oxford University Press, 1995).

5. Ronald M. Radano, "Soul Texts and the Blackness of Folk," *Modernism/Modernity* 2, no. 1 (1995): 73; Evelyn Brooks Higginbotham, "Rethinking Vernacular Culture: Black Religion and Race Records in the 1920s and 1930s," in *The House That Race Built: Black Americans, U.S. Terrain,* ed. Wahneema Lubiano (New York: Pantheon, 1997); and Ann du Cille, "Blue Notes on Black Sexuality: Sex and the Texts of Jessie Fauset and Nella Larson," *Journal of the History of Sexuality* 3, no. 3 (January 1993): 418–19.

6. Tera Hunter, *To 'Joy My Freedom: Southern Black Women's Lives and Labors after the Civil War* (Cambridge, Mass.: Harvard University Press, 1997), 169.

7. See Daphne Duval Harrison, *Black Pearls: Blues Queens of the 1920s* (New Brunswick, N.J.: Rutgers University Press, 1988); Hazel Carby, "It Just Be's Dat Way Sometime: The Sexual Politics of Women's Blues," in *Unequal Sisters: A Multicultural Reader in U.S. Women's History,* ed. Vicki L. Ruiz and Ellen Carol DuBois, 2d ed. (New York: Routledge, 1994), 238–49; and Angela Y.

Davis, *Blues Legacies and Black Feminism: Gertrude "Ma" Rainey, Bessie Smith, and Billie Holiday* (New York: Pantheon Books, 1998).

8. Manthia Diawara, "Afro-Kitsch," in *Black Popular Culture,* ed. Gina Dent (Seattle: Bay Press, 1992), 290. For Diawara, blackness "is a compelling performance against the logic of slavery and colonialism by those people whose destinies have been inextricably linked to the advancement of the West, and who, therefore, have to learn the expressive techniques of modernity—writing, music, Christianity, industrialization—in order to become uncolonizable."

9. The Four Jumps of Jive, "It's Just the Blues," composed by Richard Jones and Jimmy Gilmore, recorded in Chicago, September 12, 1945, on *The Mercury Rhythm and Blues Story, 1945–1955* (Mercury Records, 314–528–292–2).

10. Willie Dixon with Don Snowden, *I Am the Blues: The Willie Dixon Story* (New York: Da Capo Press, 1989); Jim O'Neal, "It's Just the Blues," liner notes, *The Mercury Rhythm and Blues Story, 1945–1955.* Both Willie Dixon and Richard M. Jones had worked in gospel settings as well. See Horace Clarence Boyer, *How Sweet the Sound: The Golden Age of Gospel* (Washington, D.C.: Elliott and Clark Publishing, 1995), 37. For good descriptions of the various musical styles designated by the term *rhythm and blues,* see Charlie Gillett, *The Sound of the City: The Rise of Rock and Roll,* revised and expanded edition (1970; New York: Pantheon Books, 1983), 119–51; and William Barlow and Cheryl Finley, *From Swing to Soul: An Illustrated History of African-American Popular Music from 1930 to 1960* (Washington, D.C.: Elliot and Clark Publishing, 1994), 90–119.

11. O'Neal, "It's Just the Blues," liner notes.

12. See Evelyn Brooks Higginbotham, *Righteous Discontent: The Women's Movement in the Black Baptist Church, 1880–1920* (Cambridge, Mass.: Harvard University Press, 1993); Higginbotham, "Rethinking Vernacular Culture," 157–77; Kevin K. Gaines, *Uplifting the Race: Black Leadership, Politics, and Culture in the Twentieth Century* (Chapel Hill: University of North Carolina Press, 1996); Lawrence Levine, "The Concept of the New Negro and the Realities of Black Culture," in Levine, *The Unpredictable Past: Explorations in American Cultural History* (New York: Oxford University Press, 1993), 86–106.

13. Anthony Heilbut, " 'If I Fail, You Tell the World I Tried': William Herbert Brewster on Records," in *"We'll Understand It Better By and By": Pioneering African American Gospel Composers,* ed. Bernice Johnson Reagon (Washington, D.C.: Smithsonian Institution Press, 1992), 234.

14. Jackson also claims authorship of the song. See Bernice Johnson Reagon, "William Herbert Brewster: Rememberings," in *"We'll Understand It Better By and By,"* ed. Reagon, 201.

15. Reagon, "William Herbert Brewster," 201.

16. Horace Clarence Boyer, liner notes, *Mahalia Jackson: Gospels, Spirituals, and Hymns* (Columbia Records, 1991, C2T 47083); Michael W. Harris, *The Rise of Gospel Blues: The Music of Thomas A. Dorsey in the Urban Church* (New York: Oxford University Press, 1992), 241. For an excellent example of performance-oriented folklore, see Ray Allen's *Singing in the Spirit: African-American*

Sacred Quartets in New York City (Philadelphia: University of Pennsylvania Press, 1991).

17. Reagon, "William Herbert Brewster," 191–92.

18. Horace Clarence Boyer, "William Herbert Brewster: The Eloquent Poet," in *"We'll Understand It Better By and By,"* ed. Reagon, 212.

19. Brewster quoted in Reagon, "William Herbert Brewster," 201.

20. Laurraine Goreau, *Just Mahalia, Baby* (Waco, Tex.: Word Books, 1975), 55, emphasis in original; see also Harris, *The Rise of Gospel Blues*, 258.

21. Harris, *The Rise of Gospel Blues*, 194.

22. On Jackson's initial commercial successes, see Anthony Heilbut, *The Gospel Sound: Good News and Bad Times*, reprint (1975; New York: Limelight Editions, 1985), 64–73; Viv Broughton, *Black Gospel: An Illustrated History of the Gospel Sound* (Poole, Dorset: Blandford Press, 1985), 54–56; and Goreau, *Just Mahalia, Baby*, 108–17.

23. John F. Watson, *Methodist Error* (an excerpt from the 1819 book), in *Readings in Black American Music*, ed. Eileen Southern (New York: W. W. Norton, 1971), 63; emphasis in original.

24. George W. Crawford, "Jazzin' God," *Crisis* 3 (February 1929): 45.

25. Jim Haskins, *Queen of the Blues: A Biography of Dinah Washington* (New York: William Morrow, 1987).

26. Arnold Shaw, *Honkers and Shouters: The Golden Years of Rhythm and Blues* (New York: Collier Books, 1978), 144; Haskins, *Queen of the Blues*, 18.

27. Lionel Hampton with James Haskins, *Hamp: An Autobiography* (New York: Warner Books, 1989), 87.

28. Hampton, *Hamp*, 86–87.

29. Shaw, *Honkers and Shouters*, 145.

30. Shaw writes that Washington's penetrating vocal style converged a range of idioms: "Master of all the devices of blues and gospel shading—the bent notes, the broken notes, the slides, the anticipation, and the behind-the-beat notes—she handled them with an intensity that came from her early church training. In time she developed a style of expressive phrasing that was as unique as Sinatra's" (see *Honkers and Shouters*, 146). Nelson George notes the same breadth in Washington's musical palette: "In any given performance, Washington was capable of projecting gospel fervor and jazzy saxophone like phrasing into her achingly bittersweet delivery. This combination made Washington, with the possible exceptions of Billie Holiday and Aretha Franklin afterward, the most poignant female balladeer in American music." See Nelson George, *Death of Rhythm and Blues* (New York: E. P. Dutton, 1989), 74.

31. Phil Hardy and Dave Laing, *The Faber Companion to 20th-Century Popular Music* (London: Faber and Faber, 1990), 825. Shaw observes about this period: "Dinah could do no wrong, even with country ballads like Hank Williams' 'Cold, Cold Heart' and 'I Don't Hurt Anymore,' a Hank Snow hit" (see Shaw, *Honkers and Shouters*, 146). Her endeavors in the pop market over the years reached their zenith in 1959 with the release of the ballad "What a Difference a Day Makes," easily her most commercially successful hit.

32. "Back Water Blues," *The Essential Dinah Washington: The Great Songs* (Verve, 314512905–4). Dinah Washington with the Terry Gibbs Sextet, recorded July 6, 1958, at the Newport Jazz Festival.

33. Haskins, *Queen of the Blues,* 63.

34. Quoted in Shaw, *Honkers and Shouters,* 74.

35. George, *Death of Rhythm and Blues,* 20. Nickelodeons were jukeboxlike machines that played short films of performers on request.

36. Nelson George, *The Death of Rhythm and Blues* (New York: E. P. Dutton, 1989), 20. See also Reebee Garofalo, "Crossing Over: 1939–1989," in *Split Image: African Americans in the Mass Media,* ed. Jannette L. Dates and William Barlow (Washington, D.C.: Howard University Press, 1990), 62–63.

37. Charles Keil, *Urban Blues* (Chicago: University of Chicago Press, 1966), 64.

38. George, *Death of Rhythm and Blues,* 19.

39. Ibid.

40. Jannette L. Dates and William Barlow, "Introduction: A War of Images," in *Split Image,* ed. Dates and Barlow, 2–3.

41. John Chilton, *Let the Good Times Roll: The Story of Louis Jordan and His Music* (London: Quartet Books, 1992), 144.

42. Ibid., 138. See also Dizzy Gillespie and Al Frazer, *To Be or Not to Bop* (Garden City, N.Y.: Doubleday, 1979), 350.

43. Chilton, *Let the Good Times Roll,* 145.

44. Gunther Schuller, *The Swing Era: The Development of Jazz, 1930–1945* (New York: Oxford University Press, 1989), 403.

45. For a discussion of black bands in the early 1940s, see Scott DeVeaux, *The Birth of Bebop: A Social and Musical History* (Berkeley: University of California Press, 1997), 236–69.

46. Vern Montgomery, "Jaws Unlocks," *Jazz Journal International* 36 (July 1983): 14. The tour probably set the stage for Fitzgerald's collaboration with the Ink Spots on the hit record "Into Each Life a Little Rain Must Fall," which sold over a million copies in the mid-1940s.

47. Dave Penny, liner notes, *Billy Eckstine and Cootie Williams 1944: Rhythm in a Riff* (Harlequin, HQ 2068).

48. Francis Paudras, liner notes, *Early Years of a Genius,* vol. 1 (Mythic Sound, MS6001–2). Charlie Holmes, an alto saxophonist with Williams until 1945, also recalled that reading skills in the band were moderate. Stanley Dance, *The World of Swing* (New York: Charles Scribner's Sons, 1974), 255–56. In his IJS Oral History interview, Williams claimed that Monk himself brought the arrangement to a rehearsal.

49. This version can be heard on *The Bebop Era* (Columbia Records, CK 40972). According to Eddie "Lockjaw" Davis, who joined Williams in 1943, "Epistrophy" was the group's theme song. See Montgomery, "Jaws Unlocks," 14.

50. Schuller, *The Swing Era,* 403. Guy played with Monk and Clarke on the live Minton's session recordings from 1941. Some of these recordings can be

heard on *Charlie Christian: Live Sessions at Minton's Playhouse* (Jazz Anthology, 550012).

51. The scripts in the musical examples were taken from *The Real Book*, a legally questionable fake book with which scores of musicians learned many jazz standards like "Epistrophy." For many jazz musicians of my generation and younger, the immediately familiar sight of these handwritten scores conjures memories of the "woodshed," a metaphorical space of practice, dedication, and concentration through which we socialized ourselves into becoming jazz musicians.

52. See, for instance, "Cootie Williams and Band Score at N.Y. Savoy," *Chicago Defender*, April 3, 1943, 18. An appendix to Dance, *The World of Swing*, 404–16, carries a listing of the bands employed in Harlem theaters between March 1931 and March 1945. According to the list, Williams held one-week engagements at the Savoy Ballroom in May and October 1942; January, May, July, and November 1943; and January 1945. The list was compiled by Walter C. Allen and Jerry Valburn from advertisements in the *New York Age* and *New York Amsterdam News*, two publications aimed at the black community. Although helpful, this list cannot be regarded as complete, since Williams probably performed at the Savoy more often than the compilation indicates.

53. *Billboard*, December 16, 1944, 21; January 6, 1945; and February 10, 1945. I thank Scott DeVeaux for these references.

54. Olly Wilson, "Black Music as an Art Form," *Black Music Research Journal* (1983): 7.

55. Gillespie and Frazer, *To Be or Not to Bop*, 484–85.

56. Ibid., 179.

57. Ibid., 192.

CHAPTER 4. "IT JUST STAYS WITH ME ALL OF THE TIME"

1. Arjun Appadurai, *Modernity at Large: Cultural Dimensions of Globalization* (Minneapolis: University of Minnesota Press, 1996), 8.

2. Ibid., 3, 4.

3. These interviews took place in the home of Marjorie. My mother, Celia, and my uncle Bob—the youngest of the siblings—responded to my request to record their stories. Their other brother, Mallie, Jr., declined the interview; their sister Dorothy was deceased at the time of the interviews.

4. Patricia Hill Collins, *Black Feminist Thought: Knowledge, Consciousness, and the Politics of Empowerment* (Boston: Unwin Hyman, 1990), 10.

5. Ibid., xiii.

CHAPTER 5. "WE CALLED OURSELVES MODERN"

1. Marshall Berman, *All That Is Solid Melts into Air: The Experience of Modernity* (New York: Simon and Schuster, 1982), 5.

2. Tera Hunter, *To 'Joy My Freedom: Southern Black Women's Lives and*

Labors after the Civil War (Cambridge, Mass.: Harvard University Press, 1997), 169; see also Lawrence Levine's discussion of the rise of secular song in Levine, *Black Culture, Black Consciousness* (New York: Oxford University Press, 1977), 190–297.

3. George Lipsitz, *Rainbow at Midnight: Labor and Culture in the 1940s* (Urbana: University of Illinois Press, 1994), 22; Dizzy Gillespie and Al Frazer, *To Be or Not to Bop* (Garden City, N.Y.: Doubleday, 1979), 201. For an overview of the social and cultural changes in postwar America, see Lary May's introduction to *Recasting America: Culture and Politics in the Age of the Cold War*, ed. Lary May (Chicago: University of Chicago Press, 1989), 1–16. For discussions on the relationship of bebop to postwar American society, see LeRoi Jones, *Blues People: Negro Music in White America* (New York: William Morrow, 1963), 188–201; Leslie B. Rout, Jr., "Reflections on the Evolution of Postwar Jazz," in *The Black Aesthetic*, ed. Addison Gayle, Jr. (New York: Anchor Books, 1971), 143–53; Eric Lott, "Double V, Double-Time: Bebop's Politics of Style," *Callaloo* 11 (1988): 597–605; Robin D. G. Kelley, "The Riddle of the Zoot: Malcolm Little and Black Cultural Politics during World War II," in Kelley, *Race Rebels: Culture, Politics, and the Black Working Class* (New York: Free Press, 1994), 161–81.

4. See Acklyn Lynch, *Nightmare Overhanging Darkly: Essays on African-American Culture and Resistance* (Chicago: Third World Press, 1993), 53–107, which offers an informative overview of artistic developments among black writers and musicians during the 1940s.

5. These developments in the marketing of black music registered the dramatic economic and social shifts in other realms of African American culture. Black social critic Harold Cruse has discussed some of the economic, ideological, and cultural restlessness present in wartime Harlem.

> Harlem in 1940 was just beginning to emerge from the depths of the Great Depression and it seethed with the currents of many conflicting beliefs and ideologies. It was the year in which Richard Wright reached the high point of fame with *Native Son* and was often seen in Harlem at lectures. The American Negro Theater, a professional experimental group, was preparing to make its 1941 debut as a permanent Harlem institution. The Federal Theater Project had been abolished in 1939 and the echoes of that disaster were still being heard in Harlem's cultural circles. Everything in Harlem seemed to be in a state of flux for reasons that I was not then able to fully appreciate. (Harold Cruse, *The Crisis of the Negro Intellectual: From Its Origins to the Present* [New York: William Morrow, 1967], 3)

6. Russell and David Sanjek, *American Popular Music Business in the 20th Century* (New York: Oxford University Press, 1991), 81–83. See also *Amerigrove*, vol. 1, s.v. "sound recording."

7. George Lipsitz, *Time Passages: Collective Memory and American Popular Culture* (Minneapolis: University of Minnesota Press, 1990), 116–17. Lipsitz writes: "Blacks left the South in large numbers during the 1940s, and during the

war years alone 750,000 whites moved to Los Angeles and more than 200,000 moved to Detroit."

8. For an excellent essay on the relationship among the rapidly changing worlds of postwar science, literature, medicine, and music, see Charles Hamm, "Changing Patterns in Society and Music: The U.S. since World War II," in *Contemporary Music and Music Cultures*, ed. Charles Hamm, Bruno Nettl, and Ronald Byrnside (Englewood Cliffs, N.J.: Prentice-Hall, 1975), 35–70.

9. See Herbert Aptheker, ed., *A Documentary History of the Negro People in the United States*, vol. 4: *1933–45* (New York: Citadel Press, 1974), 466. The article, written in anticipation of the 1944 elections, originally appeared in Walter White et al., "A Declaration by Negro Voters," *Crisis* 51 (January 1944): 16–17. The declaration provoked much attention in the black press and received "some notice in major white newspapers" (Aptheker, *A Documentary History*, 465). For more on the changing face of black politics during the 1940s, see John Hope Franklin and Alfred A. Moss, Jr., *From Slavery to Freedom: A History of Negro Americans* (New York: McGraw-Hill, 1988), 413–15. See also Manning Marable, *Race, Reform, and Rebellion: The Second Reconstruction in Black America, 1945–1990* (Jackson, Miss.: University Press of Mississippi, 1991), 13–39. Despite the aggressive antisegregation stance described above, Marable notes that a certain dubiety existed among African Americans as they celebrated the end of World War II in August 1945. High hopes were tempered by the knowledge of history and by fears of another antiblack backlash like the "Red Summer of 1919," which followed World War I. In those uprisings many acts of violence were aimed at African Americans, including seventy lynchings and the murder of ten black veterans of World War I.

10. Stuart Hall, "What Is This 'Black' in Black Popular Culture?" in *Black Popular Culture*, ed. Gina Dent (Seattle: Bay Press, 1992), 27; Hall quoted in Susan McClary and Robert Walser, "Theorizing the Body in African-American Music," *Black Music Research Journal* 14, no. 1 (spring 1994): 79.

11. Lerone Bennett, *Before the Mayflower: A History of Black America*, 5th ed. (Chicago: Johnson Publishing Co., 1982), 541. See Jacqueline Jones, *Labor of Love, Labor of Sorrow: Black Women, Work and the Family, from Slavery to the Present*, reprint (New York: Vintage Books, 1986), 236. See also Franklin and Moss, *From Slavery to Freedom*, 403; Earl Brown, "The Detroit Race Riot of 1943," in *A Documentary History*, ed. Aptheker, 443–53; and Dominic J. Capeci, *The Harlem Riot of 1943* (Philadelphia: Temple University Press, 1977).

12. Marable, *Race, Reform, and Rebellion*, 16; Mary Frances Berry and John Blassingame, *Long Memory: The Black Experience in America* (New York: Oxford University Press, 1982), 199. The increase in employment opportunities came in several defense-related sectors of commerce, most notably, according to Franklin and Moss, the "aircraft, electronics, automotive, and chemical industries" (Franklin and Moss, *From Slavery to Freedom*, 413).

13. Marable, *Race, Reform, and Rebellion*, 16–18; Berry and Blassingame, *Long Memory*, 199.

14. Quoted in Jacqueline Jones, *Labor of Love*, 233.

15. Lipsitz, *Rainbow at Midnight*, 20.

16. Nicholas Lemann, *The Promised Land: The Great Migration and How It Changed America* (New York: Vintage Books, 1991), 6–7; Farah Griffin, "Who Set You Flowin'?" *The African-American Migration Narrative* (New York: Oxford University Press, 1995), 3.

17. See Hazel V. Carby, "Policing the Black Woman's Body in an Urban Context," *Critical Inquiry* 18 (summer 1992): 738–55; and Hazel V. Carby, "'It Just Be's Dat Way Sometime': The Sexual Politics of Women's Blues," in *Unequal Sisters: A Multicultural Reader in U.S. Women's History*, ed. Ellen Carol DuBois and Vicki L. Ruiz (New York: Routledge, 1990), 238–49; Lemann, *The Promised Land*, 99. See also E. Franklin Frazier, *The Black Bourgeoisie: The Rise of a New Middle Class in the United States* (New York: Collier Books, 1957). Many northern cities experienced similar patterns; see, for example, an anthropological and sociological discussion of class stratification in Newark, New Jersey: Linwood H. Cousins, "Community High: The Study of Race and Class in a Black Community and High School," Ph.D. diss., University of Michigan, 1994.

18. Thelonious Monk quoted in Nat Hentoff, *The Jazz Life* (1961; New York: Da Capo Press, 1975), 195.

19. See, for example, Lott, "Double V, Double-Time"; Kelley, "The Riddle of the Zoot"; Guthrie Ramsey, "The Art of Bebop: Earl Bud Powell and the Emergence of Modern Jazz," Ph.D. diss., University of Michigan, 1994; Ingrid Monson, "The Problem with White Hipness: Race, Gender, and Cultural Conceptions in Jazz Historical Discourse," *Journal of the American Musicological Society* 48, no. 3 (fall 1995): 396–422.

20. Houston A. Baker, Jr., *Modernism and the Harlem Renaissance* (Chicago: University of Chicago Press, 1987), xiv–xv. For other discussions of the ideals of freedom and literacy with regard to black expressive culture, see also Samuel A. Floyd, Jr., *The Power of Black Music* (New York: Oxford University Press, 1995), 88; and Robert B. Stepto, *From Behind the Veil: A Study of Afro-American Narrative*, 2d ed. (Urbana: University of Chicago, 1991), 167–68.

21. My discussion of modernism and its relationship to black culture is shaped by the following works: Raymond Williams, *Keywords: A Vocabulary of Culture and Society*, rev. ed. (New York: Oxford University Press, 1985), 208–9; Dick Hebdige, "After the Masses," in *Culture/Power/History: A Reader in Contemporary Social Theory*, ed. Nicholas B. Dirks, Geoff Eley, and Sherry B. Ortner (Princeton, N.J.: Princeton University Press, 1994), 222–35; Andreas Huyssen, *After the Great Divide: Modernism, Mass Culture, Postmodernism* (Bloomington: Indiana University Press, 1986), vii–xii; Baker, *Modernism and the Harlem Renaissance*; Richard J. Powell, *The Blues Aesthetic: Black Culture and Modernism* (Washington, D.C.: Washington Project for the Arts, 1989); Michele Wallace, "Modernism, Postmodernism and the Problem of the Visual in Afro-American Culture," in *Out There: Marginalization and Contemporary Cultures*, ed. Russell Ferguson, Martha Gever, Trinh T. Minh-ha, and Cornel West (Cambridge, Mass.: MIT Press in association with the New Museum of Contemporary

Art, New York, 1990), 39–50; Stepto, *From Behind the Veil;* Craig Hansen Werner, "Bigger's Blues: *Native Son* and the Articulation of Afro-American Modernism," in Werner, *Playing the Changes: From Afro-Modernism to the Jazz Impulse* (Urbana: University of Illinois, 1994), 183–211. For more specific discussions on black music and its relationship to various notions of modernity, see Samuel A. Floyd, Jr., ed., *Black Music in the Harlem Renaissance* (Westport, Conn.: Greenwood Press, 1990); Paul Gilroy, *The Black Atlantic: Modernity and Double-Consciousness* (Cambridge, Mass.: Harvard University Press, 1993), 72–110; Ronald M. Radano, "Soul Texts and the Blackness of Folk," *Modernism/Modernity* 2, no. 1 (1995): 71–95; Ronald M. Radano, "Denoting Difference: The Writing of the Slave Spirituals," *Critical Inquiry* 22, no. 3 (spring 1996): 506–44; Krin Gabbard, "Introduction: The Jazz Canon and Its Consequences," in *Jazz among the Discourses,* ed. Gabbard (Durham, N.C.: Duke University Press, 1995), 1–28; Mark S. Harvey, "Jazz and Modernism: Changing Conceptions of Innovation and Tradition," in *Jazz in Mind: Essays on the History and Meanings of Jazz,* ed. Reginald T. Buckner and Steven Weiland (Detroit: Wayne State University Press, 1991), 128–47.

22. Charles Hamm, "Modernist Narratives and Popular Music," in Hamm, *Putting Popular Music in Its Place* (Cambridge: Cambridge University Press, 1995), 1–40; David Brackett, *Interpreting Popular Music* (Cambridge: Cambridge University Press, 1995), 19. Brackett models his thinking after Simon Frith's groundbreaking sociological work in popular music studies. See, for example, Simon Frith, *Performing Rites: On the Value of Popular Music* (Cambridge, Mass.: Harvard University Press, 1996), especially 21–46.

23. William Austin, *Music in the Twentieth Century: From Debussy through Stravinsky* (New York: W. W. Norton, 1966), 289, 291.

24. Henry Louis Gates, Jr., "Authority, (White) Power and the (Black) Critic: It's All Greek to Me," in *Culture/Power/History: A Reader in Contemporary Social Theory,* eds. Nicolas B. Dirks, Geoff Eley, and Sherry B. Ortner (Princeton, N.J.: Princeton University Press, 1994), 245–68. Originally in *Cultural Critique,* no. 7 (fall 1987): 19–46.

25. Lott, "Double V, Double-Time," 597, 599, my emphasis; Cornel West, "On Afro-American Popular Music: From Bebop to Rap," in West, *Prophetic Fragments: Illuminations of the Crisis in American Religion and Culture* (Grand Rapids, Mich.: William B. Eerdmans Publishing Company, 1988), 178, my emphasis; LeRoi Jones, "Jazz and the White Critic," in Jones, *Black Music* (New York: William Morrow, 1967), 16.

26. Richard Leppert and Susan McClary, eds., *Music and Society: The Politics of Composition, Performance and Reception* (Cambridge: Cambridge University Press, 1987), xi–xix.

27. See my "Cosmopolitan or Provincial? Ideology in Early Black Music Historiography, 1867–1940," *Black Music Research Journal* 16, no. 1 (spring 1996): 11–42.

28. See Janet Wolff, "The Ideology of Autonomous Art," in *Music and Society,* ed. Leppert and McClary, 1–12, for a historical overview of the idea of

autonomy in the arts. For an insightful discussion of positivism, objectivity, and formalism in academic music study, see Joseph Kerman, *Contemplating Music: Challenges to Musicology* (Cambridge, Mass.: Harvard University Press, 1985).

29. Madhu Dubey, *Black Women Novelists and the Nationalist Aesthetic* (Bloomington: Indiana University Press, 1994), 1–32, has a helpful discussion of the relationship between black feminist literature and Black Cultural Nationalism. I thank Farah Griffin for bringing this work to my attention.

30. James Monroe Trotter, *Music and Some Highly Musical People* (1878; New York: Charles T. Dillingham, 1881), 3. See also Ramsey, "Cosmopolitan or Provincial?" 15–18; Robert Stevenson, "America's First Black Music Historian," *Journal of the American Musicological Society* 26, no. 3 (1973): 383–404; and Stephen R. Fox, *The Guardian of Boston: William Monroe Trotter* (New York: Atheneum, 1971).

31. Leppert and McClary, *Music and Society*, xiii.

32. See Ramsey, "Cosmopolitan or Provincial?"

33. For a representative sample of Martin Williams's jazz criticism, see *The Jazz Tradition*, 2d rev. ed. (New York: Oxford University Press, 1993). Gunther Schuller's 1958 essay "Sonny Rollins and the Challenge of Thematic Improvisation," which argues for a "compositional" approach in the analysis of jazz improvisation, was widely influential in the "jazz as art" movement. See Schuller, *Musings: The Musical Worlds of Gunther Schuller* (New York: Oxford University Press, 1986), 86–97. As I argue, Leonard Feather's *Inside Jazz* (1949; New York: Da Capo Press, 1977) can certainly be interpreted as a "political" document on many levels. For a brilliant discussion of Williams's and Schuller's jazz criticism, see John Gennari, "Jazz Criticism: Its Development and Ideologies," *Black American Literature Forum* 25 (fall 1991): 449–519.

34. Robert Bone, "Richard Wright and the Chicago Renaissance," *Callaloo* 9, no. 3 (1986): 446–68, marks the Chicago movement between the years 1935 and 1950. Floyd's *Power of Black Music* discusses the musical aspect of the Chicago Renaissance. See also Rae Linda Brown, "The Woman's Symphony Orchestra of Chicago and Florence B. Price's *Piano Concerto in One Movement*," *American Music* 11 (summer 1993): 185–205.

35. VéVé Clark, "Developing Diaspora Literacy and Marasa Consciousness," in *Comparative American Identities: Race, Sex, and Nationality in the Modern Text*, ed. Hortense J. Spillers (New York: Routledge, 1991), 40.

36. Ibid.

37. Nathan Irving Huggins, *Harlem Renaissance* (New York: Oxford University Press, 1971), 3.

38. Cary D. Wintz, *Black Culture and the Harlem Renaissance* (Houston: Rice University Press, 1988), 217.

39. See, for example, Wintz, *Black Culture*, 217–32. See also John A. Williams, "The Harlem Renaissance: Its Artists, Its Impact, Its Meaning," *Black World* (November 1970): 17–18; Arna Bontemps, "The Black Renaissance of the Twenties," *Black World* (November 1970): 5–9.

40. Robert A. Bone, "The Background of the Negro Renaissance," in *Black*

History: A Reappraisal, ed. Melvin Drimmer (Garden City, N.Y.: Anchor Books, 1969), 410–11; reprinted from Robert A. Bone, *The Negro Novel in America,* rev. ed. (New Haven, Conn.: Yale University Press, 1965).

41. Gilbert Osofsky, " 'Come Out from among Them': Negro Migration and Settlement, 1890–1914," in *Black History,* ed. Drimmer, 375, 411, 378; reprinted from Gilbert Osofsky, *Harlem: The Making of a Ghetto* (New York: Harper and Row, 1966).

42. Huggins, *Harlem Renaissance,* 14; Nathan Irving Huggins, ed., *Voices from the Harlem Renaissance* (New York: Oxford University Press), 45.

43. Huggins, *Harlem Renaissance,* 14, 5–6.

44. Sidney H. Bremer, "Home in Harlem, New York: Lessons from the Harlem Renaissance Writers," *PMLA* 105, no. 1 (January 1990): 48.

45. Samuel B. Charters and Leonard Kunstadt, *Jazz: A History of the New York Scene,* reprint (1962; New York: Da Capo Press, 1981), 193–205, 138–39.

46. Eileen Southern, *The Music of Black Americans: A History,* 2d ed. (New York: W. W. Norton, 1983), 400.

47. Gunther Schuller, *Early Jazz: Its Roots and Musical Development* (New York: Oxford University Press), 246.

48. The quoted phrases come from Claude McKay, *Harlem: Negro Metropolis* (New York: E. P. Dutton, 1940), 16.

49. Alain Locke, ed., *The New Negro* (1925; New York: Atheneum, 1992), xxvii.

50. Arnold Rampersad, Introduction to Locke, ed., *The New Negro,* ix–xxiii.

51. Ibid., xxi.

52. Locke, ed., *The New Negro,* xxvi.

53. Rampersad, Introduction to Locke, ed., *The New Negro,* xxiii.

54. See Paul Burgett, "Vindication as a Thematic Principle in the Writings of Alain Locke on the Music of Black Americans," in *Black Music in the Harlem Renaissance,* ed. Floyd, 29–40, for discussion of Locke's views on jazz and vernacular black music. For an alternate interpretation of the role of blues and jazz in the Harlem Renaissance dogma, see Kathy J. Ogren, *The Jazz Revolution: Twenties America and the Meaning of Jazz* (New York: Oxford University Press, 1989), 111–38.

55. In his essay "Jazz at Home," in *The New Negro: Voice of the Harlem Renaissance,* ed. Alain Locke (1925; New York: Atheneum, 1992), J. A. Rogers tersely regards Bessie Smith and other blues and jazz performers as inimitable, inventive, and skilled artists. However, throughout the rest of the piece, he values work such as theirs primarily as source material—as something to "lift and divert into nobler channels" (224).

56. Rampersad, Foreword to Locke, ed., *The New Negro,* xix–xxi.

57. Floyd, "Music in the Harlem Renaissance: An Overview," in *Black Music in the Harlem Renaissance,* ed. Floyd, 3–4.

58. See Houston A. Baker, Jr., *Modernism and the Harlem Renaissance* (Chicago: University of Chicago Press, 1987), 91–92.

59. Ibid., 71, 73.

60. Peter Guralnick, *Sweet Soul Music: Rhythm and Blues and the Southern Dream of Freedom* (New York: Harper and Row, 1986), 34.

61. See Scott DeVeaux, *The Birth of Bebop: A Social and Musical History* (Berkeley: University of California Press, 1997), for the best account of this transitional moment in jazz. See also Arnold Shaw, *52nd St.: The Street of Jazz* (1971; New York: Da Capo Press, 1977), xi.

62. Quoted in Guralnick, *Sweet Soul Music*, 60.

63. Michael Cuscuna and Michel Ruppli, *The Blue Note Label: A Discography* (New York: Greenwood Press, 1988), xi, xiii. See also Brian Priestly, *Jazz on Record: A History* (1988; New York: Billboard Books, 1991), 75.

64. Dan Morgenstern, liner notes, *The Changing Face of Harlem: The Savoy Sessions* (Savoy, SJL 2208), cited in Scott DeVeaux, "Bebop and the Recording Industry: The 1942 AFM Recording Ban Reconsidered," *Journal of the American Musicological Society* 41 (spring 1988): 152. For information on the Savoy label, see *JazzGrove*, vol. 2, s.v. "Savoy."

65. *JazzGrove*, vol. 2, s.v. "Savoy."

66. Cuscuna and Ruppli, *The Blue Note Label*, xiv.

67. Guralnick, *Sweet Soul Music*, 61.

68. DeVeaux, "Bebop and the Recording Industry," 162.

69. Ben Sidran, *Black Talk* (1971; New York: Da Capo Press, 1980), especially xxiii; Dates and Barlow, *Split Image*, 10. See also Henry Louis Gates, Jr., ed., *"Race," Writing, and Difference* (Chicago: University of Chicago Press, 1986), 1–20. Elaborating on that theme, Gates contends that, since the Enlightenment, Europeans have used formal literature, arts, and sciences to measure the so-called African "species of men." "So, while the Enlightenment is characterized by its foundation on man's ability to reason," Gates writes, "it simultaneously used the absence and presence of reason to delimit and circumscribe the very humanity of the cultures and people of color which Europeans had been 'discovering' since the Renaissance" (8). Thus, for Phillis Wheatley, an African-born American poet, and other antebellum blacks, writing became not merely "an activity of the mind, rather, it was a commodity which they were forced to trade for their humanity" (9).

70. Michael W. Harris, *The Rise of Gospel Blues: The Music of Thomas Andrew Dorsey in the Urban Church* (New York: Oxford University Press, 1992), 267; see also C. Eric Lincoln and Lawrence H. Mamiya, *The Black Church in the African-American Experience* (Durham, N.C.: Duke University Press, 1990), 356–57; Eileen Southern, "Hymnals of the Black Church," *Black Perspective in Music* 17 (1989): 20–46; and Jon Michael Spencer, *Black Hymnody: A Hymnological History of the African-American Church* (Knoxville: University of Tennessee Press, 1992).

71. Richard Crawford, *The American Musical Landscape* (Berkeley: University of California Press, 1993), 104.

72. Leonard Feather, "Goffin, *Esquire* and the Moldy Figs," in Feather, *The Jazz Years: Earwitness to an Era* (New York: Da Capo Press, 1987), 80.

73. Quoted in Feather, "Goffin, *Esquire* and the Moldy Figs," 82. *Esquire's*

progressive musical policy continued for the next four years and lauded the achievements of black jazz musicians. When *Esquire's* editorial board changed in 1947, however, the publication became a platform for the proponents of older styles of jazz, represented by Eddie Condon and others. The abrupt policy shift, which was protested strongly by many prominent black jazz musicians, observes Feather, "marked the end of the Esquire era" (89–94).

74. Robert Goffin, ed., *Esquire's 1944 Jazz Year Book* (New York: Smith and Durrell, 1944), ix.

75. Bernard Gendron, "Moldy Figs and Modernists: Jazz at War (1942–1946)," *Discourse* 15 (spring 1993): 133. Gendron describes the aesthetic discourse as "a grouping of concepts, distinctions, oppositions, rhetorical ploys, and allowable inferences, which as a whole fixed the limits within which inquiries concerning the aesthetics of jazz could take place, and without which the claims that jazz is an art form would be merely an abstraction or an incantation." The aesthetic discourse, Gendron argues, highlights "the crucial role of what Michel Foucault has called 'discursive formations' in the constitution of jazz modernism." I thank Robert Walser for this reference.

76. Feather, *Inside Jazz*, quotations from unpaginated front matter.

77. Ibid.

78. Ibid., 4, 11.

79. Ibid., 15, 25.

80. Ibid., 24.

81. See Abby Arthur Johnson and Ronald Maberry Johnson, *Propaganda and Aesthetics: The Literary Politics of African-American Magazines in the Twentieth Century* (Amherst, Mass.: University of Massachusetts Press, 1991), 125–59, 126–27. The Boyer article actually appeared in 1948; see Richard O. Boyer, "Bop," *New Yorker*, July 3, 1948, 28–37.

82. Quoted in Johnson and Johnson, *Propaganda and Aesthetics*, 150, emphasis in the original.

83. Alain Locke, "Self Criticism: The Third Dimension in Culture," *Phylon* 11 (4th quarter, 1950): 392–94, cited in Johnson and Johnson, *Propaganda and Aesthetics*, 148.

84. Feather, *The Jazz Years*, 125.

85. Gillespie and Frazer, *To Be or Not to Bop*, 311.

86. Geoffrey Jacques, "Cubop! Afro-Cuban Music and Mid-Twentieth Century American Culture," in *Between Race and Empire: African-Americans and Cubans Before the Cuban Revolution*, ed. Lisa Brock and Digna Castañeda Fuertes (Philadelphia: Temple University Press, 1991), 249–65. I thank Robin D. G. Kelley for pointing me toward this reference.

87. Quoted in Lisa Brock, "Introduction: Between Race and Empire," in *Between Race and Empire*, ed. Brock and Castañeda Fuertes, 27.

88. Ibid., 20.

89. *The Amazing Bud Powell*, vol. 1 (Blue Note, CDP 7 81503 2).

90. Gillespie and Frazer, *To Be or Not to Bop*, 206–7.

91. John Miller Chernoff, *African Rhythm and African Sensibility: Aes-*

thetics and Social Action in African Musical Idioms (Chicago: University of Chicago Press, 1979), 111–12.

CHAPTER 6. "GOIN' TO CHICAGO"

1. LeRoi Jones [later known as Amiri Baraka], *Black Music* (New York: William Morrow, 1967), 20.

2. John W. Roberts, "African American Diversity and the Study of Folklore," *Western Folklore* 52 (April 1993): 157.

3. James Brown, *Star Time*, disk 2 (Polygram Records, 849 111–2, 1993).

4. James Weldon Johnson and J. Rosamond Johnson, eds., "Lift Every Voice and Sing," in *Songs of Zion* (Nashville: Abingdon Press, 1981), 32.

5. James Brown "Santa Claus, Go Straight to the Ghetto," *James Brown's Funky Christmas* (Polygram, 31452 7988–2, 1995); originally released in December 1968.

6. The term *color-struck* refers to a once prevalent intrablack attitude of bigotry in which fairer-skinned African Americans are valued more than those with darker complexions. Although this attitude still exists among some African Americans, it was exposed during the 1960s Black Power revolution. This color prejudice may also be harbored by darker-skinned blacks against those with lighter skin.

7. David Brackett, "James Brown's 'Superbad' and the Double-Voiced Utterance," in Brackett, *Interpreting Popular Music* (Cambridge: Cambridge University Press, 1995), 121.

8. On the "cut" in black music, see James A. Snead, "Repetition as a Figure of Black Culture," in *Black Literature and Literary Theory*, ed. Henry Louis Gates, Jr. (New York: Routledge, 1984), 59–79.

9. Zora Neale Hurston, "Characteristics of Negro Expression," in *Within the Circle: An Anthology of African-American Literary Criticism from the Harlem Renaissance to the Present*, ed. Angelyn Mitchell (Durham, N.C.: Duke University Press, 1994), 80.

10. My performing experience in both of these accompaniment practices confirms for me that funk and bebop accompaniment presents a set of idiom-specific challenges for musicians that require diligent practice and discipline in order to capture the spirit and nuance in each.

11. Ron Wellburn, "The Black Aesthetic Imperative," in *The Black Aesthetic*, ed. Addison Gayle, Jr. (1971; Garden City, N.Y.: Anchor Books, 1972), 133.

12. At least two writers have characterized James Brown's "race man" status as conflicted and contradictory. Both Nelson George and Brian Ward point out that Brown's belief in bootstrap mentality led him to blindly support Richard Nixon's "black capitalism as black deliverance" mantra. George critiques Brown's machismo attitude, which paralleled that of other male Black Power advocates of the time. In my view, these factors, in truth, make Brown a pretty typical example of a race man.

13. Ann du Cille, "The Occult of True Black Womanhood," *Signs* 19, no. 3 (spring 1994): 593.

14. Madhu Dubey, *Black Women Novelists and the Nationalist Aesthetic* (Bloomington: Indiana University Press, 1994), 4. I thank Farah J. Griffin for this reference.

15. Samuel A. Floyd, Jr., "Eileen Southern: Quiet Revolutionary," in *New Perspectives on Music: Essays in Honor of Eileen Southern,* ed. Josephine Wright with Samuel A. Floyd, Jr. (Warren, Mich.: Harmonie Park Press, 1992), 6–7. Southern's subsequent research developed into a book-length project and has since encouraged additional work in the field, including musical biography and autobiography; archival and oral histories; systematic research on jazz and blues; the compilation of bibliographies and indexes; ethnographic studies; critical editions; and much more. *The Music of Black Americans* stands as an important symbol of the epoch in which it first appeared, even as it filled a glaring lacuna in American musical scholarship as a whole.

16. Southern, *The Music of Black Americans,* 1st ed. (New York: W. W. Norton, 1971), xv.

17. A suggestive sample of this work can be found in Eileen Southern, ed., *Readings in Black American Music,* 2d ed. (New York: W. W. Norton, 1983), which has several instructive essays by black composers such as Olly Wilson, T. J. Anderson, and Hale Smith. See also Gayle, ed., *The Black Aesthetic,* 1971.

18. Floyd, "Eileen Southern," 14.

19. Ibid., 7.

20. Southern, *Music of Black Americans* (1971), xvi.

21. Ibid.

22. For an excellent comparison of *Blues People* and *The Music of Black Americans,* see Richard Crawford, "On Two Traditions of Black Music Research," *Black Music Research Journal* (1986): 1–9. Each of these works, Crawford writes, "seems the most complete embodiment of its approach to the subject" (2).

23. Sidney Finkelstein's *Jazz: A People's Music* (1948; New York: Da Capo Press, 1975) also treats political economy but does not deal with the history of black music.

24. Bruce Tucker, "Editor's Introduction: Black Music after Theory," *Black Music Research Journal* 11, no. 2 (fall 1991): v; see also John Genarri, "Jazz Criticism."

25. Ralph Ellison, "Blues People," in Ellison, *Shadow and Act* (New York: Vintage Books, 1972), 247–58. In a brilliant essay titled "Looking for the 'Real' Nigga: Social Scientists Construct the Ghetto," historian Robin D. G. Kelley provides an excellent critique of "ghetto ethnographers" from the 1960s to the 1980s by questioning the "scientific" quest for and the creation of "authentic" black culture. See Kelley, *Yo' Mama's Disfunktional! Fighting the Culture Wars in Urban America* (Boston: Beacon Press, 1997), 15–42. Although Kelley does not engage Jones/Baraka's work in the essay, many aspects of *Blues People* flatten out

difference within urban black musical culture. As Kelley writes: "By conceiving black urban culture in the singular, interpreters unwittingly reduce their subjects to cardboard typologies who fit neatly into their own definition of the 'underclass' and render invisible a wide array of complex cultural forms and practices" (17). In my view, Jones was more successful in capturing a more nuanced black culture in his fictional writing such as the short story "The Screamers," in which he describes a social dance. See *The LeRoi Jones/Amiri Baraka Reader*, ed. William J. Harris (New York: Thunder's Mouth Press, 1991), 171–78.

26. Jones, *Black Music*, 20.

27. Charles Keil, *Urban Blues* (Chicago: University of Chicago Press, 1966), 1. Keil's work uses the tools of his home discipline, anthropology, but it is also informed by the tenets of black cultural nationalism, tenets that the author apparently embraced.

28. Ibid., vii.

29. Keil, *Urban Blues*, 2d ed. (Chicago: University of Chicago Press, 1991), 225.

30. Ibid., 236.

31. Schuller, *Early Jazz*, ix.

32. Ibid.

33. Schuller, *Early Jazz*, ix; Levine, *Black Culture*, xi; Dena J. Epstein, *Sinful Tunes and Spirituals: Black Folk Music to the Civil War* (Urbana: University of Illinois Press, 1977), xiii–xvii.

34. Keil, *Urban Blues* (1991), 236.

35. Levine, *Black Culture*, xiii.

36. See, for example, Portia K. Maultsby: "Music of Northern Independent Black Music," *Ethnomusicology* 19 (September 1975): 421–49; and "Black Spirituals: An Analysis of Textual Forms and Structures," *Black Perspective in Music* 4 (spring 1976): 54–69.

37. See, for example, Horace Clarence Boyer: "An Overview: Gospel Music Comes of Age," *Black World* 23 (November 1973): 42–48, 79–86; "Analysis of His Contributions: Thomas A. Dorsey, Father of Gospel Music," *Black World* 23 (July 1974): 20–28; and "Contemporary Gospel Music: Sacred or Secular?" *First World* 1 (January/February 1977): 46–49.

38. For information on the black literary magazines of the Black Arts movement, see Johnson and Johnson, *Propaganda and Aesthetics*, 161–200.

39. Jacqueline Cogdell DjeDje, *American Black Spirituals and Gospel Songs from Southeast Georgia: A Comparative Study* (Los Angeles: University of California Center for Afro-American Studies, 1978).

40. For an extensive listing of this area of scholarship, see Irene V. Jackson, *Afro-American Religious Music—A Bibliography and Catalogue of Gospel Music* (Westport, Conn.: Greenwood Press, 1979).

41. Olly Wilson, "The Significance of the Relationship between Afro-American Music and West African Music," *Black Perspective in Music* 2, no. 1 (spring 1974): 3–22; and Pearl Williams-Jones, "Afro-American Gospel Music: Crystallization of the Black Aesthetic," *Ethnomusicology* 19 (1975): 373–85. Kofi

Agawu, "The Invention of African Rhythm," *Journal of the American Musicological Society* 48, no. 3 (fall 1995): 380–95, questions the validity of earlier conceptions of rhythm in conventional views of "African music" and forwards one that he believes is "phenomenologically truer to the African experience" (395).

CHAPTER 7. SCORING A BLACK NATION

1. Winfrey has even exercised power over literary discourse in this country. Whenever she identified a book for her televised "book club," sales skyrocketed. This influence over what many Americans read is ironic when one considers the case of the eighteenth-century black female poet Phillis Wheatley, who had to prove to her detractors that a black woman could indeed even write.

2. For an excellent collection of essays that discuss an African American "style" in music, sports, and other expressive practices, see Gina Dagel Caponi, ed., *Signifyin(g), Sanctifyin', and Slam Dunking: A Reader in African American Expressive Culture* (Amherst: University of Massachusetts Press, 1999).

3. Tricia Rose, *Black Noise: Rap Music and Black Culture in Contemporary America* (Hanover, N.H.: University Press of New England, 1994), 34.

4. For important book-length studies on rap music and hip-hop culture, see Rose, *Black Noise;* David Toop, *Rap Attack 2: African Rap to Global Hip-Hop,* 2d ed. (1984; London: Blackstock Mews, 1991); William Eric Perkins, ed., *Droppin' Science: Critical Essays on Rap Music and Hip-Hop Culture* (Philadelphia: Temple University Press, 1996); and James G. Spady et al., *Street Conscious Rap* (Philadelphia: UMUM Press, 1999).

5. The Sugarhill Gang, "Rapper's Delight," *Hip-Hop Greats: Classic Raps* (Rhino, R270957).

6. Ralph Ellison, "The Shadow and the Act," in Ellison, *Shadow and Act* (New York: Vintage Books, 1972), 275.

7. *Do the Right Thing,* written and directed by Spike Lee (film, Universal City Studios, 1989); *Boyz N the Hood,* written and directed by John Singleton (film, Columbia Pictures, 1991); *Love Jones,* written and directed by Theodore Witcher (film, New Line, 1997).

8. Robin D. G. Kelley, *Yo' Mama's Disfunktional! Fighting the Culture Wars in Urban America* (Boston: Beacon Press, 1997), 44.

9. Quoted in Henry Louis Gates, Jr., "Must Buppiehood Cost Homeboy His Soul?" Arts and Leisure Section, *New York Times,* March 1, 1992, 12.

10. Ibid.

11. Ibid, 13.

12. Michele Wallace, "Boyz N the Hood and Jungle Fever," in *Black Popular Culture,* ed. Gina Dent (Seattle: Bay Press, 1992), 123.

13. Valerie Smith, "The Documentary Impulse in Contemporary African American Film," in *Black Popular Culture,* ed. Dent, 58.

14. Lisa Kennedy, "The Body in Question," in *Black Popular Culture,* ed. Dent, 110.

15. Claudia Gorbman, *Unheard Melodies: Narrative Film Music* (Bloomington: University of Indiana, 1987), 6.

16. Anahid Kassabian, *Hearing Film: Tracking Identifications in Contemporary Hollywood Film Music* (New York: Routledge, 2001), 1.

17. Ibid., 2.

18. Gorbman, *Unheard Melodies*, 4.

19. *In This Our Life*, directed by John Huston, with a score by Max Steiner (film, Warner Brothers, 1942).

20. Kassabian, *Hearing Film*, 3.

21. Ibid.

22. Ibid., 44–45.

23. S. Craig Watkins, *Representing: Hip Hop Culture and the Production of Black Cinema* (Chicago: University of Chicago Press), 108.

24. Victoria E. Johnson, "Polyphony and Cultural Expression: Interpreting Musical Traditions in *Do the Right Thing*," in *Spike Lee's Do the Right Thing*, ed. Mark A. Reid (Cambridge: Cambridge University Press, 1997), 50–72.

25. The original score is played by the Natural Spiritual Orchestra, William Lee, conductor. It is configured as a string orchestra and jazz combo, featuring Branford Marsalis, Terrance Blanchard, Kenny Barron, Jeff Watts, and other noted jazz musicians.

26. Johnson, "Polyphony and Cultural Expression," 52.

27. Gorbman, *Unheard Melodies*, 3.

28. bell hooks, *Yearning: Race, Gender, and Cultural Politics* (Boston: South End Press, 1990), 181.

29. I thank ethnomusicologist Kyra Gaunt for her assistance in naming some of these dance steps.

30. See Juan Flores, "Puerto Rocks: New York Ricans Stake Their Claim," in *Droppin' Science: Critical Essays on Rap Music and Hip-Hop Culture*, ed. William Eric Perkins (Philadelphia: Temple University Press, 1996), 85–105.

31. James Brown, "Lickin' Stick," *James Brown: Star Time* (Polydor, 8491082).

32. Frances R. Aparicio, *Listening to Salsa: Gender, Latin Popular Music, and Puerto Rican Cultures* (Hanover, N.H.: University Press of New England, 1998), 188.

33. Lee's uncomplicated construction of Radio Raheem (and that of other characters in many of his films) has been flatly criticized by critics such as bell hooks and Stanley Crouch. Upbraiding the filmmaker for his use of stereotypes, hooks wrote that while Lee "provides many characters, they have no complexity." For an example of critiques of Lee's characterization, see bell hooks, *Yearning*, 176; Stanley Crouch, *Notes of a Hanging Judge: Essays and Reviews, 1979–1988* (New York: Oxford University Press), 237–44.

34. Smith, "The Documentary Impulse in Contemporary African American Film," 59.

35. New Jack Swing describes a dance-oriented style that combines hip-hop production techniques and the traditions of soul and rhythm and blues singing.

36. Watkins, *Representing*, 233.

CHAPTER 8. "SANTA CLAUS AIN'T GOT NOTHING ON THIS!"

1. Sidney W. Mintz and Richard Price, *An Anthropological Approach to the Afro-American Past: A Caribbean Perspective* (Philadelphia: Institute for the Study of Human Issues, 1976), quoted in Hans A. Baer and Merrill Singer, *African-American Religion in the Twentieth Century: Varieties of Protest and Accommodation* (Knoxville: University of Tennessee Press, 1982), 1.

2. See Susan McClary, *Conventional Wisdom: The Content of Form* (Berkeley: University of California Press, 2001).

3. See Robert Walser, "Rhythm, Rhyme, and Rhetoric in the Music of Public Enemy," *Ethnomusicology* 39, no. 2 (spring–summer 1995): 193–218.

4. The term *Signifyin(g)* is capped throughout this chapter for consistency with Gates's usage.

5. David Brackett, "James Brown's 'Superbad' and the Double Voiced Utterance," *Popular Music* 11 (1992): 309–23; Samuel A. Floyd, Jr., *The Power of Black Music: Interpreting Its History from Africa to the United States* (New York: Oxford University Press, 1995); Ingrid Monson, "Doubleness and Jazz Improvisation: Irony, Parody, and Ethnomusicology," *Critical Inquiry* 20 (winter 1994): 283–314; Robert Walser, "Out of Notes: Signification, Interpretation, and the Problem of Miles Davis," *Musical Quarterly* 77 (summer 1993): 343–65.

6. Matthew Richard Baumer, "Handel's Messiah: A Soulful Celebration and the Analysis of Contemporary Gospel Music," master's thesis, University of North Carolina at Chapel Hill, 1995.

7. Ibid., 10.

8. Quoted in Charles Hamm, *Music in the New World* (New York: W. W. Norton, 1983), 100.

9. Bernice Johnson Reagon, "Searching for Tindley," in *"We'll Understand It Better By and By": Pioneering African American Gospel Composers,* ed. Bernice Johnson Reagon (Washington, D.C.: Smithsonian Institution Press, 1992), 44.

10. Floyd, *The Power of Black Music,* 85.

11. Henry Louis Gates, Jr., *The Signifying Monkey: A Theory of Afro-American Literary Criticism* (New York: Oxford University Press, 1988), 46.

12. Ibid., 45, 49.

13. Floyd, *The Power of Black Music,* 6.

14. Baumer, "Handel's Messiah," 93.

15. Gates, *The Signifying Monkey,* 66.

16. Ibid., xxvii.

17. Liner notes, *Handel's Messiah: A Soulful Celebration* (Reprise Records, 9 6980-2).

18. Floyd, *The Power of Black Music,* 92, 94.

19. W. E. B. Du Bois, *The Souls of Black Folk* (1903; New York: Dover Publications, 1994), 2.

20. Walter Pitts, "Like a Tree Planted by the Water: The Musical Cycle in the

African-American Baptist Ritual," *Journal of American Folklore* 104 (summer 1991): 318–19, 328.

21. Morton Marks, "Uncovering Ritual Structures in Afro-American Music," in *Religious Movements in Contemporary America,* ed. Irving I. Zaretsky and Mark P. Leone (Princeton, N.J.: Princeton University Press, 1974), 61–62.

22. Baumer, "Handel's Messiah," 61–75.

23. Ibid., 64.

24. Reagon, "Pioneering African American Gospel Composers," in *"We'll Understand It Better By and By,"* ed. Reagon, 18.

25. Albert Murray, *Stomping the Blues* (1976; New York: Da Capo Press, 1987), 90.

26. Ibid., 27.

27. Horace Clarence Boyer, *How Sweet the Sound: The Golden Age of Gospel* (Washington, D.C.: Elliott and Clark, 1995), 125–27.

28. Pearl Williams-Jones, "Afro-American Gospel Music: Crystallization of the Black Aesthetic," *Ethnomusicology* 19 (September 1975): 373–86.

29. Ibid., 373.

30. Ibid., 376, 384.

31. Ibid., 382–83.

32. Anthony Heilbut, *The Gospel Sound: Good News and Bad Times,* revised and updated ed. (1971; New York: Limelight Editions, 1985), 250.

33. Jacqui Malone, *Steppin' the Blues: The Visible Rhythms of African American Dance* (Urbana: University of Illinois Press, 1996).

34. Murray, *Stomping the Blues,* 27.

35. Ibid., 27, 30.

36. Albert Murray, *The Hero and the Blues* (1973; New York: Vintage Books, 1995). The book is based on Murray's Paul Anthony Brick Lectures on Ethics at the University of Missouri in 1972. See Barry Shank, "Albert Murray," in *The Oxford Companion to African-American Literature,* ed. William L. Andrews, Frances Smith Foster, and Trudier Harris (New York: Oxford University Press), 1997.

37. Albert Murray, *The Omni-Americans: Some Alternatives to the Folklore of White Supremacy* (1970; New York: Da Capo, 1990).

38. Ibid., 3.

39. *Kirk Franklin and the Family Christmas* (GospoCentric, GCD2130).

EPILOGUE. "DO YOU WANT IT ON YOUR BLACK-EYED PEAS?"

1. Jill Scott, *"Who Is Jill Scott?"* (Hidden Beach Recordings, EK 62137).

2. Sonia Sanchez, "This Is Jill Scott," *Essence* 32 (January 2002): 86.

3. Robert Payne II, telephone conversation with author, December 13, 2001.

Selected Bibliography

Abu-Lughod, Lila. "Writing against Culture." In *Recapturing Anthropology: Working in the Present*, ed. Richard G. Fox, 137–62. Santa Fe, N. Mex.: School of American Research Press, 1991.

Agawu, Kofi. "The Invention of African Rhythm." *Journal of the American Musicological Society* 48, no. 3 (fall 1995): 380–95.

Allen, Ray. *Singing in the Spirit: African-American Sacred Quartets in New York City*. Philadelphia: University of Pennsylvania Press, 1991.

Angelou, Maya. *Singing' and Swingin' and Gettin' Merry Like Christmas*. New York: Bantam, 1976.

Aparicio, Frances R. *Listening to Salsa: Gender, Latin Popular Music, and Puerto Rican Cultures*. Hanover, N.H.: University Press of New England, 1998.

Appadurai, Arjun. *Modernity at Large: Cultural Dimensions of Globalization*. Minneapolis: University of Minnesota Press, 1996.

Aptheker, Herbert, ed. *A Documentary History of the Negro People in the United States*, vol. 4, *1933–45*. New York: Citadel Press, 1974.

Austin, William. *Music in the Twentieth Century: From Debussy through Stravinsky*. New York: W. W. Norton, 1966.

Baer, Hans A., and Merrill Singer. *African-American Religion in the Twentieth Century: Varieties of Protest and Accommodation*. Knoxville: University of Tennessee Press, 1992.

Baker, Houston A., Jr. *Modernism and the Harlem Renaissance*. Chicago: University of Chicago Press, 1987.

Baldwin, James. *Nobody Knows My Name: More Notes of a Native Son*. New York: Dial Press, 1961.

Barlow, William, and Cheryl Finley. *From Swing to Soul: An Illustrated History of African-American Popular Music from 1930 to 1960*. Washington, D.C.: Elliott and Clark Publishing, 1994.

Barz, Gregory F., and Timothy J. Cooley, eds. *Shadows in the Field: New Perspectives for Fieldwork in Ethnomusicology*. New York: Oxford University Press, 1997.

Baumer, Matthew Richard. "Handel's Messiah: A Soulful Celebration and the Analysis of Contemporary Gospel Music." Master's thesis, University of North Carolina at Chapel Hill, 1995.

Bennett, Lerone. *Before the Mayflower: A History of Black America.* 5th ed. Chicago: Johnson Publishing Co., 1982.

Berman, Marshall. *All That Is Solid Melts into Air: The Experience of Modernity.* New York: Simon and Schuster, 1982.

Berry, Mary Frances, and John Blassingame. *Long Memory: The Black Experience in America.* New York: Oxford University Press, 1982.

Bone, Robert A. "The Background of the Negro Renaissance." In *Black History: A Reappraisal,* ed. Melvin Drimmer, 410–11. Garden City, New York: Anchor Books, 1969. Reprinted from Robert A. Bone, *The Negro Novel in America,* rev. ed., New Haven, Conn.: Yale University Press, 1965.

———. "Richard Wright and the Chicago Renaissance." *Callaloo* 9, no. 3 (1986): 446–68.

Bontemps, Arna. "The Black Renaissance of the Twenties." *Black World* (November 1970): 5–9.

Boyer, Horace Clarence. "Analysis of His Contributions: Thomas A. Dorsey, Father of Gospel Music." *Black World* 23 (July 1974): 20–28.

———. "Contemporary Gospel Music: Sacred or Secular?" *First World* 1 (January/February 1977): 46–49.

———. *How Sweet the Sound: The Golden Age of Gospel.* Washington, D.C.: Elliott and Clark Publishing, 1995.

———. *Mahalia Jackson: Gospels, Spirituals, and Hymns.* Liner notes. Columbia Records, 1991.

———. "An Overview: Gospel Music Comes of Age." *Black World* 23 (November 1973): 42–48, 79–86.

Boyer, Richard O. "Bop." *New Yorker,* July 3, 1948, 28–37.

Brackett, David. *Interpreting Popular Music.* Cambridge: Cambridge University Press, 1995.

———. "James Brown's 'Superbad' and the Double-Voiced Utterance." In Brackett, *Interpreting Popular Music,* 108–56. Cambridge: Cambridge University Press, 1995.

Bremer, Sidney H. "Home in Harlem, New York: Lessons from the Harlem Renaissance Writers." *PMLA* 105, no. 1 (January 1990): 46–56.

Brock, Lisa. "Introduction: Between Race and Empire." In *Between Race and Empire: African-Americans and Cubans before the Cuban Revolution.,* ed. Lisa Brock and Digna Castañeda Fuertes, 1–32. Philadelphia: Temple University Press, 1991.

Brown, Earl. "The Detroit Race Riot of 1943." In *A Documentary History of the Negro People in the United States,* vol. 4, *1933–45,* ed. Herbert Aptheker, 443–53. New York: Citadel Press, 1974.

Brown, Rae Linda. "The Woman's Symphony Orchestra of Chicago and Florence B. Price's *Piano Concerto in One Movement.*" *American Music* 11 (summer 1993): 185–205.

Burgett, Paul. "Vindication as a Thematic Principle in the Writings of Alain Locke on the Music of Black Americans." In *Black Music in the Harlem Renaissance: A Collection of Essays,* ed. Samuel A. Floyd, Jr., 29–40. New York: Greenwood Press, 1990.

Capeci, Dominic J. *The Harlem Riot of 1943.* Philadelphia: Temple University Press, 1977.

Caponi, Gina Dagel, ed. *Signifyin(g), Sanctifyin', and Slam Dunking: A Reader in African American Expressive Culture.* Amherst: University of Massachusetts Press, 1999.

Carby, Hazel. " 'It Just Be's Dat Way Sometime': The Sexual Politics of Women's Blues." In *Unequal Sisters: A Multicultural Reader in U.S. Women's History,* ed. Vicki L. Ruiz and Ellen Carol DuBois, 330–41. 2d ed. New York: Routledge, 1994.

———. "Policing the Black Woman's Body in an Urban Context." *Critical Inquiry* 18, no. 4 (summer 1992): 738–55.

Charters, Samuel B., and Leonard Kunstadt. *Jazz: A History of the New York Scene.* Reprint. 1962; Da Capo Press, 1981.

Chase, Gilbert. *America's Music: From the Pilgrims to the Present.* Rev. 3d ed. Urbana: University of Illinois Press, 1987.

Chernoff, John Miller. *African Rhythm and African Sensibility: Aesthetics and Social Action in African Musical Idioms.* Chicago: University of Chicago Press, 1979.

Chilton, John. *Let the Good Times Roll: The Story of Louis Jordan and His Music.* London: Quartet Books, 1992.

Clark, VéVé. "Developing Diaspora Literacy and Marasa Consciousness." In *Comparative American Identities: Race, Sex, and Nationality in the Modern Text,* ed. Hortense J. Spillers, 40–61. New York: Routledge, 1991.

Cohen, Sara. "Ethnography and Popular Music Studies." *Popular Music* 12 (May 1993): 123–38.

Collins, Patricia Hill. *Black Feminist Thought: Knowledge, Consciousness, and the Politics of Empowerment.* Boston: Unwin Hyman, 1990.

"Cootie Williams and Band Score at N.Y. Savoy." *Chicago Defender,* April 3, 1943, 18.

Cousin, Linwood H. "Community High: The Study of Race and Class in a Black Community and High School." Ph.D. diss., University of Michigan, 1994.

Crawford, George W. "Jazzin' God." *Crisis* 3 (February 1929): 45.

Crawford, Richard. *The American Musical Landscape.* Berkeley: University of California Press, 1993.

———. "On Two Traditions of Black Music Research." *Black Music Research Journal* (1986): 1–9.

Crouch, Stanley. *Notes of a Hanging Judge: Essays and Reviews, 1979–1988.* New York: Oxford University Press, 1990.

Cruse, Harold. *The Crisis of the Negro Intellectual: From Its Origins to the Present.* New York: William Morrow, 1967.

Cuscuna, Michael, and Michel Ruppli. *The Blue Note Label: A Discography*. New York: Greenwood Press, 1988.

Dance, Stanley. *The World of Swing*. New York: Charles Scribner's Sons, 1974.

Dates, Jannette L., and William Barlow, eds. *Split Image: African Americans in the Mass Media*. Washington, D.C.: Howard University Press, 1990.

Davis, Angela Y. *Blues Legacies and Black Feminism: Gertrude "Ma" Rainey, Bessie Smith, and Billie Holiday*. New York: Pantheon Books, 1998.

DeVeaux, Scott. *The Birth of Bebop: A Social and Musical History*. Berkeley: University of California Press, 1997.

Diawara, Manthia. "Afro-Kitsch." In *Black Popular Culture*, ed. Gina Dent, 285–91. Seattle: Bay Press, 1992.

Dixon, Willie, with Don Snowden. *I Am the Blues: The Willie Dixon Story*. New York: Da Capo Press, 1989.

DjeDje, Jacqueline Cogdell. *American Black Spirituals and Gospel Songs from Southeast Georgia: A Comparative Study*. Los Angeles: University of California Center for Afro-American Studies, 1978.

Drake, St. Clair, and Horace R. Cayton. *Black Metropolis: A Study of Negro Life in a Northern City*. 1945; Chicago: University of Chicago Press, 1993.

Dubey, Madhu. *Black Women Novelists and the Nationalist Aesthetic*. Bloomington: Indiana University Press, 1994.

du Cille, Ann. "Blue Notes on Black Sexuality: Sex and the Texts of Jessie Fauset, and Nella Larson." *Journal of the History of Sexuality* 3, no. 3 (January 1993): 418–44.

———. "The Occult of True Black Womanhood." *Signs* 19, no. 3 (spring 1994): 591–629.

Ellison, Ralph. *Shadow and Act*. New York: Vintage Books, 1972.

Epstein, Dena J. *Sinful Tunes and Spirituals: Black Folk Music to the Civil War*. Urbana: University of Illinois Press, 1977.

Fabre, Geneviève, and Robert O'Meally. *History and Memory in African American Culture*. New York: Oxford University Press, 1994.

Feather, Leonard. *Inside Jazz*. 1949; New York: Da Capo Press, 1977.

———. *The Jazz Years: Earwitness to an Era*. New York: Da Capo Press, 1987.

Fischer, Michael M. J. "Ethnicity and the Postmodern Arts of Memory." In *Writing Culture: The Poetics and Politics of Ethnography*, ed. James Clifford and George E. Marcus, 194–233. Berkeley: University of California Press, 1986.

Flores, Juan. "Puerto Rocks: New York Ricans Stake Their Claim." In *Droppin' Science: Critical Essays on Rap Music and Hip-Hop Culture*, ed. William Eric Perkins, 85–105. Philadelphia: Temple University Press, 1996.

Floyd, Samuel A., Jr., ed. *Black Music in the Harlem Renaissance*. Westport, Conn.: Greenwood Press, 1990.

———. "Eileen Southern: Quiet Revolutionary." In *New Perspectives on Music: Essays in Honor of Eileen Southern*, ed. Josephine Wright with Samuel A. Floyd, Jr., 3–15. Warren, Mich.: Harmonie Park Press, 1992.

———. "Music in the Harlem Renaissance: An Overview." In *Black Music in the Harlem Renaissance: A Collection of Essays*, ed. Samuel A. Floyd, Jr., 1–27. New York: Greenwood Press, 1990.

———. *The Power of Black Music: Interpreting Its History from Africa to the United States*. New York: Oxford University Press, 1995.

———. "Ring Shout! Literary Studies, Historical Studies, and Black Music Inquiry." *Black Music Research Journal* 11, no. 2 (fall 1991): 265–87.

———, ed. *Black Music in the Harlem Renaissance*. Westport, Conn.: Greenwood Press, 1990.

Fox, Stephen R. *The Guardian of Boston: William Monroe Trotter*. New York: Atheneum, 1971.

Franklin, John Hope, and Alfred A. Moss, Jr. *From Slavery to Freedom: A History of Negro Americans*. New York: McGraw-Hill, 1988.

Frazier, E. Franklin. *The Black Bourgeoisie: The Rise of a New Middle Class in the United States*. New York: Collier Books, 1957.

Frith, Simon. *Performing Rites: On the Value of Popular Music*. Cambridge, Mass.: Harvard University Press, 1996.

Gabbard, Krin. "Introduction: The Jazz Canon and Its Consequences." In *Jazz among the Discourses*, ed. Krin Gabbard, 1–28. Durham, N.C.: Duke University Press, 1995.

Gaines, Kevin K. *Uplifting the Race: Black Leadership, Politics, and Culture in the Twentieth Century*. Chapel Hill: University of North Carolina Press, 1996.

Garofalo, Reebee. "Crossing Over: 1939–1989." In *Split Image: African Americans in the Mass Media*, ed. Jannette L. Dates and William Barlow, 57–121. Washington D.C.: Howard University Press, 1990.

———. *Rocking Out: Popular Music in the United States*. Boston: Allyn and Bacon, 1997.

Gates, Henry Louis, Jr. "Authority, (White) Power and the (Black) Critic: It's All Greek to Me." In *Culture/Power/History: A Reader in Contemporary Social Theory*, ed. Nicolas B. Dirks, Geoff Eley, and Sherry B. Ortner, 245–68. Princeton, N.J.: Princeton University Press, 1994. Originally published in *Cultural Critique* 7 (fall 1987): 19–46.

———. *Colored People: A Memoir*. New York: Vintage Books, 1994.

———. "Lifting the Veil." In *Inventing the Truth: The Art and Craft of Memoir*, ed. William Zinsser, 141–58. Boston: Houghton Mifflin, 1987.

———. "Must Buppiehood Cost Homeboy His Soul?" Arts and Leisure Section, *New York Times*, March 1, 1992, 12–13.

———. *The Signifying Monkey: A Theory of Afro-American Literary Criticism*. New York: Oxford University Press, 1988.

———. "The Trope of a New Negro and the Reconstruction of the Image of the Black." *Representations* 24 (fall 1988): 129–55.

———, ed. *"Race," Writing, and Difference*. Chicago: University of Chicago Press, 1986.

Gendron, Bernard. "Moldy Figs and Modernists: Jazz at War (1942–1946)." *Discourse* 15 (spring 1993): 130–57.

Gennari, John. "Jazz Criticism: Its Development and Ideologies." *Black American Literature Forum* 25 (fall 1991): 449–519.

George, Nelson. *The Death of Rhythm and Blues*. New York: E. P. Dutton, 1989.

Gillespie, Dizzy, and Al Frazer. *To Be or Not to Bop: Memoirs*. Garden City, N.Y.: Doubleday, 1979.

Gillett, Charlie. *The Sound of the City: The Rise of Rock and Roll*. Revised and expanded ed. 1970; New York: Pantheon Books, 1983.

Gilroy, Paul. *The Black Atlantic: Modernity and Double-Consciousness*. Cambridge, Mass.: Harvard University Press, 1993.

Goffin, Robert, ed. *Esquire's 1944 Jazz Year Book*. New York: Smith and Durrell, 1944.

Gorbman, Claudia. *Unheard Melodies: Narrative Film Music*. Bloomington: University of Indiana, 1987.

Goreau, Laurraine. *Just Mahalia, Baby*. Waco, Tex.: Word Books, 1975.

Griffin, Farah Jasmine. *"Who Set You Flowin'?" The African-American Migration Narrative*. New York: Oxford University Press, 1995.

Guralnick, Peter. *Sweet Soul Music: Rhythm and Blues and the Southern Dream of Freedom*. New York: Harper and Row, 1986.

Gwaltney, John Langston, ed. *Drylongso: A Self Portrait of Black America*. 1980; New York: New Press, 1993.

Hall, Stuart. "Ethnicity: Identity and Difference." *Radical America* 23, no. 4 (1987): 9–20.

———. "What Is This 'Black' in Black Popular Culture?" In *Black Popular Culture*, ed. Gina Dent, 21–33. Seattle: Bay Press, 1992.

Hamm, Charles. "Changing Patterns in Society and Music: The U.S. Since World War II." In *Contemporary Music and Music Cultures*, ed. Charles Hamm, Bruno Nettl, and Ronald Byrnside, 35–70. Englewood Cliffs, N.J.: Prentice-Hall, 1975.

———. "Modernist Narratives and Popular Music." In *Putting Popular Music in Its Place*, ed. Charles Hamm, 1–40. Cambridge: Cambridge University Press, 1995.

———. *Music in the New World*. New York: W. W. Norton, 1983.

Hampton, Lionel, with James Haskins. *Hamp: An Autobiography*. New York: Warner Books, 1989.

Hardy, Phil, and Dave Laing. *The Faber Companion to 20th-Century Popular Music*. London: Faber and Faber, 1990.

Harris, Michael W. *The Rise of Gospel Blues: The Music of Thomas A. Dorsey in the Urban Church*. New York: Oxford University Press, 1992.

Harrison, Daphne Duval. *Black Pearls: Blues Queens of the 1920s*. New Brunswick, N.J.: Rutgers University Press, 1988.

Harvey, Mark S. "Jazz and Modernism: Changing Conceptions of Innovation and Tradition." In *Jazz in Mind: Essays on the History and Meanings of Jazz*, ed. Reginald T. Buckner and Steven Weiland, 128–47. Detroit: Wayne State University Press, 1991.

Haskins, Jim. *Queen of the Blues: A Biography of Dinah Washington.* New York: William Morrow, 1987.

Hebdige, Dick. "After the Masses." In *Culture/Power/History: A Reader in Contemporary Social Theory,* ed. Nicholas B. Dirks, Geoff Eley, and Sherry B. Ortner, 222–35. Princeton, N.J.: Princeton University Press, 1994.

Heilbut, Anthony. *The Gospel Sound: Good News and Bad Times.* Revised and updated ed. 1971; New York: Limelight Editions, 1985.

———. "'If I Fail, You Tell the World I Tried': William Herbert Brewster on Records." In *"We'll Understand It Better By and By": Pioneering African American Composers,* ed. Bernice Johnson Reagon, 233–44. Washington, D.C.: Smithsonian Institution Press, 1992.

Hentoff, Nat. *The Jazz Life.* 1961; New York: Da Capo Press, 1975.

Higginbotham, Evelyn Brooks. "African-American Women's History and the Metalanguage of Race." *Signs* 17, no. 2 (winter 1992): 251–74.

———. "Rethinking Vernacular Culture: Black Religion and Race Records in the 1920s and 1930s." In *The House That Race Built: Black Americans, U.S. Terrain,* ed. Wahneema Lubiano, 157–77. New York: Pantheon, 1997.

———. *Righteous Discontent: The Women's Movement in the Black Baptist Church, 1880–1920.* Cambridge, Mass.: Harvard University Press, 1993.

Hobsbawm, Eric, and Terence Ranger, eds. *The Invention of Tradition.* Cambridge: Cambridge University Press, 1983.

Holloway, Joseph, ed. *Africanisms in American Culture.* Bloomington: Indiana University Press, 1990.

hooks, bell. *Yearning: Race, Gender, and Cultural Politics.* Boston: South End Press, 1990.

Huggins, Nathan Irving. *Harlem Renaissance.* New York: Oxford University Press, 1971.

———, ed. *Voices from the Harlem Renaissance.* New York: Oxford University Press, 1995.

Hunter, Tera. *To 'Joy My Freedom: Southern Black Women's Lives and Labors after the Civil War.* Cambridge, Mass.: Harvard University Press, 1997.

Hurston, Zora Neale. "Characteristics of Negro Expression." In *Within the Circle: An Anthology of African-American Literary Criticism from the Harlem Renaissance to the Present,* ed. Angelyn Mitchell, 79–94. Durham, N.C.: Duke University Press, 1994.

Huyssen, Andreas. *After the Great Divide: Modernism, Mass Culture, Postmodernism.* Bloomington: Indiana University Press, 1986.

Jackson, Irene V. *Afro-American Religious Music—A Bibliography and Catalogue of Gospel Music.* Westport, Conn.: Greenwood Press, 1979.

Jacques, Geoffrey. "Cubop! Afro-Cuban Music and Mid-Twentieth Century American Culture." In *Between Race and Empire: African-Americans and Cubans Before the Cuban Revolution,* ed. Lisa Brock and Digna Castañeda Fuertes, 249–65. Philadelphia: Temple University Press, 1991.

Johnson, Abby Arthur, and Ronald Maberry Johnson. *Propaganda and Aes-*

thetics: The Literary Politics of African-American Magazines in the Twentieth Century. Amherst: University of Massachusetts Press, 1991.

Johnson, James Weldon, and J. Rosamond Johnson. "Lift Every Voice and Sing."
In Songs of Zion, 32. Nashville, Tenn.: Abingdon Press, 1981.

Johnson, Victoria E. "Polyphony and Cultural Expression: Interpreting Musical
Traditions in Do the Right Thing." In Spike Lee's Do the Right Thing, ed.
Mark A. Reid, 50–72. Cambridge: Cambridge University Press, 1997.

Jones, Jacqueline. Labor of Love, Labor of Sorrow: Black Women, Work and the
Family, from Slavery to the Present. Reprint. New York: Vintage Books,
1986.

Jones, LeRoi. Black Music. New York: William Morrow, 1967.

———. Blues People: Negro Music in White America. New York: William Morrow, 1963.

Kassabian, Anahid. Hearing Film: Tracking Identifications in Contemporary
Hollywood Film Music. New York: Routledge, 2001.

Keil, Charles. Urban Blues. Chicago: University of Chicago Press, 1966.

Kelley, Robin D. G. "Notes on Deconstructing the Folk." American Historical
Review 97 no. 5 (December 1992): 1400–1408.

———. Race Rebels: Culture, Politics, and the Black Working Class. New York:
Free Press, 1994.

———. "The Riddle of the Zoot: Malcolm Little and Black Cultural Politics
during World War II." In Kelley, Race Rebels: Culture, Politics, and the Black
Working Class, 161–81. New York: Free Press, 1994.

———. Yo' Mama's Disfunktional! Fighting the Culture Wars in Urban America. Boston: Beacon Press, 1997.

Kennedy, Lisa. "The Body in Question." In Black Popular Culture, ed. Gina
Dent, 106–11. Seattle: Bay Press, 1992.

Kerman, Joseph. Contemplating Music: Challenges to Musicology. Cambridge,
Mass.: Harvard University Press, 1985.

Kramer, Lawrence. Music as Cultural Practice, 1800–1990. Berkeley: University
of California Press, 1990.

Lemann, Nicholas. The Promised Land: The Great Migration and How It
Changed America. New York: Vintage Books, 1991.

Leppert, Richard, and Susan McClary, eds. Music and Society: The Politics of
Composition, Performance and Reception. Cambridge: Cambridge University Press, 1987.

Levine, Lawrence. Black Culture, Black Consciousness. New York: Oxford University Press, 1977.

———. "The Concept of the New Negro and the Realities of Black Culture." In
Levine, The Unpredictable Past: Explorations in American Cultural History,
86–106. New York: Oxford University Press, 1993.

Lewis, Earl. "Connecting Memory, Self, and the Power of Place in African-
American Urban History." Journal of Urban History 21 (March 1995): 347–
71.

Limón, José E. "Representation, Ethnicity, and the Precursory Ethnography:

Notes of a Native Anthropologist." In *Recapturing Anthropology: Working in the Present*, ed. Richard G. Fox, 115–36. Santa Fe, N. Mex.: School of American Research Press, 1991.

Lincoln, Eric, and Lawrence H. Mamiya. *The Black Church in the African-American Experience.* Durham, N.C.: Duke University Press, 1990.

Lipsitz, George. *Rainbow at Midnight: Labor and Culture in the 1940s.* Urbana: University of Illinois Press, 1994.

———. *Time Passages: Collective Memory and American Popular Culture.* Minneapolis: University of Minnesota Press, 1990.

Locke, Alain, ed. *The New Negro.* 1925; New York: Atheneum, 1992.

Lott, Eric. "Double V, Double-Time: Bebop's Politics of Style." *Callaloo* 11 (1988): 597–605.

Lynch, Acklyn. *Nightmare Overhanging Darkly: Essays on African-American Culture and Resistance.* Chicago: Third World Press, 1993.

McClary, Susan. "Constructions of Subjectivity in Schubert's Music." In *Queering the Pitch: The New Gay and Lesbian Musicology,* ed. Philip Brett, Gary Thomas, and Elizabeth Wood, 205–33. New York: Routledge, 1994.

———. *Conventional Wisdom: The Content of Form.* Berkeley: University of California Press, 2001.

———. "Paradigm Dissonances: Music Theory, Cultural Studies, Feminist Criticism." *Perspectives of New Music* 32, no. 1 (winter 1994): 68–85.

McClary, Susan, and Robert Walser. "Theorizing the Body in African-American Music." *Black Music Research Journal* 14, no. 1 (spring 1994): 75–84.

McDowell, Deborah E. *Leaving Pipe Shop: Memories of Kin.* New York: Scribner, 1996.

McGinty, Doris Evans. "Black Scholars on Black Music: The Past, The Present and the Future." *Black Music Research Journal* 13, no. 1 (spring 1993): 1–13.

McKay, Claude. *Harlem: Negro Metropolis.* New York: E. P. Dutton, 1940.

Malone, Jacqui. *Steppin' the Blues: The Visible Rhythms of African American Dance.* Urbana: University of Illinois Press, 1996.

Marable, Manning. *Race, Reform, and Rebellion: The Second Reconstruction in Black America, 1945–1990.* Jackson: University Press of Mississippi, 1991.

Marks, Morton. "Uncovering Ritual Structures in Afro-American Music." In *Religious Movements in Contemporary America,* ed. Irving I. Zaretsky and Mark P. Leone, 60–134. Princeton, N.J.: Princeton University Press, 1974.

Maultsby, Portia K. "Black Spirituals: An Analysis of Textual Forms and Structures." *Black Perspective in Music* 4 (spring 1976): 54–69.

———. "Music of Northern Independent Black Churches." *Ethnomusicology* 19 (September 1975): 421–49.

May, Lary, ed. *Recasting America: Culture and Politics in the Age of the Cold War.* Chicago: University of Chicago Press, 1989.

Merriam, Alan P. *The Anthropology of Music.* Evanston, Ill.: Northwestern University Press, 1964.

Middleton, Richard. *Studying Popular Music.* Philadelphia: Open University Press, 1990.

Monson, Ingrid. "Doubleness and Jazz Improvisation: Irony, Parody, and Eth-nomusicology." *Critical Inquiry* 20 (winter 1994): 283–314.

———. "The Problem with White Hipness: Race, Gender, and Cultural Con-ceptions in Jazz Historical Discourse." *Journal of the American Musicologi-cal Society* 48, no. 3 (fall 1995): 396–422.

Montgomery, Vern. "Jaws Unlocks." *Jazz Journal International* 36 (July 1983): 14.

Morrison, Toni. *Jazz.* New York: Plume Books, 1993.

———. "The Site of Memory." In *Inventing the Truth: The Art and Craft of Memoir,* ed. William Zinsser, 85–102. Boston: Houghton Mifflin, 1987.

Murray, Albert. *The Hero and the Blues.* 1973; New York: Vintage Books, 1995.

———. *The Omni-Americans: Some Alternatives to the Folklore of White Supremacy.* 1970; New York: Da Capo Press, 1990.

———. *Stomping the Blues.* 1976; New York: Da Capo Press, 1987.

Myrdal, Gunnar. *An American Dilemma: The Negro Problem and Modern Democracy.* 1944; New Brunswick, N.J.: Transaction Publishers, 1996.

Neal, Mark Anthony. *What the Music Said: Black Popular Music and Black Popular Culture.* New York: Routledge, 1999.

Ogren, Kathy J. *The Jazz Revolution: Twenties America and the Meaning of Jazz.* New York: Oxford University Press, 1989.

Oliver, Paul. *Songsters and Saints: Vocal Traditions on Race Records.* Cam-bridge: Cambridge University Press, 1984.

O'Neal, Jim. "It's Just the Blues." Liner notes. *The Mercury Blues and Rhythm Story, 1945–1955.* Mercury Records, 314–528–292–2.

Ortner, Sherry B. *Making Gender: The Politics and Erotics of Culture.* Boston: Beacon Press, 1996.

———. "On Key Symbols." *American Anthropologist* 75 (1973): 1338–46.

———. "Resistance and the Problem of Ethnographic Refusal." *Comparative Studies in Society and History* 37, no. 1 (January 1995): 173–94.

Osofsky, Gilbert. "'Come Out from among Them": Negro Migration and Set-tlement, 1890–1914." In *Black History: A Reappraisal,* ed. Melvin Drimmer, 375. Garden City, N.Y.: Anchor Books, 1969. Reprinted from Gilbert Osofsky, *Harlem: The Making of a Ghetto.* New York: Harper and Row, 1966.

Paudras, Francis. Liner notes. *Early Years of a Genius.* Vol. 1. Mythic Sound, MS6001–2.

Penny, Dave. Liner notes. *Billy Eckstine and Cootie Williams 1944: Rhythm in a Riff.* Harlequin, HQ 2068.

Perkins, William Eric, ed. *Droppin' Science: Critical Essays on Rap Music and Hip-Hop Culture.* Philadelphia: Temple University Press, 1996.

Pitts, Walter. "Like a Tree Planted by the Water: The Musical Cycle in the African-American Baptist Ritual." *Journal of American Folklore* 104 (sum-mer 1991): 318–40.

Porter, Lewis, and Michael Ullman, with Edward Hazell. *Jazz: From Its Origins to the Present.* Englewood Cliffs, N.J.: Prentice-Hall, 1993.

Powell, Richard J. *The Blues Aesthetic: Black Culture and Modernism.* Washington, D.C.: Washington Project for the Arts, 1989.

Priestly, Brian. *Jazz on Record: A History.* 1988; New York: Billboard Books, 1991.

Radano, Ronald M. "Denoting Difference: The Writing of the Slave Spirituals." *Critical Inquiry* 22, no. 3 (spring 1996): 506–44.

———. "Soul Texts and the Blackness of Folk." *Modernism/Modernity* 2, no. 1 (1995): 71–95.

Ramsey, Guthrie P., Jr. "The Art of Bebop: Earl Bud Powell and the Emergence of Modern Jazz." Ph.D. diss., University of Michigan, 1994.

———. "Cosmopolitan or Provincial? Ideology in Early Black Music Historiography, 1867–1940." *Black Music Research Journal* 16, no. 1 (spring 1996): 11–42.

Reagon, Bernice Johnson, ed. *"We'll Understand It Better By and By": Pioneering African American Gospel Composers.* Washington, D.C.: Smithsonian Institution Press, 1992.

Ringer, Benjamin B., and Elinor R. Lawless. *Race-Ethnicity and Society.* New York: Routledge, 1989.

Roberts, John W. "African American Diversity and the Study of Folklore." *Western Folklore* 52 (April 1993): 157–71.

Rogers, J. A. "Jazz at Home." In *The New Negro: Voice of the Harlem Renaissance,* ed. Alain Locke. 1925; New York: Atheneum, 1992.

Rose, Tricia. *Black Noise: Rap Music and Black Culture in Contemporary America.* Hanover, N.H.: University Press of New England, 1994.

Rout, Leslie B., Jr. "Reflections on the Evolution of Postwar Jazz." In *The Black Aesthetic,* ed. Addison Gayle, Jr., 143–53. New York: Anchor Books, 1971.

Sanjek, Russell, and David Sanjek. *American Popular Music Business in the 20th Century.* New York: Oxford University Press, 1991.

Schuller, Gunther. *Early Jazz: Its Roots and Musical Development.* New York: Oxford University Press, 1968.

———. "Sonny Rollins and the Challenge of Thematic Improvisation." In Schuller, *Musings: The Musical Worlds of Gunther Schuller.* New York: Oxford University Press, 1986.

———. *The Swing Era: The Development of Jazz, 1930–1945.* New York: Oxford University Press, 1989.

Shank, Barry. "Albert Murray." In *The Oxford Companion to African-American Literature,* ed. William L. Andrews, Frances Smith Foster, and Trudier Harris, 515–16. New York: Oxford University Press, 1997.

Shapiro, Nat, and Nat Hentoff. *Hear Me Talkin' to Ya.* 1955; New York: Dover Publications, 1966.

Shaw, Arnold. *52nd St: The Street of Jazz.* 1971; New York: Da Capo Press, 1977.

Shibutani, T., and K. M. Kwan. *Ethnic Stratification: A Comparative Approach.* New York: Macmillan, 1965.

Sitkoff, Harvard. *A New Deal for Blacks: The Emergence of Civil Rights as a*

National Issue: The Depression Decade. New York: Oxford University Press, 1978.

Small, Christopher. *Musicking: The Meanings of Performance and Listening*. Hanover, N.H.: University Press of New England, 1998.

Smith, Michael P. "Behind the Lines: The Black Mardi Gras Indians and the New Orleans Second Line." *Black Music Research Journal* 14, no. 1 (spring 1994): 43–73.

Smith, Valerie. "The Documentary Impulse in Contemporary African American Film." In *Black Popular Culture*, ed. Gina Dent, 56–64. Seattle: Bay Press, 1992.

Snead, James A. "Repetition as a Figure of Black Culture." In *Black Literature and Literary Theory*, ed. Henry Louis Gates, Jr., 59–79. New York: Routledge, 1984.

Sollors, Werner, ed. *The Invention of Ethnicity*. New York: Oxford University Press, 1989.

Southern, Eileen. "Hymnals of the Black Church." *Black Perspective in Music* 17 (1989): 20–46.

———. *The Music of Black Americans: A History*. 1st ed., New York: W. W. Norton, 1971; 2d ed., New York: W. W. Norton, 1983.

———, ed. *Readings in Black American Music*, 2d ed. New York: W. W. Norton, 1983.

Spady, James G., et al. *Street Conscious Rap*. Philadelphia: UMUM Press, 1999.

Spencer, Jon Michael. *Black Hymnody: A Hymnological History of the African-American Church*. Knoxville: University of Tennessee Press, 1992.

Stepto, Robert B. *From Behind the Veil: A Study of Afro-American Narrative*. 2d ed. Urbana: University of Illinois Press, 1991.

Stevenson, Robert. "America's First Black Music Historian." *Journal of the American Musicological Society* 26, no. 3 (1973): 383–404.

Toop, David. *Rap Attack 2: African Rap to Global Hip-Hop*. 2d ed. 1984; London: Blackstock Mews, 1991.

Trotter, James Monroe. *Music and Some Highly Musical People*. 1878; New York: Charles T. Dillingham, 1881.

Tucker, Bruce. "Editor's Introduction: Black Music after Theory." *Black Music Research Journal* 11, no. 2 (fall 1991): iii–vii.

Vincent, Rickey. *Funk: The Music, the People, and the Rhythm of One*. New York: St. Martin's Griffin, 1995.

Wallace, Michele. "Boyz N the Hood and Jungle Fever." In *Black Popular Culture*, ed. Gina Dent, 123–31. Seattle: Bay Press, 1992.

———. "Modernism, Postmodernism and the Problem of the Visual in Afro-American Culture." In *Out There: Marginalization and Contemporary Cultures*, ed. Russell Ferguson, Martha Gever, Trinh T. Minh-ha, and Cornel West, 39–50. Cambridge, Mass.: MIT Press in association with the New Museum of Contemporary Art, New York, 1990.

Walser, Robert. "Out of Notes: Signification, Interpretation, and the Problem of Miles Davis." *Musical Quarterly* 77 (summer 1993): 343–65.

————. "Rhythm, Rhyme, and Rhetoric in the Music of Public Enemy." *Ethnomusicology* 39, no. 2 (spring–summer 1995): 193–218.

————. *Running with the Devil: Power, Gender, and Madness in Heavy Metal Music.* Hanover, N.H.: University Press of New England, 1993.

Ward, Brian. *Just My Soul Responding: Rhythm and Blues, Black Consciousness, and Race Relations.* Berkeley: University of California Press, 1998.

Watkins, S. Craig. *Representing: Hip Hop Culture and the Production of Black Cinema.* Chicago: University of Chicago Press, 1998.

Watson, John F. "Methodist Error." In *Readings in Black American Music,* ed. Eileen Southern, 62–64. New York: W. W. Norton, 1971.

Wellburn, Ron. "The Black Aesthetic Imperative." In *The Black Aesthetic,* ed. Addison Gayle, Jr., 126–42. 1971; Garden City, N.Y.: Anchor Books, 1972.

Werner, Craig. "Bigger's Blues: *Native Son* and the Articulation of Afro-American Modernism." In *Playing the Changes: From Afro-Modernism to the Jazz Impulse,* 183–211. Urbana: University of Illinois Press, 1994.

————. *A Change Is Gonna Come: Music, Race, and the Soul of America.* New York: Plume, 1999.

West, Cornel. *Prophetic Fragments: Illuminations of the Crisis in American Religion and Culture.* Grand Rapids, Mich.: William B. Eerdmans Publishing, 1988.

Wexler, Jerry, and David Ritz. *Rhythm and the Blues: A Life in American Music.* New York: Alfred A. Knopf, 1993.

White, Walter, et al. "A Declaration by Negro Voters." *Crisis* 51 (January 1944): 16–17.

Williams, John A. "The Harlem Renaissance: Its Artists, Its Impact, Its Meaning." *Black World* (November 1970): 17–18.

Williams, Martin. *The Jazz Tradition.* 2d rev. ed. New York: Oxford University Press, 1993.

Williams, Raymond. *Keywords: A Vocabulary of Culture and Society.* Rev. ed. New York: Oxford University Press, 1985.

Williams-Jones, Pearl. "Afro-American Gospel Music: Crystallization of the Black Aesthetic." *Ethnomusicology* 19 (1975): 373–85.

Wilson, Olly. "The Significance of the Relationship between Afro-American Music and West African Music." *Black Perspective in Music* 2, no. 1 (spring 1974): 3–22.

Wintz, Cary D. *Black Culture and the Harlem Renaissance.* Houston: Rice University Press, 1988.

Wolff, Janet. "The Ideology of Autonomous Art." In *Music and Society: The Politics of Composition, Performance and Reception,* ed. Richard Leppert and Susan McClary, 1–12. Cambridge: Cambridge University Press, 1987.

Woodard, Komozi. *A Nation within a Nation: Amiri Baraka (LeRoi Jones) and Black Power Politics.* Chapel Hill: University of North Carolina Press, 1999.

DISCOGRAPHY

The Bebop Era. Columbia Records, CK 40972.

Brown, James. "Lickin' Stick." *James Brown: Star Time.* Polydor, 849 108 2.

————. "Santa Claus, Go Straight to the Ghetto." *James Brown's Funky Christmas.* Polygram Records, 31452 7988–2.

————. *Star Time.* Disk 2. Polygram Records, 849 111–2.

Christian, Charlie. *Live Sessions at Minton's Playhouse.* Jazz Anthology, 550012.

The Four Jumps of Jive. "It's Just the Blues." Composed by Richard Jones and Jimmy Gilmore. Recorded in Chicago, September 12, 1945. *The Mercury Rhythm and Blues Story, 1945–1955.* Mercury Records, 314 528 292–2.

Franklin, Kirk. *Kirk Franklin and the Family Christmas.* GospoCentric, GCD2130.

Powell, Bud. *The Amazing Bud Powell,* vol. 1. Blue Note, CDP 7 81503 2.

The Sugarhill Gang. "Rapper's Delight." *Hip-Hop Greats: Classic Raps.* Rhino, R270957.

Washington, Dinah. "Back Water Blues." *The Essential Dinah Washington: The Great Songs.* Verve, audiocassette, 314512905–4.

————. *Dinah Washington on Mercury,* vol. 1. Mercury, compact disk, 832 444–2.

FILMOGRAPHY

Boyz N the Hood. Written and directed by John Singleton. Columbia Pictures, 1991.

Crooklyn. Written and directed by Spike Lee. University City Studios, 1994.

Do the Right Thing. Written and directed by Spike Lee. Universal City Studios, 1989.

In This Our Life. Directed by John Huston and with a score by Max Steiner. Warner Brothers, 1942.

Love Jones. Written and directed by Theodore Witcher. New Line, 1997.

ARCHIVAL SOURCES

Cootie Williams, Interviews, Jazz Oral History Project at the Institute for Jazz Studies, Rutgers University, Newark, N.J.

Acknowledgments

More individuals, communities, and institutions than I can name here contributed to the writing of this book. Generous support for my intellectual endeavors at various stages has helped me considerably. I am grateful for the Thurgood Marshall Dissertation Fellowship at Dartmouth College, a Ford Foundation Postdoctoral Fellowship for Minority Scholars, and for the visiting scholar residency at the W. E. B. Du Bois Institute at Harvard University. For professional and personal support at the University of Michigan I thank Willis Patterson, Ed Sarath, Faye Burton, Judith Becker, Louise Toppin, William Banfield, Stephen Newby, Charles and Maria Neal, Pam and Christopher Amos, Timothy East, Jeffery Magee, Phil and Kathy Munoa, and Jeffery Taylor.

I have warm memories of the academic year I spent at Dartmouth College because of the hospitality and lively discussions of my neighbors Jerry and Sue Auten. Robert Walser's mentoring and scholarly prowess helped to make my time in Hanover, New Hampshire, productive; his considerable racquetball skills, competitive edge, and chicken wings got me through the long New England winter. Susan McClary's close readings, honest critiques, peach cobbler, and encouragement continue to stay with me. Dartmouth's Music Department provided a collegial atmosphere that supported my research and writing activities. The soldiers in Dartmouth's 1993–1994 Gospel Choir provided spirit, faith, and even childcare and hair-braiding sessions for my daughters on occasion.

All of my former colleagues at Tufts University provided a supportive environment. Michael Ullman, in particular, offered friendship, wit, musical insights, and access to the record collection of life. His productive skepticism keeps me honest. Historians Jeanne Penvenne and Gerald Gill lent ready ears to my ideas and were "quick to the draw" when I requested references.

Liz Ammons was the model activist, scholar, and cultural worker. I will never forget her advocacy for my personal and professional well-being, the results of which I am still experiencing today. The STARS organization provided my family with a safe haven. I am especially indebted to my colleague Linda Loury for her invitation, practicality, and quiet determination. Tina and David Clayton's friendship, cookouts, and our Saturday soccer marathons will remain among my fondest memories of my time in Boston. I could not have succeeded without their faithful, selfless support.

At the University of Pennsylvania I have found a wonderful community of great citizens, scholars, and musicians. The creative energy and intellectual discourse that circulate among my colleagues in the music department continue to inspire me to elevate my game on all levels. The department's support staff at Penn, Maryellen Malek, Margaret Smith, Alfreda Frazier, and Regina Christian, have come to my rescue on too many occasions to count. Their efficiency, know-how, and telepathy have covered a multitude of my own sins. Librarian Marjorie Hassen has quickly and professionally answered my requests for materials. Kim Gallon has graciously tracked down citations with her considerable knowledge of African American bibliography. I am grateful to them both.

Several research assistants have greatly facilitated my work throughout the process of writing this book. To Carmen Harden, Anthony Peebles, Phillip Goff, and Monica McPherson I extend my gratitude. To Haley Thomas, a graduate student in folklore, I owe the greatest debt. Her transcriptions were impeccable, and her gifts for description impressive. During numerous conversations she shared insightful suggestions for making the manuscript better.

I have been blessed to have fruitful relationships with truly great musicians. Lonnie Plaxico, Rod McGaha, Kenny Campbell, Wardell Campbell, Kenny Davis, and Malcolm Banks taught me diligence, commitment, passion, and about "the concept." Von Freeman and Elder Willie James Campbell were inspirational mentors in jazz and gospel, respectively. In Philadelphia, Lucky Thompson, Lonnie Henson, Denise King, Sam Reed, Napoleon Black, Val Ray, Lee Smith, and Sam Jones continue to serve up good jazz, and I'm grateful to be in their circle. I am particularly thankful to drummer Kazeem Shaheed for insisting that I spend more time on the bandstand.

My lifetime mentors Karen Fruits, Claire Boyce, and Aaron Horne continue to inspire and guide despite the passage of time and the distance that separates us. As a freshly minted graduate with a B.A., I was taken under the wing of Samuel A. Floyd, Jr., who directed me toward this life of the mind.

He then sent me to the University of Michigan, and there, Richard Crawford did the dirty work and heavy lifting that involved training me. Rich's patience, respect for the music, passion for writing, ability to see the humor, and insistence that scholars do a musical work justice have changed me.

The "Americanists" on the national scene of musicology have blazed trails and provided intellectual and personal sustenance. Scott DeVeaux, Susan Cook, Mark Tucker, Ronald Radano, Ann Dhu, Carol Oja, Tammy Kernodle, Leonard Brown, Charles Hamm, Dale Cockrell, Karen Alquist, Lisa Barg, Kitty Preston, Ingrid Monson, Wayne Shirley, and Catherine Parsons Smith have encouraged and inspired me.

To my writing group "The Couch" (Bill Lowe, Daphne Brooks, Salim Washington, and Farah Griffin) I extend heartfelt gratitude and admiration. I learned much from this tight circle of common sense, artistic flair, and good vibes. Bill provided a sage, long view on any issue literary or musical. Daphne gave us inspiration from the younger generation and the "left coast" with brilliance beyond her years. My man from the "Motor City," Salim, contributed measured, incisive, honest, and correct critiques. Farah Griffin's theoretical acumen, intellectual range, musical curiosity, and on-point "baby sistah" signifying became the spirit behind the whole enterprise. Talking to her is always like "going home." My association with this group has made me better.

I received close readings from scholars I count as devoted friends. David Brackett has spent lots of time over the years helping me to refine my ideas. Rae Linda Brown, my "big sister" in the discipline, has been a model of professionalism and quiet grace, always there, always supportive, willing to correct. Robin D. G. Kelley has counted among my strongest supporters since the dissertation days. He has patiently read my work, commented on its strengths, and helped me to shore up its weaknesses. I feel very fortunate to have this brother in my corner. Timothy D. Taylor, one of the smartest musicologists I know, has been my most thorough reader. The honesty of his reactions has paid me the highest compliment and provided me direction at crucial points in my scholarly journey. Kyra D. Gaunt (my li'l sis in the discipline) has been a loyal friend, "home biscuit," meticulous critic, and great dance partner. She's read (and heard!) many versions of my ideas and can take a good share of the credit for any worth this book may have.

To my "Boyz": Lesly Antoine, Rahul Harris, Americus "Duece" Reed II, and the University City Grays, thanks for making Philadelphia feel like home. Ronald Daymon, you've been a staunch supporter and a great friend who's taught me how to be a father even in the eye of the storm. Linwood Cousins, your steadfast friendship, productive conversations, and enthusiasm for things academic have truly been one of the great gifts of my life. Tukufu Zuberi, you're the scholar I admire most: I thrive on your brilliance, zest for life, Cala-bama accent, problack politics, and "I got 'cha back" swagger. To my main man and road dog in Philly, Kevin Clark, you've taught me how to balance work and play and how to live more in the moment. And while many of those moments have been spent yelling on baseball diamonds and basketball courts, I knew we would be "boyz" when you said that something I had given you to read was a "literary travesty." Thanks for the trump-tight friendship, bro.

To both sides of my extended family (in vernacular terms, "my whole generation"), I love you all. Ma-dear, I've inherited your restless quest for knowledge. Thank you. To my twin, Cynthia (skinny legs and all), thanks for a lifetime of love, secrets, and arguments, and thanks especially for the keys to your car during my Chi-town research trips. Ernest, my cherished "cuz-o," your support and sojourns to "the office," the rink, and other spots sustain me between my visits back home. One love, cuz. Cousin Sina, your belief in me gives me courage and assurance. Brenda and Robert Payne, the big pot on the stove, the warmth, the musical environment, the bid whisk, and hearty laughter all remind me why I love being a Ramsey from the Windy City.

My immediate Ramsey clan has simply endured all things great and small because of my life in the academy. They've moved constantly, adjusted to starkly different subcultures—ivory tower Michigan, rural New Hampshire, suburban Boston, inner-city Philadelphia—with the verve, style, and determination of pros. Your influence and the lessons you've taught me about life and, by extension, music can be felt on literally every page of this book. To Bernadette for years of support and sacrifice and to Robert Guthrie (truly my main man), Candace Yvette (my great inspiration), and Bridget Yvonne (my heart), I dedicate this book with love and appreciation.

Index

Page numbers in italics indicate figures.

Abrams, Muhal Richard, xi
Abu-Lughod, Lila, 43
acculturation, intrablack, 133
Adderley, Cannonball, 4
aesthetics: academic discourse on, 157;
of bebop, 73, 107; of blues, 161; code-
fusion, 49, 50; of house parties, 147–
48; of jazz, 123, 161, 237n75
Africa: and Afro-modernism, 98; in
black musical tropes, 28; in black
vernacular music, 48; role of, in
African American culture, 28–29.
See also diaspora, African
African Americanists: and Black Power
movement, 19; study of music by, 18
African Americans: agency of, 41–42;
class structure of, 104; "color-struck,"
153, 238n6; in cotton industry, 103–
4; cultural politics of, 149; cultural
resistance by, 64, 110; designations
for, 219n3; double consciousness of,
198–99; educational opportunities
for, 102; expressive culture of, 35,
100, 116, 163, 191, 215; in films,
166–67; historical consciousness of,
46; in labor unions, 103; literacy of,
108; in mass media, 67; meaning of
modernity for, 97; in mid-twentieth-
century society, 130; modernist outlook of, 46, 47, 48; political influence
of, 103; public image of, 44; religious
practices of, 190; in situation comedies, 163; social assimilation of, 38;
social status of, 101, 110, 148, 158; in
sports, 163; stereotypes of, 45, 64,
156; veterans, 102, 231n9; as voters,
101, 231n9; during World War II,
101, 231n12. *See also* musicians,
African American; women, African
American
Afro-internationalism, 130
Afro-modernism, xii, 27–30; African
past in, 98; bodily celebration in, 73–
75; and classic modernism, 106; and
class struggle, 162; gender relations
and, 162; of gospel music, 52–53, 54;
and Great Migration, 162; hybridity
of, 218; improvisation in, 96; influences on, 162; international element
in, 128; of "It's Just the Blues," 51; of
late twentieth century, 187; in mass
media, 119; of mid-twentieth
century, 130; narratives of, 64, 67; of
1940s, 98, 101; north-south rhetoric
in, 64, 97, 98, 162; and politics of
integration, 120–23; as renaissancism, 106; revisionism in, 73; social
energies of, 97

263

Text: 10/13 Aldus
Display: Aldus
Compositor: BookMatters, Berkeley
Printer and Binder: Sheridan Books, Inc.